Gender and Sexuality in Weimar Modernity

⌒

Film, Literature, and "New Objectivity"

Richard W. McCormick

palgrave

GENDER AND SEXUALITY IN WEIMAR MODERNITY: FILM, LITERATURE, AND "NEW OBJECTIVITY"
© Richard W. McCormick, 2001

First published 2001 by PALGRAVE™
175 Fifth Avenue, New York, N.Y.10010 and
Houndmills, Basingstoke, Hampshire RG21 6XS.
Companies and representatives throughout the world

PALGRAVE is the new global publishing imprint of St. Martin 's Press LLC Scholarly and Reference Division and Palgrave Publishers Ltd (formerly Macmillan Press Ltd).

ISBN 0-312-29298-8 hardback

Library of Congress Cataloguing-in-Publication Data
McCormick, Richard W.,
    Gender and Sexuality in Weimar Modernity: Film, Literature, and "New Objectivity"/by Richard W. McCormick
    p. cm.
    Includes bibliographical references and index.
    ISBN 0-312-29298-8
    1.

JV6271 .M45 2001
325'.1'01—dc21   2001032760

A catalogue record for this book is available
from the British Library.

Design by Westchester Book Composition, Danbury, Connecticut, U.S.A.

First edition: December 2001
10 9 8 7 6 5 4 3 2 1

Printed in the United States of America.

For Joan, Isa, and Susana

Contents

Acknowledgments

This book has been a long time in the making, and so there are many scholars, institutions, and friends to thank for their help. First of all, I would like to thank Anton Kaes for the advice he has offered, for his scholarship on Weimar film and culture, and for the scholarship of so many others whom he has supported and inspired. There are a number of other scholars who have also been willing to provide feedback and/or support at the various stages of the development of this manuscript, and whose scholarship on topics relevant to this book has been of invaluable assistance: Mary Ann Doane, Lynne Frame, Atina Grossmann, Sabine Hake, Andreas Huyssen, Alice Kuzniar, Susan Linville, Judith Mayne, Vibeke Petersen, Patrice Petro, Karl Prümm, Kathy Roper, Julia Sneeringer, and Janet Ward.

Other scholars who have provided important assistance (through advice, feedback, sharing their scholarship, their work organizing conferences or panels, or other support) include Steve Brockmann, Jon Clark, Geoff Eley, Katherine Goodman, Randall Halle, Dagmar Herzog, Peter Hohendahl, Barbara Kosta, Dagmar Lorenz, Maria Makela, Maggie McCarthy, Jonathan Munby, Klaus Phillips, Carol Poore, Linda Schulte-Sasse, and Bob Shandley.

At my "home" institution, the University of Minnesota, my colleagues Ruth-Ellen Joeres and Jack Zipes deserve thanks for their mentorship and help with respect to this book (and many other things); other colleagues whose feedback, support, and friendship deserve mention include Dan and Maria Brewer, Frank Hirschbach, M.J. Maynes, Patrizia McBride, Charlotte Melin, Leslie Morris, Jim Parente, Jochen Schulte-Sasse, Eileen Sivert, Arlene Teraoka, Ray Wakefield, Gerhard Weiss, Eric Weitz, and Monika Zagar. Hanna Schissler, a scholar and friend whom I also met at the University of Minnesota, must also be mentioned—and thanked. A number of students and former students who worked for me as Research Assistants over the (long) course of the development of this book also must be thanked: Angelika Rauch, Peter Mühle, Beth Kautz, Alison Guenther-Pal, Beth Muellner, Barbara Drescher, and Gundolf Graml. I cannot neglect to mention those students and former students whose own research on Weimar culture was of great help to me: Beth Kautz, Kristin Makholm, Syd Norton, Britt Abel, Lorna Sopcak, and Barbara Drescher. Research papers on Weimar cinema by Martina Anderson, Jeff Baldwin-Bott, Sonja Fritzsche, and Alison Guenther-Pal were also helpful.

Film archives in Germany that deserve mention and have my gratitude for their assistance include the Film Museum Berlin (formerly the Stiftung Deutsche Kinemathek, or SDK), the Bundesarchiv-Filmarchiv in Berlin, and the Deutsches Institut für Filmkunde in Frankfurt. At the Film Museum Berlin, I am especially grateful to Hans Helmut Prinzler, Wolfgang Jacobsen, Gero Gandert, Wolfgang Theis, Rosemarie van der Zee, and Christa Schahbaz. At the Bundesarchiv-Filmarchiv, I want especially to thank Helmut Morsbach. I wish to thank the American Council of Learned Societies (ACLS) for a year-long stipend to do research for this book, as well as the German Academic Exchange Service (DAAD) for support of my research in Germany. The McKnight Foundation has also supported my research. The Graduate School and the College of Liberal Arts at the University of Minnesota were also generous in funding research assistance and leaves, as has been my home department there, the Department of German, Scandinavian and Dutch, and the Center for German and European Studies. The Center for Advanced Feminist Studies has long been another important source of intellectual community and support for me at the University of Minnesota. I want to thank Stephanie Debner for her work on the book's index and my copy editor at Westchester Publishing, Christine Hafer. Thanks also to Roee Raz, Donna Cherry, and Kristi Long at Palgrave.

Leslie Pahl has provided intellectual support as well as friendship to me for many years. Another person whose ideas, intellectual energy, and friendship have been important to me is Heidrun Suhr. My friends Anne Lalk, Susanne Stoye and Volker Groß, and Roland Ladage have hosted me in Germany on various research trips there; their friendship and interest in discussing a variety of political and cultural issues has always provided support and stimulus. Finally, I want to thank Joan Clarkson and our children, Isabel and Susana, for their creativity, warmth, intelligence, love, laughter, and support. I dedicate this book to them.

Chapter 1 ✍

Introduction
Blurred Boundaries: Modernity, Crisis, and Emancipation in the Culture of the Weimar Republic

> The radio and the telephone
> And the movies that we know
> May just be passing fancies
> And in time may go
> But oh my dear
> Our love is here to stay.

> —Ira Gershwin, 1938

Why open a book on the culture of Germany's Weimar Republic (1918–1933) with a quote from the lyrics of a Gershwin tune from America's "Tin Pan Alley"? Given that the topic of this book is the relationship between gender, sexuality, modernity, and culture, it is a fairly transparent choice. These lyrics express the hope that amidst the constant change brought about by the technical and cultural innovations of the modern age, it is romantic love that can anchor us. This is an understandable dream, albeit naive—or perhaps tongue-in-cheek. For gender and sexual relations, too, were—and are—undergoing at least as much change in modern, mass societies as any other less symbolic aspect of life. Indeed, one destabilizing factor in modern gender relations may have been precisely the popularization of much older, bourgeois ideals of romantic, heterosexual love, directed through mass culture more at the lower than at the middle classes. If so, this particular destabilization is especially ironic, given that those romantic ideals were originally meant to reinforce the concept of a stable, intimate private sphere that was "timeless," immune to the changes that the rise of the bourgeoisie and capitalism were instigating in the public realm of modern life.

A second reason that a piece of American popular music is appropriate for opening a book on the Weimar Republic: American popular culture represented for Germany during this period a special model for the development of a mass popular culture (and culture industry). Indeed, what was called "Americanism" in Germany was more or less equivalent to the "New Objectivity," the embrace of modernity and mass culture championed by many artists and intellectuals during the Weimar Republic.[1] But the German embrace of what were considered American models of democracy, modernity, and mass culture was marked by ambivalence. One notes mixed feelings even among the most enthusiastic elements of its liberal and leftist intelligentsia, not to mention among more conservative (and more powerful) forces in German society. Some of Henry Ford's ideas may have appealed to those on the Right (such as his anti-Semitism), but otherwise they considered "Americanism" for the most part a dangerous, foreign barbarism that appealed only to "rootless, cosmopolitan" intellectuals of the "asphalt" metropolis, Berlin.[2]

"Americanization" in Weimar was also equated with "feminization," especially by its opponents (Lüdtke, Marßolek, and von Saldern 21; Rosenhaft, "Lesewut," 124–27, 140). One of the ideals associated with America was the concept of the "girl," a new model of an athletic, relatively emancipated young womanhood somewhat related to the American concept of the "flapper," but in Germany definitely conflated with the so-called "New Woman," the partly mythical notion of a sexually emancipated working woman that so fascinated the illustrated press in Germany, as Patrice Petro and others have demonstrated. And it was "Girlkultur"[3] and other discourses about new models of gendered behavior (especially for women) that were the occasion of some of the greatest German ambivalence about modernity, even among male intellectuals otherwise enthusiastic about modernization and technology, let alone among conservative and nationalist forces.

EMANCIPATION AS CRISIS: GENDER, SEXUAL, AND SOCIAL DYNAMICS IN WEIMAR CULTURE

This book is a study of selected cultural texts from the Weimar Republic with an emphasis on films and literary works produced in the middle and later years of the Republic. In analyzing these texts, I attempt to situate them within a historical context defined by the destabilization of traditional social, gender, and sexual identities that characterized the first German Republic. With the collapse of Germany's authoritarian monarchy upon its defeat in history's first mechanized war on a mass scale, World War I, the first extended German experiment with democracy was initiated in November 1918. The resulting Republic would forever be associated with the city of Weimar because its constitution was ratified there in July 1919. But the Weimar Republic was threatened by revolution and counter-revolution from the beginning—indeed, it was fear of revolutionary masses in Berlin that caused the constitution to be ratified in provincial Weimar and not in the modern metropolis we always associate with the Republic. Economically burdened first with heavy war reparations and then with the onset of hyper-inflation, the Republic finally experienced a period of relative stability (1924–1929), but it was also a period of rapid modernization and industrial rationalization, accompanied by the growth of consumerism and a modern mass culture that became especially influential. The strain that such changes exerted on traditional conceptions of culture and identity only worsened in the final years of the Republic, when, beginning in late 1929, economic depression and then increasing political polarization led to its ultimate demise in 1933.

A key element in this identity crisis was gender. The onset of political democracy in Germany had brought with it suffrage and constitutional equality for women, and existing trends toward an increasing presence of women in the workforce and public life accelerated. The "shock of modernity" in Germany was often experienced as a crisis of traditional male authority, agency, and identity. But traditional conceptions of female identity were undergoing just as much strain—if not more. Female identity was thematized and debated in the culture not just in terms of male anxieties about modernity and the "New Woman," but also because women themselves were confronted with new choices and opportunities as well as many new stresses and burdens (usually doubled—if not tripled).

Anxiety about changing notions of gender roles and sexuality permeated Weimar culture, and this book investigates specific articulations of that anxiety in two competing forms of culture: literature, traditionally associated with "high" bourgeois culture, and film, the embodiment of modern mass culture, although in the 1920s precisely this distinction between "high" and "low" was under attack by artists and intellectuals (whose own traditional status and income was also under siege). This questioning of traditional aesthetic distinctions occurred in connection with a broader cultural sensibility evident in popular fashions and "lifestyles" as well as in painting, literature, theater, film, photography, design, and architecture: the

New Objectivity, a "sober" and unsentimental embrace of urban modernity, in contrast to Expressionism's horror of technology and belief in "auratic" art. And the general crisis of gendered identity in Weimar is also a key to its dominant cultural sensibility: while nothing symbolized the New Objectivity better than the working, sexually emancipated, unsentimental "New Woman," she also seemed to represent both an excess of modernity and the ultimate crisis of mastery that male intellectuals and artists—as well as social engineers—were attempting to overcome and control through "sober," "rational" documentation. Yet female social workers and sex reformers were also engaged in the same social engineering project; meanwhile women artists as well attempted to engage the new debates about female identity that raged around the "New Woman."

Much work on the culture of the Weimar Republic has followed the tendency to see its psychosexual dynamics in terms of a teleology similar to that first proposed by Siegfried Kracauer in his famous 1947 book on Weimar cinema, *From Caligari to Hitler*—a postwar study that examined Weimar cinema and culture for evidence of the predispositions in the "German psyche" that would lead to fascism in the 1930s. I began my own work on Weimar culture believing in a variation on this "Kracauerian" teleology , one that is perhaps best exemplified by Klaus Theweleit's *Male Fantasies*—that is, I tended to look at Weimar culture for evidence of negative, exclusively reactionary and misogynistic discourses that were part of the trajectory that led to the Third Reich. Within that culture there is certainly much that deserves just such an interpretation, but as my exploration of the history and culture of both the Weimar Republic and the Third Reich has continued, I have come to appreciate the Weimar Republic and its culture much more. While both Weimar and the Third Reich were in a number of ways misogynistic, one has to evaluate more positively the relatively open acknowledgement of male anxieties about gender and sexuality in Weimar, in spite of the often misogynistic impulses behind it. Weimar was a culture of male "hysteria" as much as mere misogyny, and one that allowed (in part by admitting male insecurities) a certain amount of space for women to deal with their anxieties about gender and modernity, too. Some of what was most threatening—especially, though by no means exclusively, to men—consisted of the blurring of traditionally gendered roles and behavior. It is this blurring that is precisely what was most emancipatory about Weimar culture—emancipatory, even "queer," although this cultural blurring was by no means an indication that power relations had become all that enlightened and egalitarian.[4]

This book has been influenced and enriched by the excellent feminist work on Weimar culture that was initiated by scholars like Atina Grossmann and Patrice Petro and continued by scholars such as Katharina von Ankum, Anke Gleber, Janet Ward, and Kerstin Barndt.[5] Most of this work has focused primarily on women in Weimar: women as the topic of much anxious discourse in the culture, but also women as artists and intellectuals who helped to produce, and as readers and spectators who responded to that culture. As von Ankum argues (*Women in the Metropolis,* 6), this focus on women does not mean that the volume she edited is "only" about women, given how much male projection and anxiety in Weimar culture dominated the public discourse on women. In this book I attempt to use an approach informed by such feminist scholarship and to apply it to the examination of both femininity and masculinity in Weimar culture, as constructed discursively in the culture generally, and as depicted in specific films and literary texts by both men and women, with attention to how such texts addressed and were received by men and women. The construction of both masculinity and femininity in a society are obviously interrelated—indeed, they represent "complementary" parts of one system—systems that vary from society to society but that have been generally oppressive and patriarchal, in my opinion.

The system of gender and sexuality in Weimar Germany was however under siege. The "shock of modernity" had placed traditional notions of gender in crisis, both male and female, and much attention was paid to both in that culture. In addition, things were complicated further by the new public attention in this period to what Magnus Hirschfeld (the famous German sexologist—and homosexual activist—of the era) called the "third sex," that is, to homosexuals. Thus it would seem that the binary division between what was clearly "masculine" and what was "feminine" was becoming especially blurred. This is precisely why one notes such a demand for clear boundaries and distinctions on the part of many Germans during this era—a demand that arguably led to a more brutal "clarity" on these issues in the Third Reich.

Therefore I want to make a point of affirming as emancipatory the blurring of fixed gender and sexual identities—not just to take a position that is now much more acceptable, but because the enmity to such blurring seems to me clearly connected to the crimes of the Third Reich. In this I differ with more canonical interpretations of Weimar "decadence": in my opinion what ought to be celebrated includes precisely that which has been derided as decadence and "effeminate weakness" by many writers on the left—work in the postwar era on Weimar culture by Peter Gay and by Siegfried Kracauer come to mind.[6] Alexander and Margarethe Mitscherlich's discussions of mourning and the postwar family in West Germany are also in the same tradition. In many ways they seem to blame the rise of fascism on the weakening of the bourgeois family and the ascendance of a narcissistic personality type clearly related to "effeminacy" and male homosexuality; Andrew Hewitt has demonstrated persuasively about how this same conflation of homosexuality with fascism can also be found in the writings of Theodor Adorno.[7]

I disagree strongly with this interpretation both of Weimar culture and of "decadence." The comparison with the Third Reich is instructive, however, for in that regime "decadence" was denounced as biological degeneracy, a denunciation that was clearly connected not only to anti-Semitism but to misogyny and homophobia as well.[8] As opposed to the open anxieties about gender expressed in Weimar culture, Nazi misogyny was embodied in a cultural politics that had much less space for any acknowledgement of male weakness (except in submission to the state) or for any confusion on the part of either sex about "natural" gender roles—not to mention confusion about "race." It ought to be obvious today that this drive for clear boundaries and identities led only to barbarism.

In contrast, I want to emphasize again that what was most emancipatory about Weimar's crises of identity was precisely the blurring and confusion of traditional categories of identity. We find in Weimar culture a relatively open discussion of the hollowness—indeed, cynicism—of the masquerade that prescribed roles and identities seemed to demand. Here we find similarities between character types that otherwise seem very different—the "masculine" women intellectuals who hid behind a "feminine masquerade" (as discussed in Joan Riviere's famous 1929 essay), and the male intellectuals who assumed the mask of what Helmut Lethen calls the "cold persona" in order to conceal all human emotion and ("feminine") vulnerability. In both types of masquerade one notes an anxious attempt to conceal any deviation from traditional norms for gendered behavior. This anxiety in turn can be interpreted as a tacit admission of what Judith Butler has called the performativity of gender roles, a concept that involves the realization that there is no underlying "essence" to them at all: "If gender attributes and acts, the various ways in which a body shows or produces its cultural signification, are performative, then there is not a preexisting identity by which an act or attribute might be measured; there would be no true or false, real or distorted acts of gender, and the postulation of a true gender identity would be revealed as a regulatory fiction."[9]

Implicit in this insight into the emptiness lurking behind such regulatory fictions—or "masks"—is a powerful and terrifying threat to groups invested in brutally clear, "biological" identities according to racial, gender, and sexual categories. This threat is so powerful, indeed, that the slightest intimation of this threat by such groups may well have motivated and facilitated their seizure of power at the end of the Weimar Republic. Admitting this possibility, however, does not mean that such reactionary forces were "right" about culture and identity; nor are they right today.

"NEW OBJECTIVITY"

Given that many canonical pronouncements on Weimar culture have emphasized the importance of Expressionism—influential works such as Peter Gay's *Weimar Culture* and Lotte Eisner's art-historical study of Weimar cinema, *The Haunted Screen*—it is necessary to explain why I focus instead on a later cultural sensibility, that of the so-called New Objectivity (*Neue Sachlichkeit*). Gay, like others, considered New Objectivity to be of lesser importance (and misreads somehow as "The Revenge of the Fathers"), and Eisner considered it the beginning of a decline from the aesthetic heights of Expressionist art. Whereas Eisner may possibly have been right about aesthetic quality, Gay is wrong to consider Expressionism as the consummate art of the Weimar Republic, just as he is wrong to maintain that Weimar only liberated "what was already there" in Wilhelminian culture, that is, the culture of the late German Empire, which ended in 1918 at the end of World War I. New Objectivity—conceived broadly at any rate—is now the term used by many scholars (especially in Germany) to describe what is actually unique to the culture of the Weimar Republic, as opposed to Expressionism, which dominated the 1910s.[10] For me, that uniqueness is epitomized in a new openness to modernity and mass culture by artists and intellectuals that is in marked contrast to the disdain for modern civilization that typifies Expressionism. The latter was an artistic movement that began in German painting around 1905, became important in literature around 1910, flourished just before and during the war (especially in the theater), but by 1920 was nearly exhausted. Only then, when this once revolutionary aesthetic had begun to degenerate into a fashionable, decorative visual style, did it enter the cinema, and by 1924 it was pretty much over there, too.[11]

David Bathrick and Andreas Huyssen are probably right to assert that Expressionism was the essential German modernism, yet for this very reason it inspired the opposition of the avant-garde beginning with the Dadaists already during the war, who attacked it for its naive and elitist faith in the power of art and the artist and its distance from modern life. What characterizes the German avant-garde of the 1920s—from the Bauhaus to Brecht, from Heartfield to Höch—is this enmity to elitist, "auratic" art, and the attempt to create an art less separated from modern life, a more democratic art that learned from mass culture.[12] And these are tendencies that I would connect to the sensibility first labeled as New Objectivity in the mid-1920s, at the beginning of the (ultimately all too brief) "stabilized period" of the Weimar Republic.

On the other hand, of course, the New Objectivity and Expressionism were in many ways merely two sides of the same "coin," as it were—a rather undialectical shift from a romantic and idealistic inwardness to a somewhat forced "unsentimental," materialistic affirmation of the external surfaces of modernity—and it was a transition made by many artists and intellectuals of more or less the same generation. Furthermore, it is clear that to the extent that this move to "sober" New Objectivity was an attempt to come down from the idealist, anti-modern heights of "auratic" art to embrace modernity, the masses, and the metropolis, it was a move that was marked by ambivalence on the part of the intellectuals and artists who engaged in it. It is also true that this move can be seen as the attempt of an endangered social group, the intelligentsia, to find a niche for itself in the emerging modern society that preserved some of its former prestige and autonomy. It was also an attempt that largely failed. The book burning in May of 1933, soon after the end of the Republic, would provide the most visible demonstration of this failure.

Because of the diverse cultural and artistic media in which the New Objective sensibility can be shown to manifest itself—architecture, design, the graphic arts, photojournalism, painting, the theater, and literature, as well as film—and because of my interest in the broader social issues in Weimar culture that contextualize such manifestations (which in turn illuminate that larger social context), I have attempted to give this book a more interdisciplinary approach. In addition to the focus on film in this book, I have also chosen to discuss literary texts. In considering literature—a drama and two novels—in addition to four films, I certainly am not intending to cater to older academic prejudices about the subordination of film to the study of the literature.

The maintenance of such a clear division between "high" literary culture and "low," popular, visual culture is particularly inappropriate to the Weimar context, when film was being embraced as the form of mass culture most appropriate to the representation of modernity, and literary authors were, if anything, trying to imitate film precisely for that reason. What clearly characterizes New Objectivity and the avant-garde in Weimar is the attempt to subvert the boundaries between bourgeois high culture and modern mass culture; for this very reason the opponents of such "American" leveling found solace in the traditional dichotomy, identifying what was specifically "German" with high culture, valorizing literature and theater over film, as Adelheid von Saldern has noted (227–30). But the actual status of literature and film during Weimar was much more complicated than this or any simple dichotomy can express. Precisely because of the move by the literary avant-garde to approximate modern qualities ascribed to film, literature often was more democratic and/or revolutionary than the pompous, big-budget art films produced by a commercial film industry still seeking bourgeois approval.

Furthermore, taking this attack on the traditional distinction between high and mass culture seriously means looking at cultural texts without the prejudices that are based on that distinction. This involves examining how a text might have interacted with its audience in ways that may have been emancipatory precisely because the text was more accessible to a wider public. At the same time, one needs to be wary of any too facile valorization of a text merely because it was popular (which maintains the high/low distinction at the same time it turns it on its head). Here too feminist work in cultural studies generally and on Weimar culture specifically has been pioneering, and this book is intended to carry on a dialogue with that work, as it has been developed by scholars like Petro, Gleber, and Barndt.[13]

FILM, LITERATURE, AND GERMAN STUDIES

I was lying in bed—actually I had still wanted to wash my feet, but I was too tired because of the evening I'd just had, even though I had just told Therese, "It never comes to anything to let yourself be approached on the street, and you have to have some respect for yourself anyway."

—Irmgard Keun, 5[14]

The above quote is taken from the very beginning of Irmgard Keun's 1932 novel, *The Artificial Silk Girl* (*Das kunstseidene Mädchen*), in which the first-person narrator Doris is supposedly writing in her diary about allowing a man to speak to her on the street and then going out with him, even though she knows that it is rarely worth it. The subsequent passage demonstrates that this time, too, it turns out to have been a waste of time.

Something quite similar happens at the very beginning of the 1929 silent film *People on Sunday* (*Menschen am Sonntag*).[15] As soon as the credit sequence ends, the film shows a Berlin street scene on a Saturday afternoon. In the midst of this documentary scene, one notices a young man and young woman near the subway entrance of the Zoo Station on Berlin's fashionable West End. After slowly circling about the dark-haired young woman, the young man finally speaks to her, and the young woman, who does not know him, goes off with him to an outside café, where they make a date to go to the beach together the next morning. On that date, the young woman learns more or less the same lesson that Keun's Doris knows: that allowing oneself to be approached by a man on the street is rarely worth the trouble.

Thus this brief scene from a 1929 film and the short passage from a 1932 novel are in a sense (unwitting) intertexts of each other. Each of the texts—both the film and the novel—cites a common behavior that alludes to other broader social and cultural discourses in late Weimar Germany about the supposedly emancipated sexual morals of young people, especially young single women of the white-collar work force. The fact that such citations of social discourses indicate a historical context important for understanding their functioning within each text does not mean that such citations are mere transparent reflections of some external social realities, or that each citation is some kind of positive "fact" that does not require interpretation within the context of the literary or cinematic text in which it operates. In fact, the two texts deploy similar discourses about the so-called "New Woman" of the Weimar Republic to very different ends: the film depicts two young women as somewhat naive victims of a womanizing salesman, whereas the novel presents the perspective of a female protagonist whose conscious strategy is to use her sexuality to get ahead, and while the limitations of this strategy become clear, Doris reflects on her exploits with self-irony, humor, and lots of insight into the social injustice of the class and gender hierarchy that restricts her options.

The tension between grounding elements of a text, be it cinematic or literary, within a social-historical context, and analyzing their operation within the text itself is, in my opinion, one of the structuring tensions of German studies as a subset of cultural studies. This necessary tension is also crucial to what I am attempting to do in this book. One might define German studies as an interdisciplinary endeavor that combines methods of textual analysis developed in literary and film studies with the kind of attention to social and cultural context more characteristic of the fields of history, sociology, or anthropology; it is an endeavor that attempts variously to overcome but also to mobilize contradictions inherent in the divisions between the humanities and the social sciences. Film and modern visual culture in general are necessary topics of investigation for German studies,

but not in order to abandon the study of literature. Just as German literature ought no longer to be studied as the crucial aesthetic and philosophical expression of a national culture, as in traditional *Germanistik,* neither
will the cinema be studied as a high art or as a formal system that tran-
scends political, economic, and cultural determinations at regional,
national, and international levels. This, too, is why I find it productive to
juxtapose literary texts and film texts against a common historical context:
not to read them solely against exclusive aesthetic traditions, or as transparent reflections of some more crucial social reality, but rather to see them as
related but distinct articulations of overlapping and often contradictory
cultural discourses.

In the issue of *New German Critique* devoted to "Cultural History and
Cultural Studies," Anton Kaes writes: "I never perceived the study of cinema to oppose or negate the study of literature. Instead, I embraced film as
a new and exciting area of inquiry that, in the wake of the semiotic revolution, allowed me to read *all* cultural products as texts. Although semiotics
provided a novel theoretical framework for analyzing the 'language' of film,
I never fully subscribed to the scientific terminology which permitted an
ostensibly objective analysis, untouched by history and interpretation. In
fact, I soon became skeptical about the uncritical and facile application of
the 'linguistic turn' to film analysis" (48). He goes on to specify how he
turned to "various models within the German tradition," such as the
Brechtian model, but also those associated with members of the Frankfurt
School: Horkheimer and Adorno, Benjamin, and of course Kracauer
(48–49). The latter's seminal study of Weimar cinema, *From Caligari to
Hitler,* became the "master narrative for the critical study of film within a
national context"; for all its faults, Kaes still finds it significant: "Although
we rejected Kracauer's claims about 'the' Germans, we were convinced by
his basic premise that films must not be separated from their political,
social, and cultural habitat. We learned that films signify something not *in
abstracto,* but concretely at a certain moment in time, at a certain place, and
for a certain audience. They offer responses to burning questions; they are
meant to resonate and have an impact" (49).

But this attention to the social contexts within which texts originate
and operate must be combined with careful attention to the texts themselves. In their introduction to the same special issue on "Cultural History
and Cultural Studies," the editors John Czaplicka, Andreas Huyssen, and
Anson Rabinbach warn of the danger that " . . . [t]he focus on context will
dissolve the text which no longer even has to be read carefully" (6). Close
textual analysis—not mere *textimmanent* or New Critical interpretation, but

rather informed by semiotic and deconstructionist approaches as well—is just as crucial to the project of German studies, and indeed, it is the skill that German departments are most qualified to teach, even as they move away from traditional *Germanistik*. The sensitive analysis of texts is one of the special contributions of the humanities to the project of interdisciplinary cultural studies.

But obviously any textual analysis implies some acknowledged or unacknowledged context into which the text is being placed for interpretation. The text/context tension is one that is both unavoidable and necessary, and it is this type of productive tension or contradiction that Teresa de Lauretis wrote was fundamental to feminism (*Technologies*, 26), with its insistence on the interconnections between the personal and the political, the subjective and the social, the psychoanalytical and the historical.[16] These interconnections are themselves fraught with tensions—for instance, between the tendency in some psychoanalytical work to make ahistorical generalizations with insufficient social and cultural specificity, and the tendency of much historical research to avoid the emotional, erotic, personal, and psychological implications of events in favor of "harder" aspects and "facts" viewed somehow as more "political." But these tensions and contradictions are productive when they are confronted, as opposed to being evaded by any too facile "victory" of one side over the other.[17]

IDENTITIES IN CRISIS

The films and literary works I have chosen to discuss in depth in this book come from the transitional periods at both ends of Weimar's "stabilized period" (1924–1929), with which New Objectivity is most often identified. I do discuss texts clearly identified with the stabilized period proper—films such as Walther Ruttmann's *Berlin, Symphony of a City* (*Berlin, Symphonie einer Großstadt,* 1927) and G.W. Pabst's *Pandora's Box* (*Büchse der Pandora,* 1929), for instance—but the texts I examine in the most depth are from the early stabilized period (1924–1926) and then from 1930 on. As far as literature is concerned, some of the most famous novels typically classified as part of the New Objectivity in fact appeared after 1929, documenting the social, economic, and political malaise from 1930 to 1933, the last years of the Republic. During these transitional periods, the class and gender dynamics of New Objectivity—and the perception of crisis—were especially transparent: that is, in the first few years of the stabilized period (which began in late 1923), which is also when the new post-Expressionist sensibility first emerges most clearly; and then again at the end of the

Republic, when the global depression that begins in late 1929 destroys economic stability, political polarization increases, and the accommodation of many groups with the Republic is upset. Once again middle-class intellectuals found themselves in a very precarious position, as did many others, including the "new class" of white-collar employees that had become so influential during the 1920s (a class that downwardly mobile intellectuals often were forced to join).

The texts I analyze in detail here were all well known during the Weimar Republic, and most of them were popular as well as critical successes, thus successfully negotiating the high/low split in a manner fully in harmony with the goals of New Objectivity and the avant-garde's attempt to play a role in the creation of a democratic popular culture. Except for Josef von Sternberg's film *The Blue Angel* (1930) and Leontine Sagan's film *Mädchen in Uniform* (1931), none of the texts explored here are very familiar to English speakers today, but most of them achieved some fame in England and North America in their day. E.A. Dupont's film *Variety* (1925) as well as *The Blue Angel* and *Mädchen in Uniform* were box office hits in the United States as well as in Germany. Erich Kästner's novel *Fabian* (1931), Irmgard Keun's novel *The Artificial Silk Girl* (*Das kunstseidene Mädchen*, 1932), and even Ernst Toller's very controversial drama *Hinkemann* (1924) were all translated into English.[18] G.W. Pabst's film *Secrets of a Soul* (1926) was certainly a critical success in Germany.

After this introductory chapter, the next two chapters attempt to sketch out the broader social contexts within Weimar culture into which the texts discussed in this book must be placed. Chapter 2 focuses on the famous crisis of male subjectivity that prevailed throughout Weimar culture, demonstrating that this crisis cannot be understood without taking into account the experiences of women and various debates about femininity in Weimar, and providing the socio-historical and psychosexual contexts that help to explain both this generalized crisis of gendered identity as well as its articulation in many of the most famous films produced in Weimar Germany. Chapter 3 examines in greater depth the cultural sensibility labeled New Objectivity in terms of its specific manifestations in literature and film, its relation to the broader crisis of gender and sexual identity in Weimar, and the extent to which it reflected the strategies adopted by mostly male middle-class intellectuals in their attempts to accommodate themselves with the ideal of mass democracy. The Weimar Republic never achieved that ideal, but imperfect as it was, it was a society in which traditional social, gender, and sexual identities were under strain, and New Objectivity can be understood as a means by which those intellectuals attempted to adjust to these strains—by accepting them, sometimes even celebrating them, but also by trying to control and contain them.

The rest of the book is devoted to in-depth readings of individual texts. Chapter 4 looks at male crisis specifically, both in its misogynistic articulations and in its potentially emancipatory acknowledgement of male weakness and of gender destabilization in modernity—topics that were bound to address women as well as men. In it I discuss the overt thematizations of male crisis in *Hinkemann, Variety,* and *Secrets of a Soul.* Chapter 5, and the texts analyzed in it, *Fabian* and *The Blue Angel,* focus as much on the "new" women who supposedly cause the crisis as on the male protagonists. The sexual (and textual) ambiguity of the situation in *The Blue Angel,* at any rate, creates a text that does much more than merely exemplify traditional male anxiety. In Chapter 6, the modern crisis of gender and sexual identity is examined from the perspectives of two texts by women artists: the novel *The Artificial Silk Girl* by Irmgard Keun and the film *Mädchen in Uniform* by stage and film director Leontine Sagan.

The title of Chapter 6, "Girls in Crisis," alludes to Kracauer's famous essay, "Girls and Crisis" (1931), and to the use of the English word "girl" in Weimar Germany, most notably in the context of Americanism and "Girlkultur." But of course not just "girls," but "boys" too were in crisis, as so many studies devoted to "male subjectivity" have demonstrated. I hope to show how the identity problems of both men and women were part of a single larger crisis in Weimar Germany—not just the economic and political turmoil of the Republic's last years, but the overall crisis of culture and identity so important to the outlook of so many intellectuals and artists of these years. That crisis is ultimately the crisis of modernity—and modernization—itself, with both emancipatory and destructive elements, a crisis that has by no means been resolved up to the present day.

But I want to stress again that there is a need to celebrate the emancipatory aspects, especially those emancipatory, indeed utopian moments of "polymorphous perversity" in Weimar culture—an emancipatory "queerness," if you will, that still fascinates us to this day. I use this term not just to imply a questioning of traditional norms with regard to gender and sexuality, but also to imply a contestation of fixed categories and identities that must be seen as crucial to the project of radical democratic politics.[19] This, I would insist, is a project important for people of all identities. What better legacy from the Weimar Republic can we salvage as we face the new millenium?

Chapter 2 ❧

From *Caligari* to Dietrich: Anxieties About Sex and Gender in Weimar Cinema and Culture[1]

What we need is not a mush, but a solid block. In mush we will sink, with a block victory and reconstruction will be a trifle . . . . We will become a block when the iron clamp of our world-view presses us together, and in its embrace everything soft and fluid will congeal into stone and fuse together. Whoever might hinder us on the way will have to step aside or allow himself to be melted down.

—Alfred Hugenberg, 1928[2]

MALE FANTASIES/FEMALE REALITIES

Only a year after Alfred Hugenberg made the above statement, Josef Von Sternberg left Hollywood and traveled to Berlin in order to direct one of Germany's first major sound films for its largest film company, "Ufa" (Universum-Film Aktiengesellschaft, or "Universe Film, Inc."), which Hugenberg owned. The film was *The Blue Angel,* certainly one of the most famous films associated with Germany's Weimar Republic (1918–1933). Hugenberg, who had rescued Ufa from bankruptcy in 1927, was a publishing magnate and an ultra-conservative ally of the Nazis in the period leading up to 1933, when Hitler became chancellor, and the Weimar Republic ended.

The Blue Angel, like the other films made in Germany between 1918 and 1933, must be understood in relation to a historical context defined both by developments in cinematic form and by sexual and social anxieties pervasive in the culture of the Weimar Republic. These anxieties are quite obvious in the language of Hugenberg's statement: an aversion to division, plurality, and especially to the "soft and fluid," and the longing for a monolithic fusion that results in the solidity of iron and stone. This language is easy to read psychoanalytically—fear of the female, fear of flaccidity, desire for a mythical phallic rigidity, combined with a somewhat "feminine"—or homoerotic—desire for fusion.[3] Such anxious desires are typical of the far right during the Weimar Republic, as Klaus Theweleit demonstrates with text after text in *Male Fantasies,* his exhaustive psychoanalytical study of German fascist texts in all their perverse misogyny; the very choice of negative images in Hugenberg's language is typical of what Theweleit found: "fluidity" and "mush."[4]

But misogyny was not limited to the right wing. The Dadaists were cultural anarchists whose attack on bourgeois art and literature was aligned with the Left in Germany. In an attempt to define Dada about ten years before Hugenberg's statement, a Dadaist manifesto proclaimed: "The sexual criminal Alton was a dadaist when he wrote in his diary: Killed today a young girl, it was fine and hot . . ." (Sloterdijk, 720). For the Dadaists—and the young playwright Bertolt Brecht—such citations of sexual brutality were meant largely to shock bourgeois morality and sentimentality. In contrast, on the far right wing of the political spectrum, Hugenberg intended to forge nationalists, anti-Semites, the military caste, and other reactionary groups into a solid block, an "iron front." As different as these projects were, they manifest a remarkably similar revulsion for anything perceived as soft or sentimental. Hugengerg's formulation barely disguises male fears of being "feminine," and the Dadaist manifesto denies that fear by embodying the scorned sentimentality in the corpse of a woman.

The misogynistic discourses of the Weimar Republic may well be anchored in what psychoanalysis would consider relatively "timeless" male anxieties about women; such discourses are nonetheless also related to a social reality specific to Germany between 1918 and 1933. As Patrice Petro has written: "The growing visibility of *women* in Weimar in fact goes a long way to explain the defensive reaction toward *woman* in the discourse of artists and intellectuals . . ." ("Modernity," 141). The constitution of the Weimar Republic not only was Germany's first democratic constitution; it also offered German women the promise of complete legal equality for the first time in history (a promise that has yet to be added to the U.S. Constitution). Although that promise was not in fact fulfilled, Weimar society was characterized by the emergence of a "New Woman" who exercised unprecedented forms of social and sexual autonomy. At the same time there was also a German women's movement debating new and traditional models of female identity. The women's movement in Germany had for years been divided into bourgeois and socialist factions, and by this point it was in something of a decline. But it was still influential, having been well established since the end of the nineteenth century.

The Weimar Republic has long been famous for the existence of relatively open lesbian and gay subcultures with their bars and coffeehouses in many of its large cities, especially Berlin.[5] There were also very visible political struggles aimed at repealing laws against abortion and homosexuality. Because such struggles are even now being waged in many countries, including the United States, Weimar culture is of more than mere academic interest today.

These political battles about gender and sexuality help to explain the psychological anxieties so prevalent in Weimar culture—anxieties that were quite overtly thematized in the cinema, an especially dominant form of popular culture during the 1920s. That the fears and fantasies of men were set into play by many films is not surprising, given the dominance of the male perspective in so much cinema, and the role that the cinema has come to play in discourse about gender and sexuality. Weimar cinema is interesting precisely for the openness with which anxious male fantasies are depicted, and many films can easily be interpreted in terms of them. These anxieties, however, should not be examined without reference to social realities—especially the increased visibility and agency of women in Weimar.

Nor can the films ultimately be understood without taking into account the actual presence of women in the cinemas as spectators—they too must have reacted to films that thematized destabilized gender roles, no matter how patriarchally determined the ideology underlying most of the films may have been. And their responses must necessarily have differed in some ways from men's, given the positioning of women in Weimar society. This chapter attempts not only to illustrate the male fantasies at work in a number of important Weimar films, but also to go beyond that focus on the male psyche by demonstrating the social and political dimension of such fantasies as well as the stakes for women involved in their deployment.

FEMINIST FILM THEORY AND WEIMAR CINEMA

Given the complex intersection of social realities and psychosexual anxieties in Weimar cinema, the study of its films demands an approach that is both historical and psychoanalytical. Weimar culture in general represents a field of study in which the benefits of bringing together the "political" and the "personal," the social and the psychological, are especially clear. This is a particularly feminist fusion of approaches that can be noted in a number of studies of the cinema.[6] However, as I stated in the introduction, there are often tensions between more psychoanalytically and more social-historically oriented approaches, the former tending at times toward ahistorical, universalizing generalizations and the latter ignoring whole realms of human experience (personal, emotional, erotic) in their preference for "harder" facts that supposedly have more political weight and substance. My intention is to try to combine the two approaches in a manner that uses such tensions productively, remaining aware of the pitfalls of each approach and attempting to avoid both types of errors.[7]

And from the perspective of feminist film theory, Weimar cinema is indeed fascinating. Not only was it often strikingly misogynistic, but many of its films openly call attention to phenomena like looking, voyeurism, the objectification of the female, and the castration anxiety of the male—topics of crucial concern in psychoanalytical feminist film theory. Castration anxiety—the psychoanalytical explanation for misogyny, the "dread of woman"—is the main danger the male spectator risks by gazing voyeuristically at the female image. It is this anxiety that "classical" narrative cinema (usually defined as the Hollywood studio film of the 1930s and 1940s) must work to repress in order to remain pleasurable for men, according to Laura Mulvey's famous 1975 essay "Visual Pleasure and Narrative Cinema." In contrast, the foregrounding of looking and voyeurism in many Weimar films brings with it the risk that the male spectator might get "caught looking" and thus become self-conscious about his voyeurism (which hinders its enjoyment). Castration anxiety is overtly thematized in many Weimar film narratives. Beyond this, the films contain as well a certain amount of sexual objectification of the *male* (which can be read as a function either of homoeroticism, of heterosexual male paranoia, of an address to heterosexual female viewers—or all of the above).

In Germany a film industry developed in the 1910s and 1920s with a stylistic repertoire distinct from the Hollywood cinema (where what film scholars call the "classical" model would not be completely consolidated until the sound film had been developed in the late 1920s and early 1930s). In the late 1910s the German film industry attempted in a few art film productions to adapt theatrical Expressionism for the cinema, most famously with the distorted sets of Robert Wiene's 1919 production of *The Cabinet of Dr. Caligari*. While the expressionist or "fantastic" phase of German cinema—characteristic of only a small but influential sector of German film production—gave way to a more realistic cinema by the mid-1920s, even this more realistic phase must be distinguished stylistically from the American cinema. Settings were more often contemporary, and the influence of

Hollywood comedies and melodramas was strong, but the German cinema was typified by frequent use of mobile camera, subjective camera shots (shots from a particular character's perspective, often a distorted perspective), noticeable, foregrounded editing, and the use of lighting to create expressive patterns of light and shadow (the chiaroscuro effect developed in the Expressionist phase).[8] The American cinema in contrast was much more reticent with "showy" lighting, editing, and camera work, preferring to keep technical virtuosity relatively "invisible," subordinated for the most part to a compelling narrative.

Yet the German cinema nonetheless exerted a tremendous influence on subsequent American cinema, due in large part to the work done in Hollywood from the 1920s into the 1950s by German émigrés like Ernst Lubitsch, F.W. Murnau, Fritz Lang, Douglas Sirk, Billy Wilder, Robert Siodmak, and William Dieterle; even the British filmmaker Alfred Hitchcock worked in Germany for awhile in the 1920s. American "film noir" is the style most obviously indebted to German cinema. In historical terms, the systems of editing and (especially) camera work that set up the gazes analyzed by feminist film theory were still being developed in the 1920s, and different developments in both Hollywood and Germany would eventually become part of the dominant, "classical" style of mainstream cinema studied by film scholars.

But the sexual politics—and misogyny—in the Weimar cinema were not merely matters of cinematic style in relation to some kind of "timeless" male psyche. Misogyny may be timeless enough, but in Germany during the 1920s social forces were in conflict about issues specific to the new role of women in German society. The relation of cinematic text to social reality is by no means simple or transparent reflection. But this does not mean that the two are unrelated; rather there is no neat way to separate them. As Teresa de Lauretis writes, "the *context* of cinema . . . is not only a discursive context or a textual co-text . . . it is the context of social practice, that human action which cinema articulates from both sides of the screen, so to speak, for both filmmakers and spectators as subjects in history" (*Alice Doesn't,* 52).[9]

Women's new political equality in the Weimar Republic was only the latest of recent gains: permitted to attend universities only in 1908, German women expanded their participation in the labor market during World War I. And the new art of the century, the cinema, depended not only on the visibility of women as actors on the screen but on their presence in front of the screen; in Germany they made up the "major audience" for the cinema (Bridenthal et al., 13; Petro, *Joyless Streets,* 8)—a presence that was from the beginning seen as subversive from the perspective of the upper classes (especially to upper-class men).[10] In the turbulent economic, political, and social chaos of the Weimar Republic, emancipated women (often grouped together in the image of the so-called New Woman) were blamed for social instability, especially by anti-democratic forces on the right, who also blamed socialists, Jews, and other groups who played new and more prominent roles in the republic. All of these groups were scapegoated as "other" in keeping with ominous ideological and psychological tendencies that would become all too clear after the Nazis came to power in 1933. The right-wing myth that helped to coalesce these tendencies was born with the Weimar Republic itself: the *Dolchstoßlegende,* the legend of the "stab in the back," according to which Imperial Germany had been humbled in World War I not on the battlefield, but on the home front by the enemy within—that is, by socialists, Jews, and women (and implicitly by other "others" such as homosexuals).

MALE ANXIETY IN THE POLITICAL AND LITERARY CULTURE OF WEIMAR

Salome, Ruth, Esther—she's standing half a story up the stairs from him. The tight skirt tucked in, her left hand on her hip, her right hand brandishing a pistol. The woman who had lured them up there with her shouting and crying. . . .

—Friedrich Ekkehard, *Sturmgeschlecht,* 1941,
ctd. in Theweleit, 87 (my translation)

This is a passage from one of the later pulp novels glorifying the Freikorps, the right-wing soldiers who put down proletarian uprisings in Germany after World War I. It depicts a confrontation between a soldier and a so-called "Flintenweib," a proletarian "rifle-woman" (here bearing only a pistol), during street fighting in Berlin in 1919. Theweleit cites the passage because it combines a number of associations typical of the Freikorps mentality. First, the woman in the tight skirt is both seductive and threatening: this is the mythical "red whore" typical of this literature, a trope in which communism and threatening sexuality are combined. The woman also carries a pistol, another instance of the recurring image Theweleit analyzes as "the woman with the penis" who is perceived to threaten the soldiers with injury, dismemberment, castration. Finally, the woman here is compared with beautiful Jewish women in the Bible: Esther, Ruth, and the infamous Salome, who demanded the head of John the Baptist. Communism, the working class, "unleashed" female sexuality, and the Jews: all the elements the fascists considered a part of a conspiracy against the German "fatherland" are here embodied in one image, a fusion of political and psychological discourses that activate castration anxiety (Theweleit, 87).[11]

One might even label the male anxieties in Weimar culture a "discourse of castration." I mean this term in a broad, evocative, even hyperbolic sense, figuratively and not literally, in order to specify a complex of anxieties around loss of power, control, and mastery—ultimately issues of social, political, and economic power, not sexuality, yet often as not discursively represented as a type of castration. What do these mainly social anxieties have to do with men's sexual fears? In them sexual potency and sexual identity are confused with power over women and social power in general (the power over anyone seen as "less" than masculine). Related to this confusion is the tendency to blame women for any lack of social power experienced by men.

Male attitudes about issues of power in Weimar were not only determined by centuries of patriarchal social relations. Anxieties were triggered by economic, social, and political modernization in Germany and other nations of the West. The supposed autonomy of the individual—so central to Western ideology since the enlightenment—was increasingly threatened by industrialization, technology, and warfare in the early twentieth century. The traditional order and the individual's fixed sense of identity became de-stabilized, unleashing a new fluidity that inspired both fear and desire— fear of the new and uncertain, and desire for liberation from traditional norms. The Dadaists at the end of the World War I celebrated the new chaos, recommending in a 1918 manifesto "letting oneself be tossed about by things" (Sloterdijk, 716). In the Weimar Republic, however, the dominant attitude to this modern chaos involved the (desperate) attempt to maintain distance and autonomy (see Lethen, *Verhaltenslehren*, e.g., 133–36). What was in crisis was a primarily bourgeois conception of the subject, and the autonomy supposedly crucial to that conception was clearly understood as proper to men only. Changing gender roles in modern society were obviously a part of the perceived threat.

Male "castration" anxieties, in psychological and social terms, are obviously not unique to Weimar Germany, but they were bound up with a specific crisis of modernization that was distinctly the product of German political history. Women represented one of the groups most marginal, most archetypally "other," to a German national identity understood traditionally in authoritarian (and patriarchal) terms. Male resentment of women in Germany at this time can be connected to a more widespread "crisis of male subjectivity" in the aftermath of Germany's defeat in World War I.[12] German economic power and military strength had clearly been diminished. Forces on the right—monarchists, nationalists, militarists—perceived the nation as weakened by the defeat of German army, the abdication of the Kaiser (which ended the monarchy), and the establishment of a democratic republic. The political hegemony of the Prussian aristocratic-military caste was no longer sanctioned in law: socialists and other formerly marginalized groups enjoyed new influence; suffrage and equal rights were granted to all—including women.

Women's status had been changing due both to modernization and to feminist political agitation since the middle of the nineteenth century. The move by women into new segments of the work force during the war was unprecedented—and perceived as threatening by many men, even though most women lost these jobs at the end of the war. Because of the rights granted by the Weimar Republic's constitution, the Republic was known (and hated by anti-democratic forces) for female emancipation and other democratic and egalitarian reforms—although what was actually accomplished along these lines never lived up to the promises and hopes associated with the birth of the Republic.[13]

As if this was not bad enough from the traditionalist viewpoint, from 1918 into the early 1920s there were uprisings associated with the Communist left in Germany.[14] Meanwhile the Treaty of Versailles that set the terms for peace after World War I forced Germany to make financial reparations to the victors that were not only humiliating but burdened the already weakened economy dangerously. This situation was especially humiliating to the anti-democratic right in Germany: in a typical right-wing novel about the First World War, Franz Schauwecker's *Aufbruch der Nation* (1929), the hero considered the German surrender to be the self-castration of the nation (ctd. in Sloterdijk, 758). Even after the postwar chaos—revolution, counter-revolution, hyper-inflation—had been "stabilized," the authoritarian Right still felt humiliated and had by no means given up the hope of re-establishing the traditional order.

But a discourse of castration did not only operate in the fascist imagination; it is evident in literature produced by many writers associated with the left, which felt impotent after the revolutionary hopes of 1918 were dashed. For these hopes had been destroyed not only by the bloody activities of the right-wing Freikorps, but also by the Social Democrats, who first led the new republic and were willing to ally with the Right—indeed, to use the Freikorps—in order to put down proletarian uprisings. This willingness to work with the right showed the limits of the reforms the

Social Democrats were planning to undertake at the head of the new state. In addition, the right wing was not appeased by this Social Democratic cooperation; it continued to despise the Social Democrats and the republic. Far-right, Freikorps-allied attempts to overturn the republic included the "Kapp Putsch" in 1920 and Hitler's "beer-hall putsch" of 1923.[15]

Thus there were feelings of "emasculation" on the left as well. Ernst Toller, a leftist writer who was himself imprisoned for revolutionary activity in 1919, wrote some of the most poignant stage dramas exploring resignation and disillusionment on the German left. His 1924 play *Hinkemann* presents an honest—and literal—example of a discourse of castration, universalized to address the dilemma not of the revolutionary but of the returning veteran. It tells the story of a muscular working-class veteran whose wartime injury left him literally castrated. He is unable to find work except as a strong man and "geek" in a carnival sideshow: besides showing off his muscles he must kill rats by biting into their throats. To make the humiliation complete, his wife betrays him with another man.[16]

Hinkemann addresses typical anxieties of returning soldiers after World War I. A certain resentment of the homefront is probably understandable on the part of soldiers in any war, and combined with personal fears about possible spousal betrayal and more general fears about social changes with regard to gender roles, the potential for some virulent misogyny was created (see, e.g., Tatar, 11–13). Women had opportunities to exercise more economic and sexual autonomy during the war, and thus men's social and sexual anxieties had some actual basis in reality. But such fears of a figural "castration" had little connection to the danger of *actual dismemberment* modern soldiers face in war. Certainly women had little to do with that danger, which was primarily a function of military violence and technology.

The motif of male defeat was often coupled with sexual violence and brutal revenge against women: in Alfred Döblin's 1929 novel *Berlin Alexanderplatz* one finds a lower-class protagonist, Franz Biberkopf, who is depicted as regaining his self-esteem after release from prison by raping the sister of the woman he had murdered (Döblin, 29–34). This is only the beginning of a modernist "classic" obsessed with a lower-class milieu of pimps and criminals, where women seem to function only as brutalized objects of sexual exchange.[17] In Erich Kästner's *Fabian* (1931), the demoralizing chaos of late Weimar society is depicted again and again in terms of an aggressive and depraved female sexuality "out of control" (especially in the character of Irene Moll).[18]

This discourse of lost control and lost mastery was not just a male fantasy; it does bear some relation, however distorted, to social reality—specifically to the increasing emancipation and autonomy being exercised by many women. While some working-class women had always worked outside the home, few middle-class women had done so until recently. The opening of German universities to women in 1908 and the growing presence of women employees in the so-called "new class" of office workers presented a new threat to the bourgeois belief that proper women belonged in the home. Although most women worked in other sectors of the work force, women's employment was growing most rapidly among white-collar workers (Mason, 80–81). The new, white-collar class in and of itself blurred traditional gender roles in ways that even much of the left found threatening, given its romanticization of a muscular, vital, proletarian masculinity, and its invocation of a suffering, maternal—and constantly pregnant—working-class femininity.[19] The appearance of a certain modern androgyny is understandable in the new white-collar work sphere, in which traditional sex roles had precious little to do with the kind of work to be done.[20]

In any case, the mythical New Woman of the 1920s had a real counterpart who was most likely to be found doing office work (Petro, 109–110). But she could also be seen elsewhere in Weimar society. She was not just a convention of political, literary, or journalistic discourse, as historians Renate Bridenthal, Atina Grossman, and Marion Kaplan asserted: "The 'new women'—who voted, used contraception, obtained illegal abortions, and earned wages—were more than a bohemian minority or an artistic convention. They existed in office and factory, bedroom and kitchen, just as surely as—and more significantly than—in cafe and cabaret. . . . And it was this 'new woman' who was to become a symbol of degeneracy and modern 'asphalt culture' in Nazi propaganda" (Bridenthal et al., 11).[21]

Fascist propaganda against this New Woman was linked to the campaign against what the Nazis called "Marxist, Jewish, cosmopolitan women's rights advocates" (Bridenthal et al., 18). In spite of this linkage, however, German feminists were not necessarily positively disposed to the "New Women." Associated with the androgynous look of women's fashions in the 1920s, younger working women were considered by older, conservative feminists to be "masculinized" and unnatural; their attachment to fashion and modern consumer culture made them suspect to socialist feminists.[22] But in the German fascist imagination, all such distinctions between factions of feminists and between older feminists and emancipated younger women were meaningless. All independent-minded women were collapsed into one generalized image to be attacked. This misogynistic strategy was combined with anti-Semitism and anti-Marxism in the construction of a monolithic "other" that threatened the "fatherland."

The propaganda that originated out of such fascist paranoia both reflected and mobilized generalized male fears about the new role of women. Related sources of male paranoia to be tapped included the campaigns during the 1920s to repeal laws that prohibited abortion and homosexuality as well as the relatively open lesbian and gay subculture in Berlin and other large cities.

MALE FANTASIES IN WEIMAR CINEMA

In the way writers have often referred to a collective "German psyche," as Kracauer did in his famous book *From Caligari to Hitler,* they have meant a predominantly male consciousness (or unconscious). That male psyche, as we have seen, was haunted by paranoia that a conspiracy of "others"— women, socialists, Jews, homosexuals, foreigners—had humiliated the German "fatherland" and were hindering efforts to resurrect its power. Equating German national identity with manhood, this collective male consciousness was obsessed with the supposed loss of male power and authority. And this obsession can be found throughout Weimar cinema, as I will attempt to demonstrate here by focusing on specifically cinematic manifestations of these discourses in a number of the most famous German films of the Weimar Republic.

The cinematic depiction of male fears with regard to women, traditional gender roles, and male sexual identity undergoes a significant change in Weimar, at least if one focuses on its most famous art films. The depicted source of these fears moves "from Caligari to Dietrich," from vampire to vamp, or from feminized monster to "phallic woman."[23] In *The Cabinet of Dr. Caligari* (1920), the most famous German Expressionist film, Dr. Caligari (portrayed by Werner Krauss) is an evil hypnotist who has the young man Cesare (a "somnambulist" portrayed by Conrad Veidt) in his power (see Figure 2.1). At one point in the film, Cesare breaks into the bedroom of the film's female protagonist, Jane. Instead of killing her (as his master Caligari apparently has ordered), he carries her away. Cesare, a slender, feminized young man in black tights, seems at this point to exceed his identity as Caligari's "tool," overcome by his own desire for Jane. This is an anarchic moment in the film at which the three elements—woman, desire, and the "monster"—come together to threaten not only the stable order symbolized by the bourgeois home guarded by Jane's father but even the evil

Figure 2.1　Dr. Caligari exposes his "secret" to Jane: Werner Krauss as Caligari, Conrad Veidt as Cesare, Lil Dagover as Jane in Robert Wiene's *The Cabinet of Dr. Caligari* (1920).
Photo courtesy of Film Museum Berlin.

authority exerted by Caligari. This anarchic moment of desire detaches Cesare completely from all authority—even that of his master Caligari. Petro thus reads him as an embodiment of female desire—that is, as a double for Jane, not for the villain Caligari or the male protagonist, Francis (*Joyless Streets,* 147–49).

The same elements appear in a much less complicated relationship in a later, more popular Expressionist film: *Nosferatu,* F.W. Murnau's 1922 adaptation of Bram Stoker's *Dracula*. In the film the ineffectual male protagonist Jonathan is sent on business from his native Bremen to Transylvania in order to meet Nosferatu, who, unbeknownst to Jonathan, is a vampire. The encounter with Jonathan causes Nosferatu to travel to Bremen, bringing the bubonic plague with him. The city is saved from the vampire and the plague only by the sacrifice of a "pure woman": Nina, Jonathan's wife.[24] Nosferatu, lord of the land of phantoms, is associated with a variety of technical tricks that call attention to the cinematic medium: speeding up the action, switching the photographic image from positive to negative, and creating the illusion of movement on the part of inanimate objects. Nos-

feratu looks much more like a monster than Cesare, but he too is feminized. His face, posture, and demeanor also create a rather obvious anti-
Semitic caricature.[25] If this is interpreted to mean that a feminized Jew
brings a plague from the East to Germany, the monster can easily be read in
terms of the typical fascist association of Judaism with Bolshevism, an eastern "disease" of great concern to the German right in the 1920s. There is a
gendered aspect to this Jewish/Bolshevik threat, for the monster and his
plague come beckoned by the desire of a woman.[26] Not only does Nosferatu have a vision of Nina while still in Transylvania that makes him desire
her, but Nina seems to desire him too, long before he arrives in Bremen.

In his castle in Transylvania, Nosferatu is just about to attack Jonathan
when he has a vision of Nina. The vampire then spares Jonathan and goes
to Bremen to find Nina, bringing the plague with him. The city can only
be saved by a "pure woman" who will keep Nosferatu at her side until the
light of dawn destroys him; it is Nina who makes this sacrifice, paying with
her life. Judith Mayne argues convincingly that the logic of the editing—in
contradiction to the narrative suggested by the inter-titles—demonstrates
that Nina desires Nosferatu. When Nina, swooning in her bed in Bremen,
reaches out to Transylvania, she makes contact not with her husband
Jonathan, but with Nosferatu. Subsequently she waits at the seacoast, supposedly for her husband's arrival, yet the spectator knows that Jonathan is
returning on horseback over land, while it is Nosferatu who heads for Bremen by ship (Mayne, "Dracula," 29–30).[27]

While *Caligari* has a complex array of characters and more than one triangle of desire, *Nosferatu* instead concentrates on one triangle: the bum-
bling German husband, the monster who is so very "other," and the wife
who desires the monster (if only unconsciously). In *The Last Laugh* (1924),
Murnau's first film after his "fantastic" phase, sexual issues seem secondary.
Social mobility is the main topic, albeit in a very sentimentalized form, in
this story of an elderly hotel doorman who loses his job because of his age.
A discourse of castration, however, is fairly easy to discern: his loss of social
status is clearly symbolized by the loss of the uniform that had enabled him
to stand so straight and tall. Once he loses his job, his posture is never the
same, as portrayed in the hunched-over, somewhat grotesque (and expressionistic) performance of Emil Jannings, in one of the famous roles he
played depicting male defeat.

The film is for the most part relatively realistic in style, but at one point
in the film there is a collage of images that is the most striking departure
from realism—more striking even than any of Murnau's other technical
innovations in the film, such as the pioneering use of "unchained" (mobile)

camera and the impressive dream sequence. This collage of images exceeds visual realism, and it grounds the doorman's crisis in psychosexual terms. After a neighbor discovers his demotion, the doorman comes home to the proletarian tenement where he lives, and to reach his apartment he must walk through the building's inner courtyard. In so doing he confronts the open derision of the women there who had once looked up to him—or at least admired his uniform. At the end of this walk past the laughing women in the windows, the collage appears, consisting of many images of jeering, apparently female mouths. Here misogynistic discourses analyzed by Theweleit come to mind, in which the "gaping mouths" of proletarian women are perceived as threatening by aristocratic (and uniformed) right-wing soldiers (Theweleit, 180–86, 196).

E.A. Dupont's *Variety* (1925), like *The Last Laugh,* became internationally famous for its virtuoso use of mobile camera shots and subjective point-of-view shots, images filmed from the perspective of a particular character. In *Variety* the most effective images are shot from the perspective of characters on trapezes high above the audience. Mobile shots from various perspectives are edited together masterfully, creating many suspenseful (and dizzying) effects. At the same time, as in *The Last Laugh,* these cinematic techniques are displayed (or shown off) to such an extent that attention is called to this manipulation of seeing and looking.

Variety is a film with a contemporary setting, typical of the more realistic films that began to dominate as expressionist films declined in the mid-1920s. In one analysis of Weimar cinema, Thomas Elsaesser maintains that in the art films of the Expressionist phase, repressed anxieties about social and sexual mobility surface, but in terms of the bizarre logic of dreams and the unconscious mind—and therefore in "fantastic" forms (Elsaesser, "Social Mobility," 16–20). Indeed, he prefers to label that cinema "fantastic," not Expressionist. But the same fears appear, albeit in increasingly "realistic" forms in New Objectivity. With the move toward "realism," social fears were no longer displaced into the fantastic realm, but instead displaced onto sexual relations. Of course there is no easy separation between anxieties about social, sexual, and gender identities, and the latter two types of anxieties were also obvious if displaced in the earlier "fantastic" films. In the later films, social and sexual anxieties are not revealed anymore in fantastic narratives or mise-en-scene (that is, film images, especially with regard to set and costume design), but by other stylistic means, including an excessive, virtuoso use of camera and editing.

In *Variety* the fantastic has left the mise-en-scene (which is for the most part realistic) and instead has become totally contained in new cinematic techniques. The story itself is conventional enough, built around a sexual triangle similar to that in *Nosferatu,* albeit in more naturalistic form.[28] Emil Jannings, portraying a cuckold in this film just as he will later in *The Blue Angel* (1930), plays the good, solid German male whose passion for his exotic mistress blinds him to her betrayal of him with a slender, sophisticated (and feminized), cosmopolitan man with a southern European name: Artinelli. All three of them are trapeze artists, objects of the spectacle of the circus, and it is only by accident that Jannings's character learns to see "for himself." Then he can see what is actually going on behind the seductive spectacle of success.

But this familiar story of love betrayed is told with excessive stylistic virtuosity. Along with all the dizzying camera movement and editing effects, the film's visual excess includes another "fantastic" collage—not of mouths jeering, but of eyes watching the spectacle (see Figure 4.3 on p. 85). This emphasis on looking is also very evident in Fritz Lang's *Metropolis* (1926). Indeed, a very similar collage of eyes appears, gazing in lust at the robot Maria, an evil vamp if ever there was one. The collage of eyes in *Metropolis* occurs in the scene in which the "false Maria," the evil robot-vamp created in the image of the "true" and "good" Maria, has succeeded in fooling an audience of upper-class men; their lustful gaze at her confirms that the robot's incarnation as woman is complete, as Andreas Huyssen has argued (74–75).

Lang's film can be considered the "swan-song" of Expressionism or as a futuristic work that initiated the genre of the science-fiction film. The film depicts Metropolis, a fantastic city of the future that nonetheless still depends on cruel exploitation of its working class. The young woman Maria preaches to the workers about social justice in a very non-violent, indeed religious manner; she incurs the wrath of the Master of Metropolis anyway. He instructs his henchman, the mad scientist Rotwang, to kidnap her and use her image for a robot that will lead the workers astray. In *Metropolis,* the monster has become the woman; as Elsaesser writes, its robot "constitutes the decisive transformation, from 'medium' or Golem to vamp and woman" ("Lulu," 55). Or at any rate the monster has taken on the image of the woman: outwardly, the false, robot Maria is a vamp, a monstrous version of the New Woman. Beneath the surface, however, she is a machine, controlled by Rotwang in the service of the Master of Metropolis. She is not a "real" female of flesh and blood, but the Master's instrument of steel. At the same time she is a "phallic woman" whose power exceeds his control: she almost destroys his empire by inciting the workers to destroy Metropolis. As the Master's "tool" one might joke that the false Maria is indeed a "phallic woman." But she is so too in the psychoanalytic sense: she is powerful, seductive, threatening to the Master's power, and beyond his control.[29]

Metropolis emphasizes seeing and looking, the "cinematic gaze," like other films of the Weimar era. This is evident, for example, in the scene before the robot Maria is created, when the real Maria tries in vain to escape a shaft of light controlled by the mad scientist Rotwang. A close-up reveals the source of the light to be a large, round lamp Rotwang holds in front of his face, directly beneath his piercing stare; this beam with which his gaze is identified becomes a weapon to trap Maria, to drive her into his laboratory, where he will steal her image (in order to give it to the robot).

Weimar films often foreground seeing and looking in this way, and they call attention to many of the elements by which the cinema constructs narrative—camera, editing, lighting. Such self-reflexive references to filmmaking were indeed characteristic of Weimar "art cinema"—a genre of the commercial cinema, it should be remembered—but such self-reflexivity was not necessarily progressive, and indeed often seems to express a conservative ambivalence about modernity.[30] In any case the overt emphasis on the gaze in Weimar cinema has definite political implications concerning issues of sexuality and power.

The Blue Angel (1930) was directed by an American (the Austrian-born Josef von Sternberg, who learned filmmaking in the U.S.) but produced in Germany, and it is a film that cites some of the famous German films of the 1920s discussed above. In it the same self-reflexive emphasis on seeing and being seen can be noted; in the film's narrative, as in *Metropolis*, the figure of the "monster" lives on as a vamp. Unlike *Metropolis*, the vamp here is not a machine, but she is a character who can be compared to Dr. Caligari's somnambulist Cesare. The latter's "coming to life" is Caligari's most impressive trick before his audiences, and one that is prepared first by a two-dimensional illustration of his image. Just as Cesare starts as a two-dimensional image that then starts to move, reflecting the cinema's most important illusion (that of making a series of static images appear to be one moving image), so the vamp Lola Lola—portrayed by Marlene Dietrich—is first glimpsed as a drawn image on a poster, then as photograph on a postcard, and then from a close-up of the postcard there is finally a cut to Lola herself performing in the cabaret called the "Blue Angel." (See Figure 2.2.)

Spotlights in *The Blue Angel* are used self-reflexively, as in *Metropolis*, but whereas in the latter film Rotwang uses a beam of light to trap Maria in order to create the image of the robot/vamp, here it is the vamp's prey, the stuffy bourgeois, Professor Rath (played by Emil Jannings), who gets caught

Figure 2.2   The first live, full view of Marlene Dietrich as Lola Lola in Sternberg's *The Blue Angel* (1930). Photo courtesy of Film Museum Berlin.

in a spotlight aimed at the audience by Lola onstage, in anticipation of the seduction of Rath by Lola. At the end of the film, after his love for her has brought him only ruin and humiliation, a flashlight in the dark will seek out the destroyed Rath in the darkness. This is a direct citation of *The Last Laugh*, in which another ruined man played by Jannings is also found in the dark by a nightwatchman. But *The Blue Angel* has not only shown Rath's downfall; it has foregrounded as well the process by which the cabaret performer Lola becomes the quintessential cinematic vamp, a process not complete until the end of the film. (See cover illustration of Dietrich as Lola at the end of *The Blue Angel*; compare this image to Figure 2.2 of first full shot of Lola in the film.)[31]

FEMALE SPECTATORSHIP AND WOMEN'S SOCIAL POSITION

It is easy enough to see discourses of male humiliation and castration at work in *The Blue Angel* and many other German films of the Weimar Republic. Castration anxiety and "male subjectivity in crisis" are prevalent in many cultural texts of this era, but, as Petro and others have correctly asserted, to read Weimar cinema only in those terms is to leave out the perspective of women, who made up such a significant portion of the audience for German cinema. This is not just a problem with regard to the interpretation of films; it affects any form of historical and cultural critique informed by feminism. Should women only be discussed as objects, or is their subjectivity also to be taken into account in the study of a culture? Even Theweleit can be faulted along these lines. He calls his book *Male Fantasies,* so one should expect the main issue to be male subjectivity, but he seems to have grander ambitions in terms of a theory of fascism. He finds all previous scholarship on fascism lacking, and he ends up producing an extensive narrative on the fascist personality that grants women primarily the status of passive victims.

The meaning of the vamp in Weimar cinema is hardly exhausted by its function with regard to male castration anxieties; the vamp's relation to the political debate about female identity in Weimar society is even more significant. That debate was being waged among women as well as men. Which was the proper model for women, the one embodied by the traditional maternal type or the one exemplified by the New Woman? (The latter was often demonized as a vamp, although of course the two concepts, "New Woman" and "vamp," are distinct.) Whereas the emancipated New Woman was a cause for concern to both Left and Right in Weimar, the maternal type was exalted across the political spectrum: the right wing valorized the sturdy German mother who would bear soldiers for the fatherland, and the left wing championed the suffering proletarian mother who needed to be saved by the manly revolution of the proletariat. These "types or textual constructs," as Petro says, could take on "meanings other than male anxiety and fear when we consider their function in the address to female audiences" (*Joyless Streets,* 110). In other words, women too were addressed by these "types" of femininity propagated in political and advertising campaigns and depicted in popular films. It is only reasonable to assume that, viewing vamps (and other glamorized/demonized depictions of autonomous women) in the cinema, women would have reacted from a perspective defined at least in part by their own feelings about the role of women in German society. Certainly German feminists were debating that role, and given the controversy in Weimar about female identity, most women would have had opinions about such a central issue in their lives.

The psychoanalytical model of feminist film theory first suggested by Mulvey's "Visual Pleasure and Narrative Cinema" was pioneering for a number of reasons, including its concern with cinema's address to the spectator. It was also criticized because it defined narrative cinema solely in terms of its appeal to the psyche of the male spectator. Much subsequent work in film theory has attempted to determine what female spectatorship would mean in psychoanalytical terms.[32] The most serious problem with many such psychoanalytical models of the late 1970s and early 1980s about gendered spectatorship is the assumption that identification in the cinema is so rigidly determined by the sex of the spectator. Both Parveen Adams and D.N. Rodowick have demonstrated that, in Freud's psychoanalytical model, there is much more ambiguity about identification and sexual difference than allowed for in the binary scheme found in Mulvey and much of the psychoanalytically based film theory that followed her famous 1975 essay. Indeed, "femininity" and "masculinity," are not terms that represent fixed, opposite poles of identification ("active" vs. passive"); instead they refer to different end points on a spectrum along which oscillation constantly occurs. In addition there is no necessary separation between identification and object choice; that is, one may indeed identify with an object of desire (Adams, 68–88; Rodowick, 66–94). As Mayne observed in her discussion of psychoanalytical feminist film criticism's evolution from the 1970s through the 1980s, there was a noticeable move on the part of many critics from a model of cinematic identification that was characterized by fixed gender identity to one that emphasizes both Freud's idea of the essentially bisexual nature of the psyche and the constant shifting of the psyche between "masculine" and "feminine" positions ("Feminist Film Theory," 16; "Marlene Dietrich," 40).[33]

There are many persuasive readings of Weimar cinema that "deviate" from the perspective of strictly defined gender positions. Richard Dyer points out that some critics have read all of Murnau's work from a gay perspective, and he suggests such an interpretation for *Nosferatu* in particular, contextualizing it not merely in terms of Murnau's homosexuality but also in terms of debates waged within the gay subculture that flourished in the Weimar Republic (Dyer, esp. 7, 16, 23). Historical precedents exist for reading vampire figures as Jewish, but there is also precedent for reading them as homosexual.[34] Similarly, Dyer—following B. Ruby Rich—situates Leontine Sagan's 1931 film *Mädchen in Uniform* in relation to debates within the Weimar Republic's lesbian subculture.

Gendered spectatorship is a concept that is most productive when understood in relation to socially defined norms within a specific historical context—norms from which deviation is possible. Obviously, the social and historical positioning of spectators needs to be taken into account. Thus Petro writes of the potential for Weimar female spectators to identify with

Emil Jannings's humiliated doorman in Murnau's *The Last Laugh* precisely because of the character's "feminization" (that is, his downward mobility, his loss of power) (*Joyless Streets,* 23–25, 155, 162–63). After all, Weimar society seemed to promise social mobility to women, but at the same time it demonized such mobility and ultimately delivered little of it. Even *Metropolis* can be read differently by focusing on its potential allusion to social debates especially relevant to women; it has been suggested, for instance, that the actions of the "good Maria" in saving the worker's children in the bowels of the "mother city"—from the flood that threatens to wash them away—can be seen in connection to anxieties and conflicts around reproduction and abortion in Weimar Germany (Ratchye, *Metropolis*).

But perhaps the best evidence for the existence of responses that deviate from the dominant discourse of castration anxiety and male crisis pertains to *The Blue Angel*. Mulvey may have been right when she wrote that Sternberg turned Dietrich into the "ultimate fetish" for patriarchal cinema, but that cannot be the whole story, given that *The Blue Angel* was extremely popular in Berlin's lesbian subculture during the early 1930s—more popular even than *Mädchen in Uniform*.[35]

In considering other spectators, the possibility of other readings of cultural texts becomes clear. A "dominant" reading—one determined by the perspectives that dominate a society—cannot preclude other, more emancipatory interpretations that might resist dominant meanings. A textual reading that stresses the "closure" of a narrative—how its loose ends are wrapped up, how its various conflicts are resolved—will generally downplay the destabilizing elements in the text that the narrative supposedly works to "close off" in its resolution. For example, Judith Mayne stresses the ambiguity of the Lola character at the beginning of *The Blue Angel*— the Lola, that is, before she has been transformed into the iconic vamp she becomes by the end of the film, a figure that seems closer to a cliché of the patriarchal imaginary ("Marlene Dietrich," 29, 31–32, 37). The less iconic, more sexually ambiguous Lola of the beginning of the film appeals especially to "other" spectators less interested in patriarchal clichés, but in a reading stressing the closure of this film, this more interesting Lola would be viewed as only an element within an overall narrative strategy aimed at a closure in the service of patriarchy.

This faith in the ability of narrative closure always to be successful in its suppression of any subversive or resistant elements seems exaggerated. Such success may always be demonstrable through extensive analysis of a film's narrative structure, but does not such a process overemphasize narrative at the expense of visual spectacle? Furthermore, does such narrative analysis bear much relation to the way diverse historical spectators actually respond to a film? That most mainstream films will in some ways reinforce dominant ideology is only to be expected—and as demonstrated above, a patriarchal bias in Weimar films about gender anxiety is easy to see. But it is also reasonable to assume that dominant ideology within a film will not always be able to eliminate all traces of subversion (through narrative closure or otherwise)—and certainly not for all spectators at all times.[36]

Even if one places emphasis on the closure of a film like *The Blue Angel* in such a way that patriarchal stereotypes about vamps and cuckolds seem to triumph, however, it must be remembered that the most clichéd depictions of women in Weimar cinema bear some relation to debates about gender and sexuality in Weimar society and especially to the debate about the New Woman. Here too an address to women and *their* fantasies by the cinema must be noted, although it is not necessarily an emancipatory address. The power a glamorous but threatening vamp seems to wield over men might have had some appeal to women who identified with more "emancipated" morals and who felt insecure about status and power in ways specific to the constraints of their social positioning as women. It is understandable that some women might be attracted to the image of a powerful vamp, who seems to exert an agency that is otherwise not associated with women as they were usually depicted. One of the seductive appeals of consumer capitalism for women is precisely the idea that becoming a desirable commodity is powerful—or is there more agency to this supposed commodity status than critics have assumed? Historicizing such dynamics in films means interpreting them in terms of the cinema's historical role in the rise of consumerism—and the role for women envisioned in a consumer society.[37]

Even in its least emancipatory aspects, then, Weimar cinema cannot be understood without considering the way it appealed to women. And cinema's implication in consumerism was not entirely reactionary from a feminist perspective, because consumer capitalism, as an engine of economic and social modernization, is precisely one of the most powerful forces that has de-stabilized traditional values and gender roles. Certainly in Weimar society this was the case. Consumerism was associated very much with the New Woman, especially in terms of her supposed love of fashion, her hedonism, and her attachment to mass culture.

The New Woman was at the center of the political debates about the "proper" role of women in Weimar, debates in which German feminists also participated. Again, many bourgeois feminists emphasized the maternal role and castigated "new women" as "masculinized" and unnatural (Briden-

thal et al., 11–12).[38] Arguments that emphasized motherhood as the primary model for female identity had definite political ramifications. As
noted above, both the left and the right valorized the maternal role, but for
the right it was crucial to an explicitly anti-feminist strategy in the 1920s,
exemplified in the successful campaign by German conservative and commercial interests to establish a national "Mother's Day" in Germany. This
holiday "glorified motherhood without providing any maternal benefits,
and added weight to the insistence that women were primarily creatures of
their biology" (Bridenthal et al., 14; Hausen).[39]

The cult of motherhood instituted by the Nazis did not spring into
being with their accession to power in 1933; it obviously had its origins in
much older discourses, ones not exclusive to National Socialism. Toward
the end of the Weimar Republic, many middle-class women ignored the
obvious misogyny of Nazism, preferring to believe that Nazi promises to
value motherhood and restore "traditional values" would lead to the development of a "separate sphere" of activity for women. The conservative
wing of bourgeois German feminism especially succumbed to this delusion.
After 1933, of course, nothing of the sort was allowed by the Nazis—even
the woman appointed head of the officially sanctioned women's organization in the Third Reich, Gertrud Scholtz-Klink, had little autonomy.[40]

In terms of the "failure" of German feminism in the face of the Third
Reich, Bridenthal and Koonz make the point that "the conservatism of
Weimar women must be seen in the context of the fraudulence of their
supposed emancipation—that is, the discrepancy between the opportunis-
tic promises made to women by parties and the constitution and their
actual social situation (34). The modernization with which the Right liked
to identify women was often much harder on women than men, given the
actual weakness of most women's social and economic positions. With
respect to the ideology of motherhood, it should be remembered that pro-
natalism was a powerful policy in many nations—even in the Soviet
Union—especially between the wars. And in the 1931 German campaign
to legalize abortion, the Left stressed the benefits such a step would provide
poor mothers; it did not stress reproductive freedom. As Atina Grossman
points out, no one on either side of the abortion battle questioned the idea
that women's central role was motherhood ("Abortion," 69).

Nonetheless, in hindsight at any rate, the consequences of an attraction
to the traditional, maternal model of womanhood in late Weimar seem
clear: the danger on the right was not acknowledged by many German
feminists. And after 1933, most non-Jewish feminists did nothing to protest

what began to happen to Jewish women, who also had been part of the bourgeois feminist movement.[41]

The two positions in the social debate—the "new" vs. the maternal woman—more or less reproduce an ancient patriarchal dichotomy in the representation of woman: virgin/Madonna vs. whore, idealization vs. disparagement. This is not surprising, given the long dominance of this dichotomy. Once again, however, what is interesting is how at a particular moment of history—in Weimar Germany—exactly how such a discourse functioned, how it structured and limited the social debate, how various political forces (including feminists) formed strategic alliances in terms of it, and whether such strategies were able to renegotiate it or even undermine it.[42] And of course what was most unique to (and most emancipatory about) Weimar was the "blurring" of old dichotomies like this one with regard to feminine stereotypes, as well as others having to do with rigid conceptions of gender and sexual behavior.

The controversy about the role of women in Weimar played a role in the social and political developments leading to the creation of a fascist state in Germany. It also suggests how the political stakes for women spectators watching films about "vamps" (and other clichéd notions of womanhood) differed from those of men. This difference must be taken into account when analyzing Weimar cinema. Keeping this difference in mind cannot undo the pervasiveness of patriarchal stereotypes in that cinema, any more than pointing to the existence of surprisingly emancipatory movements within Weimar society can undo the fact that oppressive forces in that society were much more powerful, as their victory in 1933 would prove. But we should also strive to keep alive the memory of the actual complexity of Weimar culture and its emancipatory moments. For these struggles over gender, identity, and culture in modernity are hardly over.

Chapter 3 ✎

"New Objectivity": Ambivalent Accommodations with Modernity

What would a surgeon be worth if his hand trembled out of sympathy? An emotional doctor is a bad doctor. Thank God that for the most part you are only so nauseously sentimental while drinking beer, Breslauer. Just like your colleague, this surgeon—what is his name? . . . . A competent man. Cold and sober as a modern refrigerator.

—Irmgard Keun, *Nach Mitternacht* (83, 1937)[1]

MODERNITY IN WEIMAR

The whole district is like this: street leading into street of houses like shabby monumental safes crammed with the tarnished valuables and second-hand furniture of a bankrupt middle class.

I am a camera with its shutter open, quite passive, recording, not thinking.

—Isherwood, *Goodbye to Berlin*, 1

These lines from the beginning of a piece of autobiographically based fiction about life in Berlin at the end of Germany's Weimar Republic were written by an Englishman. Although Christopher Isherwood's observations were of course those of a foreigner who stood apart from what was going on, the lines above capture some significant aspects not only of Weimar culture but also of one of the predominant attitudes with regard to that culture among German intellectuals of the time.

Rather than illustrate the celebrated image of Berlin as the ultimate modern metropolis, as it was indeed seen at the time (and it is this image of

Berlin with which Isherwood's works about Berlin tend to be associated), these lines define Berlin as a visual monument to a bygone middle-class respectability. This "surface image" contradicted its "modern" image, based so much on the celebrated nightlife conducted mostly inside cabarets, cafes, and clubs. Modernization—in the form first of gaslights in the mid-nineteenth century and later of electrification—is of course what allows night life to flourish in the first place.[2] Capturing nocturnal reality with a camera has always been a technical problem. What was famously recorded on film in the 1920s were of course the displays of electric lights that transformed the workaday facade of the metropolis, but the traces of such displays tend to vanish in daylight. Of course, the very modern flow of traffic is visible in day—but this was set against the static background of the city's facade.[3]

The once pompous, now shabby facade of Berlin captured in Isherwood's description had been created during the German Empire, and the economic basis behind the image was squandered in financing the Empire's war and in the peace that followed the Empire's demise. Also implied in Isherwood's description is the ongoing German attachment to that lost status and identity, destabilized in the chaos of war, inflation, industrial rationalization, and then world depression.

The "photographic" attention to the actual surface reality of Berlin, the devotion to recording, and the disavowal of thinking evident in Isherwood's famous line beginning, "I am a camera" were attitudes quite typical of the Weimar intelligentsia. Typical as well was the implicit sense of alienation not unsurprising in a foreign observer like Isherwood yet shared in many ways by German intellectuals, no matter how hard they tried to overcome it—which went as far as this very disavowal of intellectual and ideological activity in their embrace of a passive, technological, "objective" documentation of social reality. This pose of detached observation was favored by many German intellectuals, at first enthusiastically, in harmony with the fashionable "New Objectivity" that became popular in the Weimar Republic's brief stabilized period (1924–1929), and then more helplessly in the face of the chaos of late Weimar, as the Republic neared its end (1933).

The culture of Germany's Weimar Republic—popular and intellectual—is of special interest to those interested in the study of modernity and modernization, both in general terms and in the specifically German context. With regard to economic modernization and the development of a capitalist consumer culture, the 1920s in Germany represent a crucial period. The Weimar period was characterized both by rapid industrial rationalization and by the development and the celebration of new forms of mass culture. Intellectuals across the political spectrum, precisely at the moment when their middle-class income and status was no longer secure, began to embrace a modern mass culture about which they had long been at best ambivalent. The German Left, which had long remained loyal to high bourgeois culture and suspicious of modern mass culture, began during Weimar to revise its opinion of the new medium of film, becoming aware of "a democratic potential inherent in the structure of cinematic representation" (Hansen, "Early Silent Cinema," 172). Members of the leftist avant-garde began to praise mass culture as a weapon against bourgeois culture, fascinated as they were with "Americanism" (and, even for a while, "Fordism"). But on the anti-democratic Right as well, some influential factions also gave up their ambivalence about modernization (though never about democracy), as what Jeffrey Herf calls "reactionary modernism" was being fashioned.

Many of the developments in Weimar Germany that had significant influence on subsequent twentieth-century history were typical of the stabilized period and its characteristic New Objectivity. The latter is arguably the cultural disposition most unique to Weimar—as opposed to Expressionism or Dada, which had older origins. As mentioned above, Berlin gained recognition as *the* modern European metropolis during this period, modern consumer culture took hold in Germany on a new scale, and the new class of white-collar office workers became influential. The cinema became important in a new way during this era, as the German and American film industries became ever more entwined in Dawes Plan-type financing (see Saunders). In a sense, this brief era anticipated the consumer culture that would become dominant in Western Europe and North America after World War II, which in turn led ultimately to a "postindustrial" or "third stage" of capitalism.

It is clear that studies of modernity and modernization can benefit from examination of the development of consumerism and mass culture in the Weimar Republic. For beneath the new and happily distracted consumerist culture of the Weimar Republic, of course, all sorts of anxieties were lurking, especially about its de-stabilization of traditional identities—above all class, gender, and ethnic/national identities, but also sexual identities. These anxieties would have drastic consequences after the economic bubble burst at the end of 1929. I would assert that the stabilization of such anxieties remains a problem within industrial and postindustrial modernity up to the present, and that anxiety about the destabilization of traditional gender identities plays an especially crucial role.

In Weimar Germany explicitly thematized anxiety about gender roles was characteristic of much cultural discourse, in both "high" and popular culture. The photographic gaze applied to Weimar reality was called "passive" by Isherwood, but other preferred descriptions were "sober," "cool," or "coldly discerning," even "surgical."[4] Regardless of the particular description, this gaze was considered to be a male one, but it is perhaps better understood as a defensive male strategy for retaining mastery and avoiding "feminization," the fate of the objects of that gaze—and, as Eve Rosenhaft has shown, there is textual evidence of male anxiety about becoming the object of the gaze of emancipated New Women ("Lesewut," 138–40). Anxieties about status take explicitly gendered and sexualized forms in a wide number of cultural texts produced in Germany during the 1920s—in films and literary works, the primary focus of this study, but also in paintings, photojournalism, and other media of both "high" and "low" cultures.

The emphasis on the destabilization of gender roles must be seen in turn in the context of the construction of gender in bourgeois ideology since the eighteenth century. From the beginning, the exclusion of women from the public sphere played a formative (if unacknowledged) role in that ideology, since that sphere was defined in relation to a "private" realm of subjectivity, intimacy, and domesticity identified with women. This meant in real terms the confinement of (middle-class) women within this private realm, upon which the public sphere depended, and the denial of any public agency to women, fully in accordance with the new conceptions of "natural" gender roles that also were being consolidated with the rise of the bourgeoisie.[5] Weimar culture represents a historical moment of heightened anxiety about the erosion of those "natural" roles: women were appearing in public and assuming new public roles on an unprecedented scale. And whereas the subject of the bourgeois public sphere was supposedly universal but implicitly male, in Weimar culture and especially in New Objectivity one finds an overt thematization of anxiety about gender directed (in its dominant version) at an explicitly male subject—one no longer sure of the autonomy bourgeois subjecthood was supposed to guarantee. Of course, this pronounced emphasis on gender was bound to interest women as well.

WHAT WAS "NEW OBJECTIVITY"?

"Neue Sachlichkeit," usually translated as "New Objectivity," is most often identified with the stabilized period of the Weimar Republic. This period began in 1924 with the Dawes Plan, which arranged loans from American bankers that refinanced the crippling debts Germany owed to the victors of

World War I (as required by the punitive Versailles peace treaty). The Dawes Plan facilitated Chancellor Stresemann's elimination of the hyper-inflation that had plagued Germany in the early 1920s, reaching a crisis point by late 1923. The new economic stability that began with the Dawes Plan would end with the onset of the world depression in 1929, when American bankers were forced by the Wall Street crash to call in foreign loans; Germany was thus hit very soon after the crash, and very severely.

But in 1924, the achievement of stability was quite a relief for the Weimar Republic after five chaotic years characterized by the national humiliation of the Versailles treaty, revolution from the communist Left, counter-revolution from the anti-democratic Right, and hyperinflation. In applying the term "New Objectivity" to a widespread sensibility that became dominant in the stabilized period, I am using it in its broadest sense, to characterize a cultural sensibility that connects a wide variety of social, political, and artistic attitudes and endeavors in Weimar culture. It was a period in which the "isms"—Expressionism, romantic anti-capitalism, rev-olutionary socialism, indeed any utopianism—seemed exhausted, and accommodation with capitalist modernization seemed the only pragmatic option.

There is considerable agreement that "New Objectivity" cannot be used to define a particular artistic school or movement; neither, for that matter, can it be applied to a particular political tendency.[6] In his famous study in 1970, Helmut Lethen wrote that there was much within New Objectivity to allow appropriation by conservative technocrats in West Germany in the 1950s (*Neue Sachlichkeit*, 1).[7] Certainly this is the case if it is defined strictly in relation to industrial rationalization and the "Fordism" that appealed to industrial managers and the engineers Herf stresses in his study (2–3, 152–88). But New Objectivity was hardly just a conservative or even cen-trist phenomenon. Indeed, it is difficult to restrict it to either end of the traditional political spectrum, and this confounding of ordinary left-right distinctions makes it almost "postmodern."[8] Many endeavors of Weimar's leftist avant-garde can be related to New Objectivity: Erwin Piscator's experimentation with technical innovations in the theater as well as the functionalist style of the Bauhaus after the early 1920s can certainly be considered "New Objectivist". The same can be said about Brecht, although he, like many others—including the much more centrist and "apolitical" Joseph Roth—became increasingly critical of it by the end of the 1920s. But of course, ambivalence about New Objectivity was actually quite common among those whose work can most clearly be considered New Objectivist.[9]

We can limit its definition in sociological terms: the adherents of New Objectivity were predominantly members of the intelligentsia (especially if this term is defined broadly enough to include professionals like engineers and the managerial class). In more recent studies, Lethen (1994) and Martin Lindner (1994) treat it as a stance of the historical avant-garde, but for them this group spanned a political spectrum stretching from Bertolt Brecht and Johannes R. Becher on the Left to Arnolt Bronnen and Ernst Jünger on the Right. While we tend to think of the Right as strictly anti-modern in Weimar Germany, one can also notice parallels there with New Objectivity; indeed, the reconciliation of right-wing authoritarianism with technological modernization Herf calls "reactionary modernism" is typically New Objectivist. This odd synthesis obviously anticipates the "romanticism of steel" ("stählerne Romantik") Goebbels would proclaim as the appropriate sensibility for the twentieth century (Herf, 3).[10] But it also seems to have resulted from a process of reconciliation with modernity strangely comparable to that undergone by many intellectuals and artists of the liberal left during the 1920s. Alfred Döblin, for instance, went from condemning modern civilization in a typically Expressionist fashion to an embrace of the modern metropolis as a natural, "organic" form of human society (Dollenmayer, 54–62).[11]

The origin of the term "New Objectivity" is usually traced back to its application to painting. Gustav Hartlaub at the Mannheim Museum used the term in 1923 to define the return to objective realism in German painting in the aftermath of Expressionism and Dada (Schmied, "Neue Sachlichkeit and German Realism," 9). But there is evidence that Lion Feuchtwanger was using the term "sachlich" to apply to new directions in literature as early as 1922 (Becker, 14–15). Even when just limited to painting, the term encompassed at least two trends, a socially critical, naturalistic "verism," and a more conservative "magical realism." Kracauer used the term in *From Caligari to Hitler* to refer to a sensibility of the stabilized period beginning in 1924, which Hartlaub cannot have originally intended, given the fact that he saw precedents for this trend in painting going back a decade. Nonetheless, Hartlaub's coinage only caught on in the mid-1920s, and a number of famous painters and other visual artists continued to work in a "New Objectivist" vein throughout the 1920s: Otto Dix, Christian Schad, Max Beckmann, George Grosz, Hanna Höch; indeed, this was certainly the main epoch for this type of visual art, even if older precedents can be identified.[12]

But the term was not only limited to painting; by the late 1920s it could be applied to all sorts of cultural developments—trends in architecture, lit-

erature, photography, and film, as well as political attitudes, even "emancipated" sexuality (which could mean sexual behavior that was "modern,"
unconventional, sober, cynical, or simply de-sentimentalized). And although
the "stabilized period" ends with the stock market crash in 1929, the New
Objective sensibility can be said to continue at least until 1933. This is certainly the case in literature; as Becker points out, many of the most famous
New Objective novels were written after 1929 (16–17). In late Weimar the
sensibility is perhaps most famously exemplified in (and by) Erich Kästner's
1931 novel *Fabian,* in which a supposedly "free-floating" ("freischweben-
der") intellectual documents the chaos of the end of the republic as well as
his own paralysis and impotence in the face of it.[13]

Kracauer ascribes the trend to social resignation and cynicism, and cynicism is of course the term Peter Sloterdijk uses to define the Weimar
Republic, which provides the central historical model for his critique of
Western intellectual history. But the era was much more ambiguous than
such predominantly negative terms can imply. John Willett (*Art and Politics*), for instance, defines the period much more positively, in part by trans-
lating *Neue Sachlichkeit* as the "New Sobriety," and stressing the willingness
of avant-garde artists to give up their anti-modern disdain for modern civilization, and instead to apply their skills to a modern, democratic design for
the life of the masses. This commitment to produce a functional, political
art can be seen as reflecting hopes that a truly democratic public sphere was
emerging and that its formation could be assisted and influenced by artists
and intellectuals.

This move in a pragmatic, democratic direction is typified by the
Bauhaus's shift from a mystical, organic Expressionism to a rectilinear functionalism, certainly in the ideals behind this shift if not necessarily always in
its results. Comparable too would be the activities of erstwhile Dadaist
John Heartfield, who put photomontage to practical use in his work for the
Arbeiter-Illustrierte Zeitung, or "Workers' Illustrated Newspaper," a Communist publication directed at the working class. This application of the principles of photomontage to making critical statements about modern life
can also be noted in a quite different manner in the work of Hanna
Höch[14]—she was certainly not a doctrinaire Marxist like Heartfield—as
well as in more clearly mass cultural venues, that is, in advertising and the
illustrated press, the photojournalistic context Petro explores.

Many writers were influenced by journalists and the genre of *Reportage*—
journalistic reporting as exemplified in the work of Egon Erwin Kisch, who
eventually joined the KPD, the German Communist Party—especially its
social engagement with contemporary events and its accessible style. Other

writers (like Döblin) moved toward a style that attempted to learn from mass culture by approximating filmic montage—another example of appropriating mass culture in the struggle against conventional bourgeois art, a favored avant-garde practice in the 1920s.

This avant-garde strategy—the attempt to use mass cultural forms as weapons against high culture, the kind of culture crucial to the classical bourgeois public sphere—bears a resemblance to the concept of a "counter-public sphere" as developed by Oskar Negt and Alexander Kluge in their 1972 book *Öffentlichkeit und Erfahrung* (*The Public Sphere and Experience*). Negt and Kluge saw the potential for an oppositional public sphere, as Miriam Hansen has written, "in the contradictory make-up of the late-capitalist public spheres of production" ("Early Silent Cinema," 156), that is, within the very processes of capitalist modernization that Habermas blamed for the decline of the classic bourgeois sphere. Within those processes there was the possibility of "a medium for the organization in relation to—rather than, as in the classical model, separation from—the material sphere of everyday life, the social conditions of production" ("Early Silent Cinema," 156). Of course, Negt and Kluge had no illusions about capitalist mass culture per se; they were arguing for a counter-public sphere that "was a fundamentally new structure opposed to both the classical-representative and the market-oriented types of public sphere" ("Early Silent Cinema," 156). They were not guilty of any naive optimism about mass culture.[15] Such optimism had still been possible in the 1920s, but it became much more difficult to maintain after the uses to which mass culture would be put in the 1930s by fascists and Stalinists—and capitalists in Hollywood too, one might add.

Related to this optimistic attitude toward mass culture in Weimar was an uncritical fascination with (an idea of) America, but the influence of the Soviet avant-garde, from Constructivism to Eisenstein and Vertov, was equally important. This is particularly noticeable in the German cinema. Chaplin was enormously popular with audiences and with critics,[16] and in German filmmaking there was also an obvious move in the direction of American melodramatic realism. At the same time, however, *Potemkin*'s overwhelming popular success led to many attempts to imitate Soviet cinema, especially the shock effects created by Soviet-style montage. This attraction to the cinema and especially to technical innovation in the cinema may have been naive, or doomed, like the general technological optimism of the left avant-garde, but Willett is right to stress a positive moment, even if he underplays the disillusionment and cynicism that was also undeniably related to the overall mood of the period.

As Lindner asserts, the Americanism and the modern mass culture so celebrated in New Objectivity meant above all three things: "Sport, Kino und Jazz"—that is, sports, the movies, and jazz (171). The widespread popularity of jazz included the type of entertainment personified by the Tiller Girls, an English troupe of dancers whose chorus line routines could be said to fuse the display of female legs with the mechanized ethos of the assembly line.[17] As part of the "Americanist" fascination for sports, boxing especially was valorized. Brecht liked it so much he cited it as a model for entertainment superior to the bourgeois theater (Bathrick, 132).[18] It was also a model that was arguably more public and democratic and less elitist and pseudo-religious. But sports too became a cult, one that included the glorification of all outdoor activity, including mountain climbing.[19] The cinema participated in this cult of sports, the outdoors, and youth, as can be noted in films from across the political spectrum, from Brecht and Slatan Dudow's *Kuhle Wampe* of 1932 to Hans Steinhoff's pro-Nazi *Hitler Youth Quex* of 1933. All of these elements can be considered positively as part of the rejection of "high" bourgeois art, with its inwardness, elitism, and traditionalism—and more negatively as symptoms of the new consumer culture with its commodification of leisure time and youthful narcissism.

The cult of youth complemented the fascination with the new and the modern that was a function of another main element of New Objectivity: the glamorization and fetishization of technology. Related to this phenomenon is the scientism, the rationalistic "objectivity" so typical of the era. Even Brecht, who by 1929 was making fun of the sensibility with his poem titled "700 Intellectuals Praying to an Oil Tank,"[20] nonetheless remained very keen on seeing his Marxism as a "scientific" socialism, and he would not seriously relativize his infatuation with science until he heard about Hiroshima.[21]

One element that unites most of these amorphous elements is the gendering of New Objectivity: the gender of the subject who seemingly produced it, the subject it glorified, and to whom it was addressed, was obviously, explicitly, indeed defensively *masculine*. New Objectivity is typified by engineers, technicians, scientists, journalists, boxers, athletes, and the spectators for whom the Tiller Girls displayed their legs.[22] On a visual level one can get a feeling for the hard, scientific "masculinity" of the era defined as New Objectivist just by noting the shift in the designs of the Bauhaus from the rounded, "organic" Expressionism of Erich Mendelsohn's architectural work in the early 1920s to the rectilinear functionalism of Walter Gropius's designs in the mid- and later 1920s.[23]

The obviously gendered nature of New Objectivity is not addressed or acknowledged by Kracauer, by Willett, or even by Sloterdijk, for all his attention to Weimar sexual cynicism (and the omnipresence of wounded war veterans, especially amputees, on the streets of Weimar Germany). Theweleit, who does draw attention to such dynamics in Weimar culture, does not concern himself with New Objectivity. Newer works by critics like Helmut Lethen and Martin Lindner do note the obviously gendered nature of discourses associated with New Objectivity, although it is not their main focus. Lethen, in his 1994 book *Verhaltenslehren der Kälte* (forthcoming in English translation as *Cool Conduct*), treats New Objectivity as a sensibility characteristic of the historical avant-garde from 1910 to 1930; it involved the clear rejection of the Expressionism's romantic ("feminized") cult of "authenticity," which had dominated the first decade of that period, in favor of a Baroque-inspired, coldly strategic, Machiavellian—and masculine—masquerade. In contrast to Sloterdijk, who attacks this masquerade—not really because it is male, but cynical—Lethen tends to defend it, or at least to demand that it be understood as a historical necessity, criticizing Sloterdijk for being ahistorical. While Lethen too has an acknowledged contemporary agenda behind his critique of Sloterdijk and others (140), his insistence on more attention to the original context of New Objectivity is to be welcomed. But his critique of Sloterdijk on these grounds, as persuasive as it is, is flawed by his apparent (and not very persuasive) connection of Sloterdijk with feminist and psychoanalytical positions on Weimar culture, and his defensiveness about the latter. It may indeed be too easy to psychoanalyze the "cold persona" of New Objectivity as merely the masquerade of "virile narcissism," especially if it is done with an ahistorical disregard for the specificity of its context (69–70). Yet Lethen himself both asserts—and provides a great deal of historical evidence—that it is a very "masculine" masquerade, all the while remaining defensive about a feminist analysis of the phenomenon.[24]

In the stress on more careful attention to historical context, he is allied with Martin Lindner. The latter, however, does not stress the break with Expressionism as Lethen does, but rather demonstrates how both Expressionism and New Objectivity were simply two phases in a longer historical development within the ideological disposition he calls "Lebensideologie," which I will translate as the "ideology of vitalism," which is related to, but broader than what is usually called "Lebensphilosophie" ("life-philosophy").[25] Strongly influenced by thinkers like Friedrich Nietzsche, Wilhelm Dilthey, and Georg Simmel, "Lebensideologie" according to Lindner was dominant in shaping the beliefs of the intellectual class from 1890 until 1955, a period he labels Germany's "classical modernity"

(2, 5).[26] Lindner demonstrates how crucial gendered polarities are to the polarities that constituted "Lebensideologie" (84–87), but beyond this analysis of gender's place in the ideological system created almost exclusively by male intellectuals whose ideas he surveys, Lindner does not thematize gender.[27]

It is not surprising that recent work by feminist scholars such as Adelheid von Saldern, Eve Rosenhaft, Anke Gleber, Kerstin Barndt, Katharina von Ankum, and a number of others whose essays are collected in the volume *Women in the Metropolis* (edited by von Ankum), have foregrounded the crucial role of gender in Weimar culture in a more systematic and persuasive manner than have the scholars mentioned above. In my opinion, this attention to gender helps to make sense of many of the apparently disparate ideologies, artists, and intellectuals connected to New Objectivity in Weimar. The gender dynamics at work teach us something that is more fundamental than what is attained through Lindner's exhaustive analysis and reconstruction of the paradigms of intellectual history. One concept of Lindner's that is quite useful is the idea of crisis, which he sees as crucial to New Objectivity in particular and to the larger period of "classical modernity" as a whole. For it is the modern crisis of the bourgeois subject that underlies all of the developments Lindner analyzes. Industrial modernity presented a serious threat to the proclaimed autonomy of the subject, which was always an implicitly male one. By the 1920s, the perception that this endangered subject was a male one was quite explicit, especially for the male intellectuals whose own social and economic status was specifically threatened. And that threat was quite often both perceived and depicted in gendered terms.

NEW OBJECTIVITY AND "MALE CRISIS"

In 1929, Kurt Pinthus defined New Objectivity in post-Expressionist literature specifically as "masculine" literature, in an essay with exactly that title: "Männliche Literatur." Of course nothing is more typical of modernist movements in the arts than the tendency to disparage slightly older movements as "feminine" in the attempt to stylize themselves as bold, "masculine," and revolutionary; this can be noted not just in New Objectivity's disparagement of what now seemed a romantic, sentimental Expressionism, but also in the Expressionists' vitalist/activist perspective on what they saw as an effeminate, mystical, escapist Neo-Romanticism, and in the latter's distancing of itself from the dandyist decadence of aestheticism.[28]

But Pinthus's argument is a bit less polemical; he defines the previous era of literature, from 1910 to 1925, not as "feminine" literature but as the immature literature of the "Jüngling," the male adolescent. "Masculine" literature thus means "mature" literature; oedipal crises have been resolved, and naive youthful rebellion is over.[29] The process of maturation also seems to involve coming to terms with wartime experiences (Pinthus, 328–33). Indeed, war—or anti-war—novels became one of the main genres of literary New Objectivity, Erich Maria Remarque's *Im Westen nichts neues* (*All Quiet on the Western Front,* 1929) being the most well known example.

John Willett defines the experience of World War I as central to the generation of artists whose activities he traces in his book on the "New Sobriety" (*Art and Politics,* 20). He means primarily the experience of male artists, of course: it was the male rite of passage in World War I—the horrors of the trenches and gas warfare—that cured this generation both of nationalism and romantic utopianism, Willett asserts.[30] There can be no doubt that the trauma resulting from the first mechanized war of mass destruction had a tremendous influence on postwar society (especially on war veterans).[31] But with this analysis Willett reproduces yet again the male bias that is so striking both in so much of the art from the Weimar Republic and in the discourse about Weimar art and culture that prevailed for so long (e.g., Kracauer, Gay).

The war was indeed an experience that tended to be very different depending on gender—in a way that exaggerated male distrust and resentment of women. The actual experiences of most women and everyone else on the home front during World War I were not particularly easy, however; nor did the home front provide a "stab in the back" to the German war effort, in spite of how convenient this legend became to the military and the Right after the war.[32] But, as we have noted, a certain resentment of the home front was probably inevitable. There was thus the potential for some powerful misogyny, especially given other insecurities about modernization and the changing status of women during the war: their presence in greater numbers and in new sectors of the labor market—which must in turn have made the experience of the war positive for some women, in spite of the shortages and hunger on the home front.[33] After the war, women received new rights in the Weimar constitution; the new democracy also placed in question the old system of social status. Inflation then destroyed middle-class savings; consumerism and mass culture overturned traditional values. Many of the resulting insecurities crystallized around fascination with and contempt for the New Woman, who was so associated with both consumerism and sexual emancipation. A new order of modern social, gender, and sexual identities threatened more traditional concepts of identity. This perceived threat caused insecurity and disorientation on the part of many, a condition that was likely further aggravated by homophobia, inspired by the open campaign for homosexual rights and fairly open urban homosexual subcultures.

New Objectivity can be interpreted as a particular response to such underlying anxieties as they manifested themselves during the stabilized period, above all for middle-class males, and especially for intellectuals. Indeed, the situation of intellectuals was so fragile after the chaos of inflation—for many whose savings, privileges, and secure positions were gone—that accommodation with mass culture, or rather the budding "culture industry," can be seen in terms of economic necessity (Kaes, *Kino-Debatte,* 12–17, 32–35). Resignation and cynicism ought only to be expected, but there was also genuine commitment on the part of some to playing a "public" role within the new society. (Probably a combination of both cynicism and commitment was also common). But the idea of the modern public still seemed to exclude women, for all their increased (and controversial) public presence. Women—especially "new" ones—were seen primarily as an obstacle to public rationality. In New Objectivity there is an obvious gesture of disavowal of the underlying anxieties about gender and modernity, an attempt to re-achieve "masculine" mastery through objectivity, science, technology. The hope was to master chaos, anxiety, and the specific social and economic problems plaguing intellectuals and artists—all of which tended to get subsumed under the supposed threat of women and the fear of male impotence or "feminization." Mastery would be regained by documenting the anxieties of modernity "objectively" and "soberly" with the help of modern technology and/or "scientific" methods.

Artistic mastery was also at stake—a certain modernist hubris, as it were. Willett, for example, summarizes the advice of a 1928 primer on photography by the Berlin Constructivist Werner Graeff with the assertion that "there is no reason on earth for the camera to obey the same laws of perspective and balance as the human eye. It can twist, foreshorten, superimpose, blur and cut; *all that matters is that the photographer should remain in control*" (my emphasis; Willett, *Art and Politics,* 140–41). This is an attitude toward the camera Willett finds "astonishingly up to date"; it is interesting in this context precisely for its emphasis on control and mastery—qualities that the increasingly marginalized modern artist seems here to be able to reclaim. Graeff gives advice that is by no means aimed at a merely "realistic" or "documentary" use of the camera—that is, the aesthetic associated with the most common (and more narrow) understanding of New Objectivity. But its relation to the fetishization of technology and the underlying quest to regain mastery is also clear.

NEW OBJECTIVITY AND THE CINEMA

The "excess" occasioned by joy in the mastery of new technology is very typical of German cinema in these years. What meaning does New Objectivity have for the German cinema? The German cinema that became internationally famous after World War I was the "Expressionist" or "fantastic" cinema epitomized in films like Robert Wiene's *The Cabinet of Dr. Caligari* (1920) and F.W. Murnau's *Nosferatu* (1922), the first film adaptation of Bram Stoker's *Dracula*. This type of cinema represented a small segment of German film production in the early Weimar years (Kaes, "Film in der Weimarer Republik," 46); even among films belonging to the "Autorenkino," or the "cinema of authors/auteurs," the small but prestigious art film sector of film production in this period,[34] by no means can all films be called Expressionist. Thomas Elsaesser has asserted that the so-called Expressionist cinema actually functioned like a genre ("Secret Affinities," 35), an apt term if only for the reminder that Expressionist (and other types of art films) were produced by the commercial film industry in Germany.[35] It should also be noted that Expressionism came to the cinema when it was just about exhausted already in the theater, and it had long been moribund in painting—although of course many painters who became famous during the heyday of Expressionism before World War I continued to paint, but rarely in a style still considered "Expressionist." Otto Dix is a good example of someone whose style by the mid-20s is categorized as New Objectivist.

In *Caligari*, "fantastic" effects are achieved primarily by mise-en-scene, the painted false perspective of the theatrical, "Expressionist" sets (although the style has also been called "cubist"—cf. Budd). A few years later, in *Nosferatu*, much of the film is shot outdoors, on location, and the fantastic effects are more properly cinematic—negative footage, fast-motion and other special effects—all of which are associated with the monster. As the German cinema became more technologically advanced, there was a move toward more realistic stories in more contemporary settings; this is already true of Murnau's *The Last Laugh* (*Der letzte Mann,* 1924), which, again, was famous for its use of mobile and subjective camera. The development accelerated in the stabilized period by the apparent attempt to approximate American filmmaking.

Even in the less fantastic, more realistic films of the middle and later Weimar years, a certain technical "excess" remains. This is true even of films by its most "realistic" directors, such as G.W. Pabst, whose best work is traditionally lauded for its "social realism" and who indeed is the only film director Kracauer discusses in the chapter in which he defines the New Objectivity (*Caligari*, 165–80). This excess is probably what most clearly distinguishes Weimar realism from Hollywood realism—or for that matter from the entertainment cinema of the Third Reich. In that excess one can perhaps note some resistance to the homogenizing tendencies toward the "classical" model of realist cinema that would become consolidated in the 1930s in Hollywood (a model the German cinema of the Third Reich would for the most part emulate).

New Objectivity for the German cinema, then, meant this move toward realism, contemporary settings, combined with a technical virtuosity in camera work, optical printing, and editing that was not completely subordinated to the story. The influence of American-style melodrama is evident, but so are Soviet montage and a somewhat brutal social realism that would seem to have its origins in German theatrical Naturalism.[36] The move in literature toward Reportage and the experimentation on the stage with "documentary" theater found cinematic parallels in somewhat conservative cultural documentaries, the so-called "Kulturfilm,"[37] and in more progressive "city films" like the avant-gardist Walter Ruttman's Berlin-montage *Berlin, die Symphonie einer Großstadt* (*Berlin, Symphony of a City*, 1927) or *Menschen am Sonntag* (*People on Sunday*, 1929), a collaboration by Robert Siodmak, Billy Wilder, Fred Zinneman, and others.

Even Fritz Lang's *Metropolis*, made in 1926, released in 1927, and often considered the last gasp of Expressionism, is perhaps more properly described as "futurist." If anything, it is the last gasp of the big-budget art film of the mid-1920s, since it bankrupted Ufa and drove its producer, Erich Pommer, to Hollywood for a few years. Andreas Huyssen has interpreted it not as an Expressionist denunciation of technology but rather a New Objectivist reconciliation with technology, for in it the threat of technology is displaced onto a female robot/vamp who eventually is burned at the stake: technology thus is purged of its threat (Huyssen, 81). The technical excess in cinematic New Objectivity is not merely a formal or stylistic matter; it is intricately related to the gender anxieties foregrounded in this book. This is evident with regard to the special effects used for the creation of the robot in *Metropolis*, as well as to the most frantic moment of montage at the heart of the urban "documentary" film *Berlin, Symphony of a City*, in which one finds the staged suicide of a despairing woman (cf. Petro, *Joyless Streets*, 43). As Lethen asserts, film and photography were exemplary of New Objectivity's concern with surface reality, its disavowal of "inwardness," and its obsession with surveillance (*Verhaltenslehren*, 50–51). Lethen admits that New Objectivity was an overwhelmingly masculinist sensibility. Of course, the obsession with a controlling gaze was as much (if not more) an anxiety about being exposed to such a gaze as it was about the desire to wield that gaze—hence the concern with masks.

WOMEN AND NEW OBJECTIVITY

Women caused particular concern in this process of "disenchantment"—the introduction of the "new objectivity" (*Neue Sachlichkeit*)—into daily life. Women, after all, had traditionally been understood as the embodiment of the irrational. They were thought to resist discipline, organization, and instrumental rationality and to remain need-oriented in the service of human needs. The new rationalized woman seemed particularly threatening at the same time she was absolutely necessary if women could continue to fulfill their womanly and maternal duties in the new age. But if New Women learned to practice the speed and utilitarian values of rationalization in their own homes, who would provide the home to succor and replenish workers from the rigors of rationalized industry?

—Atina Grossmann, "*Girlkultur,*" 75–76

Women—especially "emancipated" women—were, of all the threatening "Others" in Weimar society, the one group that many male intellectuals across the political spectrum found especially disturbing—and as Grossmann points out, concerns about "controlling" them motivated sex reformers, social scientists, and social workers (and many of this last category were themselves women). Even though the New Woman and emancipated sexuality were very much associated with the era, indeed in some ways were seen to represent New Objectivity and Americanism more than any other phenomena, in general they remained "problems" to be solved by rational engineering, or a symptom to be analyzed under the inspection of a "sober" male gaze.[38]

Kracauer, for instance, treats them in exactly this way in his writings in the 1920s and 1930s—that is, as symptoms. The Tiller Girls are discussed as symptomatic of modern mass culture—indeed, as emblematic of the logic of capitalism—in his article "Das Ornament der Masse" ("The Mass Ornament," 1927), and another troupe of dancers is discussed as symptomatic of the irrelevancy of Americanism after the Wall Street crash in his "Girls und Krise" ("Girls and Crisis," 1931). Women tend to become identified with New Objectivity (and Americanism) especially once these sensibilities begin to fall into discredit; in disparaging New Objectivity, critics disparage it too as being feminized and decadent or degenerate, no longer masculine and scientific.

Technology and science—as glorified in the justification for industrial rationalization, as thematized in literature and the cinema, and as manifested in new photographic and cinematic techniques—were also invoked in the examination and control precisely of the destabilization women were seen to represent. Emancipated women were considered decadent excesses of modernity that if not controlled would threaten the stable, rational, scientific modernity with which the male subject was now identified (as well as endangering the old-fashioned intimate sphere necessary for its reproduction). Stabilizing modernity gets equated with stabilizing threats to male subjectivity, and male anxieties become foregrounded in very explicit ways as part of this project of "curing" them. It is also interesting how many German "art films" of this era openly thematize male anxieties about women—projecting onto images of women supposedly "private" anxieties that represent social anxieties as much as (if not more than) purely psychological or sexual anxieties.

The excess in the films of the era seems ultimately to represent an admission of instability and a lack of resolution for which there would be little if any room in Nazi culture. Indeed, perhaps in the end all this excess occasioned by attempts to represent anxieties about gender in modernity did have a positive function—one that might correspond to something like a genuine public debate on gender. It was certainly no debate among "equals," given the obvious masculine bias of German culture at this time—from the literary world to the film industry that was producing such films—but the very thematization of social anxieties about gender was bound to interest those less invested in such bias—above all women. The open acknowledgement of such anxieties (even if only for exploitative purposes) is indeed typical of Weimar cinema, and it becomes much less customary in the Third Reich (in which it was less permissible to admit weakness).

In any case, it is the explicit depiction of male anxieties in cinematic and other cultural texts of the Weimar era that enacts a destabilization not adequately contained, excessive to narrative closure. This is one of the reasons why Patrice Petro finds Weimar cinema to be interesting from the perspective of female spectators—the *female* subject absent in so much discussion of Weimar culture. The marking of males in crisis as "impotent" or "feminized" in Weimar cinema, which from the dominant heterosexual male perspective represented anxieties about loss of power, would necessarily be received somewhat differently by women, whose relation both to power and to social constructions of what "femininity" entails was obviously different (Petro, e.g., 25). The excess associated with the destabilization of traditional gender and sexual identities in Weimar culture also "exceeds" male paranoia and any misogynistic intentions. To some extent, then, the cinema served a public function in addressing spectators of both genders and of various classes concerned about their roles and status within Weimar society. There is thus something potentially emancipatory about the depiction of weak males, but this is a very contradictory dynamic, given the relationship of such male anxieties about power to the misogynistic depiction of violence against women of the sort Maria Tatar investigates.[39]

A further complication of the meaning of such excess is the obvious potential for a homoerotic reception of "feminized" males and "masculinized" females in Weimar texts, in spite of the male and heterosexual paranoia that seem so often to motivate such depictions. The potential for a homoerotic reception cannot have been overlooked—and from what we know of Carl Froelich's efforts in producing the 1931 film *Mädchen in Uniform,* the benefits and dangers of this reception were openly calculated.[40] This is not surprising, given the public awareness of homosexuality in Weimar due to the overt political campaigns on behalf of homosexual rights and to the not very covert lesbian and gay subcultures in Berlin— indeed, some of their bars and cafes were listed in tourist guides to Berlin's risqué night life.

Beyond the obvious significance of female subjects in Weimar culture with regard to questions of address and reception, there were also women involved in its production. There were a number of women authors in the Weimar Republic: to name only a few, Else Lasker-Schüler, Ricarda Huch, Anna Seghers, Marieluise Fleißer, Irmgard Keun, Vicki Baum, and Thea von Harbou (most famous for the screenplays she wrote for Fritz Lang's films). There were also two women who directed famous films in the years just before 1933—Leontine Sagan, who directed *Mädchen in Uniform,* and Leni Riefenstahl, who directed *The Blue Light (Das blaue Licht,* 1932).[41]

At first glance, neither Riefenstahl nor Sagan would seem especially New Objectivist, but they can be related to its sensibilities without much difficulty. Sagan directs a film that contrasts authoritarian with democratic values, while at the same time thematizing sexual emancipation as clearly one of the latter, central to the film's emphasis overt emphasis on lesbian love. Riefenstahl's film is after all a mountain film, a genre closely related to the cult of youth, sports, and nature. While Riefenstahl's own contribution to the genre is a fairy-tale romanticism more readily amenable to right-wing tendencies than is the case with some other mountain films, it was in fact the left-wing Bela Balasz whose assistance was so crucial to her work on the film.[42]

Even in its most narrowly defined sense, New Objectivity was not produced solely by men; indeed, Pinthus, in calling its literary manifestation "masculine," claimed for it works by Fleißer and Seghers. What did he find so "masculine" in their works? In Seghers it was an absence of sentimentality, and in Fleißer it was the de-mystification of romantic love (Pinthus, 331–32). In the 1980s Livia Wittmann noted that in the works of Fleißer and Keun all the typical formal characteristics of literary New Objectivity are to be found, and then questioned why novels by Fleißer and Keun were not canonized in postwar literary history with other classics of New Objectivity like those by Kästner or Hans Fallada. Seghers, Fleißer, and Keun were suppressed in the Third Reich. But Seghers was canonized within the Marxist tradition, whereas Fleißer and Keun were mostly ignored for most of the postwar period.[43]

Only in the late 1960s would Fleißer be rediscovered, and Keun had to wait about another ten years. Why? In part simply because they were women—a fact that has always hindered literary canonization—but also because their New Objectivist demystification of romantic love from the perspective of *female* characters was somehow more threatening than what one finds in the novels of the men, a reaction noted already in the response of contemporary critics (Wittmann, 56–63). As Lethen points out, there was a special provocation to masculinist New Objective attitudes toward gender in the creation of female characters whose identities were neither "authentic," harmonious, nor sentimental, but just as oriented to mimicry and simulation in dealing with the chaos of modernity as were many male characters (242–43).

The apparent threat posed by such writing was not unrelated to a definite trend that can be noted in the Weimar Republic after about 1930: together with the overall shift to the Right under the Brüning government as political polarization set in during the Depression, there was also evident a concerted effort to restore traditional conceptions of family and motherhood as against emancipated "New Women" and the hedonistic "Girlkultur" of Americanism. The economic collapse and the conservative shift in the government also meant the abandonment of the welfare-state experiments intended to make women's double burden easier (Grossmann, "*Girlkultur,*" 76). Emancipated and androgynous types of women were denounced all the way from the fashion magazines (cf. Petro, *Joyless Streets,* 121–24) to Kästner's *Fabian,* a novel that in terms of gender politics is definitely a nostalgic lament. In January of 1933, just days before Hitler would take power, Alice Rühle-Gerstel wrote bitterly that the restorative trend was evident not just in the media campaign directed at women, but among many women themselves as well (359–60).[44]

In New Objectivity and in late Weimar culture we note a public fascination with the instability of traditional, fixed gender identities in modernization but also already an attempt to "control" them—and that attempt seems to be related to tendencies toward homogenization and control in popular culture in general, and in the entertainment film in particular. In contrast to New Objectivity, National Socialism provided a much more definitive "answer" to such consequences of modernization as destabilized identities, subversive or divisive elements in mass culture, and other problems of national resolve. As a "reactionary modernism," fascism was an emphatic disavowal not really of modernity but rather of heterogeneity (and of course democracy) in modernity. The new managerial class whose fate was tied to modernization opted to acquiesce in this disavowal for the sake of a strong, "masculine" and homogenous national identity—an acquiescence that certainly deserves to be called cynical.

For in the Third Reich, any anxieties or doubts about "natural" roles according to gender and "race" (a category inseparable from certain "biological" assumptions about gender) would be much more forcefully disavowed. This had its effect throughout the culture, including the cinema, where, in contrast to films of the Weimar period, female characters would tend to be trivialized to the point where they would no longer be allowed even to represent any serious threat.[45] The affirmation of a homogenous national identity included, especially in the cinema, a program for a unitary, "middle-brow," and predominantly escapist mass culture in which traditional identities were not to be questioned.

But was this the inevitable end of the consumerist popular culture of the 1920s, or was it a forced co-optation of that culture by the new regime in the Third Reich? While for many years studies of the new consumer culture that became dominant in the Weimar Republic have tended to view it exclusively as a symptom of the decay of an idealized, democratic public sphere, the parallels between the concerns about such "decay" and concerns about the (post)modern blurring of idealized class and gender identities should give us pause. There were and are new developments here that deserve more than just wholesale denunciation.[46]

Chapter 4 ∽

Boys in Crisis: Discourses of Castration in the Early Stabilized Period

Here the nation has, on command and with steady aim, cut off its genitals . . . .

—Franz Schauwecker, *Aufbruch der Nation* (1928)[1]

The Carnival of Humiliation, I
Literal Castration—as Metaphor—in Ernst Toller's Drama Hinkemann *(1924)*

Peter Gay's *Weimar Culture: the Outsider as Insider* (1968) is a still canonical, if now somewhat dated study of the period. The canonical status is in many ways deserved, but one of the book's most annoying aspects is its somewhat facile Freudian analysis of Weimar culture, an analysis that unfortunately still haunts us.[2] Expressionism, which Gay defines as the dominant artistic expression of the Weimar Republic (thus placing a phenomenon primarily of the 1910s into the 1920s, a mistake that Walter Laqueur only magnifies) can be characterized as a "Revolt of the Sons," followed upon by the "Revenge of the Fathers," which encompasses the later Weimar Republic and the triumph of the Nazis in 1933. That Gay so blithely defines Weimar culture in terms of fathers and sons, in terms of an Oedipal scheme enshrining male psychic development as the touchstone for all understanding, is perhaps not so surprising; indeed, it is typical of a long tradition of scholarship on the Left about German culture. From (the postwar) Kracauer to Adorno (Hewitt, 1–78), the Mitscherlichs, and beyond, weak or "effeminate" sons and powerful mothers are more or less blamed for fascism—and also for the inability to "mourn" fascism (Linville, 3–5). This attitude is evident in Gay's reference to the many "repulsive" films of the era; he bases his remarks on Kracauer's *From Caligari to Hitler:* "again and again there are scenes in which the man puts his head, helpless, on the woman's bosom. The revenge of the father and the omnipotence of the mother were twin aspects of the Weimar scene, both equally destructive to the youth" (141–42).

One of the "weak sons" Gay actually names within a page of these remarks (140) was the writer Ernst Toller. Toller is mentioned specifically in the context of his suicide, which in fact occurred long after both Expressionism and the Weimar Republic: it occurred in 1939 in New York, after six years of exile from Hitler's Germany.[3] The plays that first earned Toller fame are certainly Expressionist dramas. Was Expressionism a literature of "sons"? To be fair to Gay (among many others), I should concede that it was of course largely a male affair; outside of Else Lasker-Schüler there are rarely any female writers mentioned in connection with it. And certainly Expressionist dramas do deal often enough with rebellions against oppressive fathers—the titles alone of Walter Hasenclever's *The Son* (*Der Sohn,* 1914) and Arnolt Bronnen's *Patricide* (*Vatermord,* 1920) reveal this preoccupation.[4]

Toller was without a doubt one of those rebellious sons, and generational conflict is thematized in his very first drama, *Transfiguration* (*Die Wandlung,* 1918). But Toller went beyond thematization of Oedipal crisis and the usual "discourses of castration" in the 1924 play that marks his move beyond Expressionism, *Hinkemann: A Tragedy* (*Hinkemann: Eine Tragödie*).[5] In that play *literal castration*—a problem so obviously specific to the male body—becomes a metaphor for the universal human condition. *Hinkemann* thus still posits a specifically male crisis as a model for all humanity. In this play, however, Toller nonetheless manages to undermine the ideology of the "strong male" that undergirds fascism—and many leftist analyses of fascism—in some very illuminating ways. As Helen Cafferty asserts: "Clearly, Toller wanted to reject the metaphor that our everyday language suggests: male potency equals national strength" (48). Yet by engaging that metaphor so directly, Toller's play unleashed a long history of negative reception.

In *Male Subjectivities at the Margins,* Kaja Silverman emphasizes "the central part which the equation of penis and phallus play in the maintenance of a certain 'reality'" (65), that is, reality as constructed in patriarchal ideologies. What in Lacanian terms Silverman calls the equation of penis to phallus can be explained as the equation of the male genitals with the principle of power in the symbolic system that underlies a certain social order, an order, that is, that limits discursive power and social agency above all to those with male bodies. But precisely because of this equation, Silverman asserts that "when the male subject is brought into a traumatic encounter with lack, as in the situation of war, he often experiences it as the impairment of his anatomical masculinity" (62). Thus Silverman finds in many American films of the immediate post–World War II era a depiction of trauma among returning veterans that openly thematizes the central equation of the male body to social power because that "dominant fiction" is in crisis (54).

That central equation is quite frankly thematized in Toller's play. Indeed, at one point in the drama, the character Hinkemann buys an antique phallic deity, referring to it bitterly as the symbol of all power and exploitation. The historical context of the play *Hinkemann* is also comparable to that of the films Silverman analyzes: the crisis of returning German veterans after World War I was in fact much more severe than anything faced by Americans after World War II. Germany had lost the war, had sustained 2.4 million casualties on the field and economic hardships at home; of the 300,000 German civilian deaths, many were caused by disease and malnutrition (Berghahn, 44). Anton Kaes has suggested that the traumatic experience of the war, especially as experienced by the German soldiers at the front who survived the horrors of mechanized and gas warfare, the trenches, shell shock, and the death of so many of their comrades, had a massive, if for many years mostly unconscious, impact on Weimar culture (and its cinema).[6]

Beyond the physical and psychic impact of the war itself was the social and political upheaval in its aftermath. Germany's dominant order—symbolized by the Kaiser and the aristocratic-military caste he represented—was deposed in 1918, beginning a chaotic period of revolution, counter-revolution, and hyperinflation that would take four years to "stabilize." The loss of orientation in post-World War I Germany is perhaps no better symbolized than in the situation of Toller's character Hinkemann, the worker who returns from the war a castrated war veteran who can get no other job than as a strong man in a freak show. What ensues is a veritable carnival of humiliation, exactly the nightmare feared by the "cold persona" described in Lethen's *Verhaltenslehren,* who tries so desperately to mask his anxieties about being exposed to such ridicule.

HINKEMANN *IN CONTEXT:* ERNST TOLLER *AND THE CRISES OF EARLY WEIMAR*

Kaiser Wilhelm II abdicated on November 9, 1918, two days before Germany surrendered, which brought World War I to an end. This act created a power vacuum in Germany, making it clear how unstable the old order had become. Morale among the troops had become an increasing problem for months, leading to some mutinies, the rebellion of sailors in Kiel being the most famous example. As troops were demobilized, enlisted soldiers joined disgruntled workers in sporadic attempts in various German cities to form councils that would be the basis of a new form of government. These councils, or *Räte*, had somewhat vague, idealistic ideas about creating a kind of just, socialist order—but they did not necessarily imply any widespread willingness to fight an armed revolution, in spite of the hopes of radical leftist groups like Spartakus, out of which in turn was founded the German Communist Party (KPD) in late 1918. At the same time Friedrich Ebert, at the head of the more reformist-minded "majority" Social Democrats, proclaimed a republic. To these moderate Social Democratic parliamentarians, the council movements, born of relatively spontaneous uprisings by workers, appeared quite threatening. Committed to order, Ebert enlisted the military generals of the old aristocratic order to protect the new parliamentary democracy by eliminating the workers' councils (Peukert, 38–41).

The regular Army and the paramilitary *Freikorps* were only too happy to attack the workers and intellectuals involved in the council movements, whom they considered dangerous revolutionaries. In a number of bloody campaigns they took control of districts where councils had attempted to assume power and ultimately destroyed the councils, in the process murdering Rosa Luxemburg and Karl Liebknecht, the heads of the Spartacists (and the KPD) in Berlin, and Kurt Eisner, the anarchist socialist who had led the *Räterepublik,* the council-republic (also known as the "Soviet Republic") set up in Munich.[7] The military forces did all this out of no great loyalty to the new democratic German republic convened in Weimar, which they generally despised, as would become clear again and again over the fifteen-year history of the republic.

Right in the middle of this defeated revolution following the end of World War I was the young writer Ernst Toller. He had indeed played a leading role in the short-lived socialist republic in Munich, and, after his capture in June 1919, he was condemned to five years in prison for his role in the revolution. During those years in prison he wrote many of his most famous plays—including *Masses and Man* (*Masse Mensch,* 1920), *The Machine-Wreckers* (*Die Maschinenstürmer,* 1922), and *Hinkemann,* which he began writing in 1921–1922. *Hinkemann* was first performed in late 1923, and then in a revised version became a major theater scandal in 1924, just as Toller himself was finally about to be released from prison. Imprisonment had not ended his literary activity, and it had not ended his political activity, either: from prison he ran as a USPD (Independent Socialist) candidate for both the Bavarian *Landtag* and the *Reichstag* in 1920, and he became an alternate delegate to both parliamentary bodies.

Thus even at the most superficial level the situation of Toller's castrated character Hinkemann would seem to offer rich parallels not just to Germany and its veterans, but also to the working-class revolutionaries of 1918–1919, and to Toller's own situation as well. He was after all a captured and imprisoned Leftist intellectual and artist who wrote his pacifist, antifascist plays in prison, addressing them to a nation that would not heed him— indeed, a nation that would eventually drive him, as both a Leftist and a Jew, into exile in 1933. Interpretations emphasizing such parallels have always been debated: against the background of which (if any) of these various larger contexts—national, social, historical, or autobiographical— ought the play *Hinkemann* to be understood? The common interpretation of the castrated figure Hinkemann as an allegory for Germany is one reason the play first became so controversial politically: the nationalist right wing interpreted it as a treasonous libel of German veterans and the German nation. Toller himself denied this interpretation, which could be found in the writings of left-wing critics as well, and in revising the play he changed its name from the original title of the 1923 version, *The German Hinkemann* (*Der deutsche Hinkemann*) to the one word title *Hinkemann* in 1924 in order to make that clear (Frühwald and Spalek, 142–43). Yet in spite of the intentions of the author, the play seems to invite numerous allegorical or metaphorical interpretations precisely because of its unusual focus on literal castration. It would seem that this disturbing theme has encouraged most critics to avoid its disturbing biological concreteness by fleeing to the distance of more universal generalization. At the same time the metaphorical "richness," as it were, of the figure of castration in the patriarchal imagination is immediately apparent, being so easily equated with other sexual metaphors such as "impotence" and "sterility," which are used so often to describe conditions of social and existential powerlessness, weakness, and futility that have (intrinsically at least) little if anything to do with biological sex.

The play *Hinkemann* is named after its protagonist, Eugen Hinkemann, an unemployed, castrated veteran. At the beginning of the play, Hinkemann frightens and confuses his wife Grete with his fits of rage and melancholy. She confesses to one of his employed proletarian friends, Paul Grosshahn, that Hinkemann is "not a man at all" ("gar kein Mann"; 1.1: 12).[8] In the 1926 English translation of the play, titled *Brokenbrow,* Grosshahn is called "Jock Rooster," but his surname is more literally translated as "big rooster," perhaps even more effectively as "big cock." Grosshahn is aptly described by Cafferty as a "macho proletarian" (51); he laughs cruelly upon learning of his friend's condition and then demands that Grete come visit him to satisfy her sexual needs. Grete, in her characteristically passive manner, submits to his command.

Meanwhile Hinkemann has found a job as a strong man in a carnival freak show, in which he must kill rats and mice with his teeth, drinking some of their blood. Hinkemann had earlier been thrown into a fit of despair about the blinding of a finch to make its song better; because of his special empathy for any creature forced to endure bodily mutilation, he is obviously sickened at the prospect of this carnival job, but jobs are scarce, and the money is too good. Above all he accepts the job out of the need to support Grete, for their relationship is the one human bond that gives him sustenance. Grete at this point is already pregnant with a child fathered by Grosshahn, and she is strolling happily through the carnival on his arm when by chance the two of them see Hinkemann's act. Grosshahn is outraged by what he considers to be a swindle: German manhood, heroism, and culture, as the carnival barker proclaims, are being represented by a man Grosshahn knows to be a eunuch. In contrast, Grete is overwhelmed by the great sacrifice Hinkemann is making for her as he bites into the necks of rats; she knows only too well how sensitive he has become to the injury of any living creature. Grosshahn, angered by her sympathy for Hinkemann, leaves her, but she is determined not to remain with him anyway. She has decided to re-dedicate herself to Hinkemann.

The next scene occurs in a working-class bar, where adherents of different ideological positions are arguing; among others there is an orthodox Communist, an anarchist, and a pious Christian. Hinkemann enters and joins the discussion: he mentions "a friend" of his who has been castrated, and he asks them how one should understand and deal with such a problem according to their various political philosophies. They all laugh; no one has much of an answer. Then Grosshahn enters the bar, telling Hinkemann that he and Grete saw him at the carnival. When Hinkemann asks how Grete reacted, Grosshahn lies and says that she laughed at him. He then tells Hinkemann not only that he has slept with Grete, but also that he will abandon her. He then relates to the other men at the bar the story of a eunuch portraying a strongman at the carnival, which makes everyone laugh. He is about to reveal the eunuch's identity when Hinkemann himself screams out that he is the eunuch. Hinkemann demands that they keep laughing, tells them how unready they are for any new, more humane society, and then rushes out of the bar, still in despair because he thinks that Grete has laughed at him.

In the street he meets his employer, the owner of the booth where Hinkemann performs. He tries to quit his job, but his boss does not take him seriously. At this point Hinkemann breaks down, and what follows is a dream sequence in which multitudes of one-armed and one-legged veterans fill the stage from all directions, singing military songs and playing accordions, moving toward the center. When no group can advance any farther, they start to sing a threatening revolutionary verse, "Down with the dogs of the reactionaries!" ("Nieder mit die Hunde [sic] von der Reaktion!"; 3.1: 38). Then the police arrive and issue orders, and the veterans do an about-face, moving in orderly groups back offstage to a military marching song. Newspaper boys come onstage shouting sensational headlines, followed by street vendors hawking medicines for impotence, Freikorps recruits with rubber truncheons, and prostitutes who fight over the collapsed Hinkemann.

In the final scene Hinkemann comes home with the Priapus he has found in an antique shop. He offers a bitter prayer to this symbol of naked power, which in his despair he considers the only god. Finally Grete arrives, wanting to atone for her adultery in humble submission. At first she does not understand that Hinkemann is angry with her only for laughing at him, but she is willing to acknowledge that sin as well, even though it is not true. Eventually Hinkemann realizes that she is as miserable and helpless as he is, and he forgives her, but he still sees no future for them together. He feels defeated, and he wants her to go on her own, still healthy in body, to continue the struggle for a better world. Grete does not understand him and is afraid of being left alone; she leaves the apartment sadly, and shortly Hinkemann thereafter learns that she has jumped out a window to her death. At the end of the play he is alone with her corpse, not knowing what to do.

This ending is one of the major changes Toller made in his 1924 revision of the original version that premiered in September 1923. In the original version the play ends with Hinkemann making the same speech about the arbitrariness of fate that ends the newer version, but meanwhile he prepares a noose to hang himself.[9] Toller changed the ending in response to Marxist criticisms that the play was too pessimistic (Frühwald, 67). As mentioned above, the title of the play had been changed from *The German Hinkemann,* as the play was called at its Leipzig premiere on September 19, 1923, to *Hinkemann,* its title when staged in Dresden on January 17, 1924. This was Toller's attempt to respond to the charge that the play was too "allegorical" (largely in response to Alfred Kerr's critique of the 1923 premiere).[10]

In spite of these changes the play became one of the great theater scandals of 1924. As Frühwald reminds us (89–93), the play had caused no scandal at its premiere in Leipzig in September 1923—at that time Brecht's *Baal* was causing the scandal (89). By January 1924, however, the production of *Hinkemann* in Dresden became the target of right-wing protests, and this had largely to do with external political developments that had occurred between September 1923 and early 1924. Among these was the failed right-wing putsch by Hitler in Munich in November 1923. Hitler's ("beer hall") putsch was defeated at just about the same time that a left-wing coalition government of Communists and Social Democrats in Saxony was forcibly ended by national troops. So while the Right had failed in Bavaria, the Left had been thwarted in Saxony. Saxony thus became a place where the Right would be able to find an opportunity to make up for the humiliating blow it had suffered in Bavaria. A play by Toller of all people, who was still in prison for his revolutionary activities, made a perfect target for the nationalist right wing, and after the protests in Dresden, the play would continue to be a target in other cities over the next few months.

As accurate as Frühwald may be in his insistence that external conditions caused the scandals, one cannot deny that Toller's play itself was a special provocation to the Right, at the same time being not all that popular with critics on the Left. *Hinkemann* struck a nerve, and that is an important historical fact, whether or not the play was being misinterpreted by critics, political activists, or any other members of the public. As Brockmann points out, the "allegorical" equation of Hinkemann and Germany is made explicitly in the play itself by Hinkemann's boss, who advertises Hinkemann as "*The* German hero! The German culture! The manly fist of Germany!" ("D e r deutsche Held! Die deutsche Kultur! Die deutsche Männerfaust!"; 2.3: 18). Grosshahn is angered by that equation, which he finds fraudulent, since he knows that "*the* German hero" is actually a eunuch (2.3: 30). These two characters are clearly marked as negative in the play, and Cafferty's point is well taken that it "is not surprising that conservative nationalists accepted Grosshahn's interpretation," given that they "share the same assumptions about sex and power" (49). Nonetheless the play is definitely thematizing these false assumptions. They are precisely what the play attempts to question, and it would seem that the play's reception has never recovered from this affront to the masculinist ideology so dear both to the militarist Right and to the Left's macho cult of proletarian manhood.

HINKEMANN *AND MALE CRISIS IN WEIMAR MODERNITY*

The machine doesn't push me around. I am the master and not the machine. When I stand at the machine, I am overcome with a devilish glee: You have to make this slave feel that you're the boss! And then I drive that howling, humming, and groaning thing to the limit of its power, until it sweats blood . . . so to speak . . . and I laugh and enjoy myself while it torments itself and slaves away. So, my little beast, I yell, you must obey! Obey! And I make the machine swallow the roughest piece of wood and have it form it according to my command! Be a man, Eugen, then you are the master. (1.1: 9–10)[11]

—Ernst Toller, *Hinkemann*

The above quote ends with Paul Grosshahn's advice to Hinkemann, before he knows that his friend has been castrated and that precisely this equation of mastery with masculinity has become especially problematic for him. In response to Hinkemann's—typically Expressionist—critique of the machine as the principle of the exploitation and oppression of human labor, Grosshahn responds with these remarks about the machine that are emblematic of the cult of the machine typically associated with New Objectivity. At the same time they demonstrate the stakes for the male subject in this accommodation with modernization. What is at stake is mastery, of course: the supposed autonomy of traditional male subject is especially threatened by modernization and technology, as was demonstrated so concretely in the first modern war, World War I, and in an especially humiliating way for the German Empire. But in New Objectivity the male subject seeks to regain mastery precisely through technology. Toller's text demonstrates through the proletarian Grosshahn's expression of this ideology both how masculinist it is and how little it differs from the fascist modernism of Ernst Jünger; indeed, *Hinkemann* shows us how close such ideas are to the fascist ideal of the soldier as machine.[12]

If this quest for mastery depends on denial of the threatening consequences of modernization and the recent world war in the Weimar Republic, as Brockmann convincingly argues, then Hinkemann embodies an especially disturbing threat to such denial, as a living reminder of the power of modern warfare to wound masculine pride at the site of its symbolic identity. Thus what *Hinkemann* provides is an allegory of humiliation, the most intense provocation possible to what Lethen calls the "cold persona" of New Objectivity, that very masculine response to the turbulence of postwar reality by means of which all feelings of insecurity would be masked. It is fear of humiliation, fear of appearing ridiculous ("lächerlich") that is the ultimate motivation for the development of such a type.[13] And as Toller wrote in a 1923 letter to Stefan Zweig, in *Hinkemann* he wanted specifically to confront the condition of being ridiculous ("Lächerlichkeit," *Briefe,* 153). Given that Toller intended to confront the humiliation and ridicule that the reigning sensibility so feared, it should be no surprise that the play was so often rejected across the political spectrum, and indeed that another German playwright, one much more in tune with the "cold persona" of New Objectivity, Brecht, began to usurp Toller's position as Germany's most well-known dramatist from just about this point in the 1920s.

The play *Hinkemann* can be said to mark Toller's move beyond Expressionism (Frühwald, 87). The elements that signal this move are the more naturalistic characters and setting; still reminiscent of Expressionism are the allegorical/typological names given to the characters and the fantastic dream sequence, which consisted of separate scenes in the second and third acts in the 1923 version of the play. These scenes were however consolidated into one scene in the third act (3.1: 38–41) in the definitive 1924 version of the play (Frühwald, 85). Nonetheless, *Hinkemann* retains a humanist skepticism about modernization typical of Toller's earlier works and Expressionism in general. In the same way, his 1927 drama *Hoppla! That's Life! (Hoppla, wir leben!)* is a text that documents Weimar's "stabilized period" so well, and its premiere, directed by Piscator, was the epitome of "New Objective" experiments in the theater with projections, film, and "documentary" theater. But *Hoppla* is no celebration of the new era; rather, it is a pessimistic critique of its amoral cynicism (cf. Sloterdijk, 889). But it should be emphasized that this mixture of documentary theater and critique is not, however, so unusual; literary New Objectivity was rarely an uncritical celebration of modernity.[14] From our position today, at any rate, Toller's skepticism about Weimar modernity seems justified; his linkage of the cult of the machine with a brutal "heroic" masculinity in *Hinkemann* seems especially prophetic.

While he does critique this linkage, the gender politics of *Hinkemann* are not entirely unproblematic, of course. Although Silverman finds the American films she analyzes in the aftermath of World War II significant for their open admission of male insecurities, she asserts that they ultimately work to recuperate male subjectivity. While such a verdict would perhaps be unfair to *Hinkemann,* it is in any case necessary to look more closely at the role Grete, Hinkemann's wife, has in the play. In large part her role is determined by her function in the drama of male humiliation: her seduction by Grosshahn is an important stage in the tragedy, as well as a "natural" consequence—and illustration of—her husband's castration.

It is not Grete's sexual betrayal of Hinkemann that is most painful to him, however; it is rather the fact that, believing Grosshahn's malicious lie, he thinks that she laughed at him when she saw him onstage at the freak show. This Grete never understands. Her role is thus passive to an almost astounding degree: she submits quite passively to Grosshahn's seduction, consisting of her meek acquiescence to his forceful demand that she visit him. This again is transformed into a much more serious betrayal by Grosshahn, who finds the way to hurt Hinkemann most by lying about Grete's reaction to his carnival performance. In this light Grete seems merely an instrument through which Grosshahn can humiliate Hinkemann, an object of exchange in a sadistic competition between men.

Yet precisely at the moment when, according to Grosshahn, Grete was supposedly laughing at her husband, what she actually does is to stand up to Grosshahn: realizing the extent of her husband's sacrifice on her behalf, she is determined to return to him, and she ends her relationship with Grosshahn: "Why do you threaten me, Paul? I'm not going to come with you" ("Warum drohst du mir, Paul? Ich komm doch nicht mit dir"; 2.3: 21). It is true that this is followed by an admission that she is not in control: "My life never belonged to me" ("Mein Leben gehörte niemals mir"); furthermore, her decision to leave Grosshahn is made so that she can offer herself completely to the service of her husband, that is, completely in the spirit of passive, self-sacrificing martyrdom. Nonetheless she does stand up to the proud, bullying Grosshahn, and rebuff him; this rejection wounds his pride enough to make him want to hurt Hinkemann as severely as he can—hence he invents the lie that covers up Grete's true reaction to her husband's humiliating spectacle onstage.

As I have indicated, this single example of agency on Grete's part does not really contradict her otherwise generally passive behavior. This is even more true of her final decision to kill herself, an act based on her inability to understand why Hinkemann does not accept her offer of self-sacrificing atonement, why he will not allow her to stay with him. Cafferty asserts that the drama provides a critique of Grete's passivity as much as it does of Grosshahn's selfish assertiveness, that it is an attack on traditional gender stereotypes, especially the association of masculinity with bullying aggression and of femininity with passive acceptance (51–53). While this argument is persuasive, it would seem that the situation is more complicated.

At the height of his rage at her, Hinkemann suddenly sees in Grete's eyes "the eyes of a harassed creature, beaten, punished, tortured" ("die Augen der gehetzten, der geschlagenen, der gepeinigten, der gemarterten Kreatur"; 3.2: 50–51), and this makes him recognize himself. He realizes that Grete is no better off than he is, that she is just as scared and powerless—that they both share vulnerability and lack, the lack that is the basis of the human condition. Nonetheless he wants her to leave him, for she is healthy and can continue the struggle for a better life, and he is too tired and has seen too much (3.2: 52–53). She does not understand him, and she walks away with heavy steps and commits suicide. Upon learning this, Hinkemann in the original version of the play himself prepares to commit suicide, either succumbing to the same resignation, or out of guilt that he was not able to offer enough strength to Grete.

In the second, less "pessimistic" version of the play, Hinkemann does not completely succumb to resignation; he does not kill himself, in spite of his despairing knowledge of human weakness, denial, and cruelty. He does not imitate Grete's suicide. Is this merely another example of a very old pattern in literature, according to which the death of a woman functions to facilitate growth in the male protagonist? The problem with such an interpretation is that this second ending of the play does not demonstrate all that much growth. Furthermore, Grete's suicide can only be a lesson to Hinkemann to the extent that he identifies with her and decides that she has made the wrong choice. And of course he has identified with her upon seeing in her eyes the same feelings of fear and powerlessness he knows himself.

It is this identification of the castrated male with the powerless, frightened female that is perhaps the most interesting aspect of the play. A similar identification between male and female victims occurs in Toller's *Transfiguration* (*Die Wandlung*), as Cafferty notes (49–50): the skeletons of dead male soldiers welcome the skeleton of a thirteen-year old girl who has died in a gang rape by other soldiers, greeting her with the statement: "We have all been violated" ("Wir sind alle geschändet").[15] In Toller's second play, *Masses and Man* (*Masse Mensch*), the protagonist is a humanist intellectual who leads revolutionary workers and who tries to resist mass violence with a pacifist insistence on the value of each human individual. This protagonist is female, called indeed "The Woman," but her (proletarian) male rival, "The Nameless One," advocates violent revolution, equating bloodshed with sex and deriding her as a nun for her pacifism. The class politics here are interesting: pacifism is associated with the bourgeois intellectual—appearing as a woman—in contrast to a vital, bloodthirsty masculinity associated with the working class.

Also clear is Toller's apparent identification with figures who are "less than male." This may have had some relation to his Jewishness, which of course was often considered "feminized" in an anti-Semitic society.[16] In

Transfiguration Jewish identity is thematized,[17] and there of course the male protagonist is a savior figure who is "above sex." Later, of course, in *Hoppla! That's Life!*, we find a male protagonist who does seek monogamous sexual love, only to be set straight by his "objective," cold, emancipated former girlfriend, for whom sex is entirely functionalized.

What appears progressive to us today in this tendency is the attempt to question the connection between vitalist masculinity and power, but it is combined with a corresponding, somewhat sentimentalized, bourgeois vision of a civilizing but asexual femininity. The evils of modernity are clearly identified with sexual license in *Hinkemann,* as demonstrated by the speeches of his employer at the carnival director both in front of the crowd (2.3: 17–18) and to Hinkemann personally (3.1: 36). The headlines the newspaper boys scream in the dream also make it clear that "naked dancing" ("Nackttänze") and films with titles like "Sex Murderess of Forty Men" ("Lustmörderin der vierzig Männer") are crucial ingredients of modern insanity (3.1: 39). Both examples focus primarily on female sexual excess, with the film title exemplifying the common fantasy of a murderous female sexuality—even though male sex murderers were undoubtedly much more prevalent, as well as fantasies of identification with them, or so one must surmise from many representations produced by male artists of the Weimar avant-garde, as Beth Irwin Lewis and Maria Tatar have demonstrated so well.

Thus the critique of Grete's passive femininity in *Hinkemann* may be a much more class-biased critique than it is an example of emancipatory thinking about gender. Aggressive proletarian masculinity and passive proletarian femininity are critiqued from the standpoint of a castrated hero who embodies the virtues of a somewhat androgynous and enlightened (male) intelligentsia. Gender dynamics are complicated in Toller's works and not necessarily progressive or even consistent. Certainly the proletarian women Toller depicts in *Machine-Wreckers* (*Maschinenstürmer,* 1922) seem negative not for any passivity but rather precisely for their insufficient (bourgeois) femininity; it is their "masculine" character that for Toller connects them to irrational revolutionary violence. And in *Hoppla!* (1927), the female intellectual character, Eva, is the embodiment of "cold," emancipated, desentimentalized sexuality that is part and parcel of the cynical modernity being critiqued.

It is thus a sentimentalized concept of femininity that Toller seems to valorize, and it is a femininity that is embodied rarely if at all by any actually female characters in his plays. Indeed, it is probably best embodied by Hinkemann himself, in some kind of perfect synthesis of masculine and feminine polarities that appealed so to male intellectuals in the sway of what Lindner calls *Lebensideologie* (the "ideology of vitalism").

Evaluated in terms of the author's other works, then, and perhaps in terms of authorial intention as well, the play is (not surprisingly) limited by class and gender biases all too typical of the age. Yet there is still something quite subversive about such an androgynous project, I would argue, especially in an era when there was such anxiety about the blurring of all boundaries, above all in terms of gender. Similarly, the play's embrace of the suffering "creature" at the core of every human being is all the more astounding in a decade when so much energy went into masking that "feminine" vulnerability, especially on the part of the male avant-garde who attempted to hide behind what Lethen calls the "cold persona." With Toller it is above all the open thematization—even to some extent the valorization—of male lack that is provocative, even more so because it is combined with an insistence that the basic "lack" in human existence is not gendered at all.

Nowhere is this provocation clearer than in *Hinkemann,* and the resulting scandal was evidence that the provocation disturbed certain sectors of the German public, especially the more reactionary ones, but not merely those. As Eve Rosenhaft has written, the representation of masculinity was at issue, and this occupied the Left in Weimar as well as the Right in defensive maneuvers that demonstrate how unstable traditional identities had become—and how concerns about disempowerment were fused with anxieties about loss of manhood ("Lesewut," 133, 139, 141). The play thus provoked its public far beyond what its author intended, illustrating both the extent to which the blurring of traditional identities had progressed and how threatening that process was to Weimar society. And yet precisely in exposing the "impotence" of traditional identities, the play hints at a more humane vision of the possibilities that lie beyond them.

The Carnival of Humiliation, II

Sex & Social Mobility, Mass Spectacle & Reflexivity
in E.A. Dupont's Film Variety *(1925)*

The film *Varieté* premiered in Berlin in November 1925. Directed by Ewald Andre Dupont and produced by Erich Pommer, the film starred Lya de Putti and Emil Jannings. Both Siegfried Kracauer (*Caligari*, 125–27) and Lotte Eisner (278–84), in their canonical books on the German cinema of the 1920s, considered *Variety* (as it was called in its American release) to be a key film in the transition from Expressionism in German cinema to the type of realism associated with the New Objectivity. It was definitely a product of the German "art cinema," but it was also a huge box office hit, in Germany as well as the United States.

It was an "art film" that nonetheless recalled in certain ways the sensational, lurid, and much more "low-brow" early German cinema. Perhaps it is this citation of early German cinema (that is, the cinema before 1918)[18] that helps to make *Variety* such a rich text, one that provides both a mixture of— and reflection upon—mass entertainment, innovative cinematic technique, and male insecurities about female autonomy—both sexual and economic. As is true of many famous films made during Germany's Weimar Republic (1918–1933)—from Karl Grune's *The Street* (1923) and F.W. Murnau's *The Last Laugh* (1924) to G.W. Pabst's *Pandora's Box* (1929) and Josef von Sternberg's *The Blue Angel* (1930)—this film tells a story of male humiliation.[19] In a plot that resembles *The Street, Pandora's Box,* and *The Blue Angel,* a male protagonist is seduced and then cuckolded by a woman who embodies an interesting mixture of exotic vamp and ambitious working woman. She betrays him with an effeminate, sophisticated, foreign cosmopolitan. The manner in which this familiar story of humiliation and revenge is told, however, indicates a deeper ambivalence about modernity—and about the very mass spectacle that the film itself reproduces.

Variety can readily be related to the emerging New Objectivity of the "stabilized period" of the Weimar Republic (1924–1929). Aspects of the film that are arguably "New Objective" include its contradictory move both toward melodrama and documentary, and its embrace—and ambivalent examination—of mass entertainment. The film uses the carnival as a metaphor for the topsy-turvy world of modernity, a metaphor that also can be noted in Expressionist films—above all in *The Cabinet of Dr. Caligari* (Robert Wiene). But here it is a very contemporary and very urban entertainment milieu captured most impressively with virtuoso camera work shot on location in Berlin's famous variety palace, the Wintergarten.

While the film celebrates the modernity of its own camera and editing techniques, it remains very ambivalent about the urban modernity, upward mobility, "Americanism," and destabilization of traditional gender identities it so sensationally depicts.[20] *Variety,* despite all its citation—and mobilization—of the forms of mass spectacle and entertainment associated with Weimar modernity, remains an "art film." The German "art cinema" of the 1920s is characterized on the one hand by a certain aesthetic conservatism that reflects the ambivalence about film and mass culture on the part of intellectuals so well documented in Anton Kaes's *Kino-Debatte* ("Debate

About the Cinema"). On the other hand, the art cinema often manifests a political conservatism typical of large German industries during the 1920s, including the film industry, which was becoming ever more concentrated throughout the decade. By "political conservativism" I mean the generally anti-democratic, class-based hierarchical elitism characteristic of the dominant social groups in the Weimar Republic. Hence the rather cynical (and strategic) contradiction of producing films ambivalent about mass culture and modernity that were themselves stunning spectacles made with all the technical expertise money could buy.

With *Variety,* one clearly has a film that was the product of Erich Pommer's special division at Ufa, the goal of which was to produce big-budget "art films" of the sort that to this day fill the film-historical canon of the Weimar cinema. At the same time, this was a film that was a box office hit both in Germany and the United States—something for which Pommer and the German industry had long been striving. It thematized popular success in the entertainment world in the way we now expect the "self-reflexive" Weimar art cinema to do. What I would like to examine more closely, however, is precisely the "self-reflexivity" in *Variety,* for this aspect of the film is more problematic than its melodramatic or sensational aspects. It is the self-reflexivity in the film that, far from being politically "progressive," betrays the film's ultimately conservative, elitist, anti-democratic distaste for the mass entertainment it is (cynically) producing.

THE TWO VERSIONS OF THE FILM

The 1925 production of *Variety* was the third film adaptation of Felix Holländer's novel, *The Oath of Stefan Huller* [*Der Eid des Stefan Huller*].[21] The first two film adaptations had been made in 1912 and 1919. That a film about sexual betrayal set in the milieu of acrobats in a variety show was made as early as 1912 is significant, since at that point the cinema in Germany had only recently extricated itself from the lower-class world of variety shows, music halls, and carnivals. In the years after the cinema's invention in 1895, films had primarily been shown in variety halls and in *Wanderkinos,* the "wandering" tent cinemas that appeared at fairs and carnivals; only in 1904 did storefront cinemas begin to compete seriously with these venues. By 1910 German films began to be exhibited in ever grander cinema "palaces," as the German film industry strove for bourgeois respectability, precisely in order to compensate for its quite recent, lowbrow origins (Schlüpmann, 8–9, 12).

A film presenting a titillating view of the demi-monde of carnival and variety performers was still considered marketable in 1925 by Erich Pommer.[22] The German "art cinema" began around 1912 and is often called an *Autorenkino,* or "cinema of authors/auteurs" (Schlüpmann 247; Elsaesser and Wedel, 113). By the 1920s, the German art film was only one of many products—and strategies—of a large, commercial film industry. It was certainly nothing very similar to the concept of a low-budget *Autorenkino* with oppositional ambitions that we associate with the "New German Cinema" of the 1970s.[23] Certainly for *Variety* it is a debatable term, at least if the director Dupont is supposed to be the film's "author"; the producer Pommer and the cinematographer Karl Freund were both arguably much more important for the film. Pommer intended *Variety* to capitalize on the mobile-camera techniques Freund had developed in *The Last Laugh,* the film Pommer had produced a year earlier with F.W. Murnau directing. Pommer wanted to use Freund again to film *Variety,* but for director he chose Dupont over Murnau, apparently because he felt that the latter was unsuited to directing a melodrama so focused on (heterosexual) sex. It was also Pommer who persuaded Dupont to film the story in the new dynamic visual style that he wanted to market (Luft, ctd. in Combs).[24]

For although *The Last Laugh* had been a critical success, and while it had wowed and intimidated Hollywood with its technical virtuosity, it had not been an overwhelming box office hit. Proving Pommer's calculations right, *Variety* did become such a hit, both in Germany and the United States. Early on German critics saw it as the film the German film industry had long awaited, one that could compete with American cinema; the German trade journal *Kinematograph* asserted that the film was sure to conquer "even the aloof Americans" ("*Varieté:* Der grosse deutsche Film"). Many American critics agreed, and so did American audiences. 1926 headlines about the film's New York reception in another German trade journal, *Lichtbild-Bühne,* tell the story: "Thunderous Success of *Variety* in New York" and "Record Box Office for *Variety*" ("Stürmischer Erfolg"; "Rekord-Einnahmen").

Variety was for a long time the one great success Ufa managed to achieve in the United States (Esser, 165). It had the technical virtuosity of *The Last Laugh* with a story about sexual betrayal so lurid, at least by American standards, that Famous Players Lasky cut it drastically; the version released in the United States in all but New York and a few other large cities was about half an hour shorter.[25] It is this amputated version that is still available today in the United States (and in Great Britain as well—see Combs).[26] Because it is the shorter version with which most North American viewers are familiar, it is worth comparing the two. The longer "German" original is not only sexually more explicit than the "American" version, it also depicts greater social distance between Boss's humble status at the beginning of the film and the success he earns as a star of the Wintergarten later in the film.

Both the original German version and the American version begin in prison. Boss Huller, who has spent ten years in prison for murder, is called to see the prison director. The director has received a petition to grant the prisoner clemency, and therefore he asks that Boss break his long silence and tell his story. In a flashback, Boss does so. In the German version of the film, the flashback depicts Boss Huller as someone who runs a troupe of tawdry female dancers in a Hamburg carnival. His tired and worn-out wife plays piano for the show; Boss appears to be the more energetic and nurturing parent to their infant son. He longs to return to his old career as a trapeze artist, but his wife refuses to allow him to do so. A mysterious, exotic young dancer known as Berta-Marie joins the troupe, and Boss falls in love with her. He runs away with her to a carnival in Berlin, where he resumes his career on the trapeze with Berta-Marie as his partner. Their success leads to an offer from a world-famous trapeze artist, Artinelli, to leave the carnival behind for the more prestigious world of Berlin's internationally famous Wintergarten. They form a trio with Artinelli and are very successful, but now Boss is himself betrayed by the sophisticated and devious Artinelli, who after a somewhat brutal "seduction" of Berta-Marie carries on a sexual liaison with her. When Boss learns that he has been betrayed, he fantasizes dropping Artinelli during the trapeze act, but instead he kills him later in a knife fight in Artinelli's dressing room. Boss then turns himself in to the police. Here the flashback ends, and the prison director, moved by Boss's story, grants him freedom; the film ends with the gates of the prison opening up to beautiful, sunny skies.

The American version retains the frame of the prison scenes around the main flashback, but in the flashback plot the scenes in Hamburg, including wife and child, are cut. The story begins with Berta-Marie and Boss as trapeze artists at the carnival in Berlin, just as they are about to be discovered by Artinelli. Berta-Marie becomes in this version Boss's wife, not his mistress; Boss has not abandoned his family for her but rather is blameless until he murders Artinelli. Berta-Marie is a faithless wife who succumbs to a clever womanizer, rather than the exotic vamp who seduces Boss away from hearth and home only to betray him for the more wordly and handsome Artinelli.

VARIETY AND "NEW OBJECTIVITY":
DOCUMENTARY, MELODRAMA, AND REFLEXIVITY

Eisner credits Dupont for his adroit use of "the last vestiges of Expression-ism" in the prison sequences that frame the film (278); Kracauer also notes "traces of expressionism" in the same scenes (*Caligari*,127; 71). The open-ing high angle shot shows prisoners in white uniforms moving in a circle against a dark, cavernous background. Emphasis is placed on the number 28 on Boss's back—his face is never shown until the flashback begins; only then does he acquire an identity. This is another convention of Expression-ist staging, which stressed nameless and faceless masses in ornamental forms, and characters named only by an external designation and a num-ber:"prisoner number 28."

But both critics see the film as having achieved something other than Expressionism.[27] Kracauer writes that *Variety* indulges in the "new realism" that was becoming dominant in 1925 (*Caligari*, 125). It is this "realism" that aligns the film with the shift in artistic sensibility of the mid-1920s that came with the waning of Expressionism in the German art cinema, an art movement notable for its emphasis on interiority and subjectivity and its anxiety about technology and modernization, and the rise of the so-called New Objectivity ("Neue Sachlichkeit"), with an emphasis on documenting the external surfaces of reality and a more affirmative attitude about tech-nology, the city, and modern mass culture. This transition from obsessive, subjective interiority and distorted, anxious perspectives on modernity to a fetishization of "objectivity," technology, and the "surface" of modern real-ity is a bit too extreme (or binary) not to be somewhat suspect, and indeed it is belied by certain stylistic and attitudinal continuities—notably an ambivalence about modernity that one finds beneath both Expressionist anxieties about, and New Objective celebrations, of modern mass culture.[28]

Although Kracauer writes about the film's "realism," neither the film's rather generic melodramatic plot nor the dizzying effects of its camera work and editing for the trapeze sequences appear to today's sensibilities to be especially "realistic." Kracauer is right, however: in 1925 *Variety* was famous precisely for its realism. This reputation had much to do with its impressive "documentary" shots of Berlin and Hamburg: for example, the carnival in Hamburg's St. Pauli district, and in Berlin the Friedrichstrasse railway station, certain street scenes, and the interior shots of the Winter-garten (see "*Varieté: Der grosse deutsche Film*"). Shooting on location was still relatively rare in the German art film, which was famous primarily for its carefully constructed studio sets that could be illuminated so precisely and expressively. In this way *Variety* is clearly related to New Objectivity and associated trends of the middle and later 1920s in German film, photography, theater, literature, and painting, in which the attempt to move toward a documentary approach was noted.[29]

But the film is connected to such trends not merely because of the presence of some documentary footage; what the footage actually depicts is even more significant: carnival scenes, the hectic night life on Berlin's streets, and above all, famous international variety acts in the Wintergarten—which was not only the venue where the most popular mass entertainment form of the late nineteenth century, the variety show, had its most glamorous home, but it was also the very hall where the first films by the Skladanowsky brothers had been exhibited in 1895.[30] *Variety* captured a number of variety acts inside (and outside) the Wintergarten, and one of them was the Tiller Girls, the most famous of many troupes of chorus-line dancers who toured Europe during the 1920s and were all the rage, especially in Berlin.[31] Indeed, although the "Tiller Girls" were originally an English troupe (and one that spawned many imitations with the same name), they symbolized "Americanism" in Germany as much as other phenomena like "jazz" or "Hollywood" did.

Americanism—and the ideal of success represented by America—are also crucial to Berta-Marie's "betrayal" of Boss. Artinelli first lures her into his room with a telegraph he has received that contains an offer from America for the trio of acrobats; then he attempts to coerce her sexual compliance with the argument that she owes him her upward mobility—her rise from sleazy carnival performer to the toast of the internationally famous Wintergarten. America represents the pinnacle of achievement in the world of variety shows (or vaudeville, as it was called in the United States). America is also connected—in this film at any rate—to loose sexual morals and other "unhealthy" effects of quick upward mobility and the celebrity offered by modern mass culture. For *Variety,* despite all its citation—and mobilization—of the forms of mass spectacle and entertainment associated with Weimar modernity, remains an "art film," and thus its depiction of modernity, democracy, and class mobility is for the most part negative.

The American critic in Berlin for the U.S. trade journal *Variety* called the style of the German film *Variety* "modernistic" (Trask). Writing in the *New Republic* in 1926, Evelyn Gerstein went so far as to compare its technique to Leger, Picasso and Stravinsky. But as Kracauer wrote in *Die Angestellten* ("The White Collar Employees," 1929), the secret of New Objectivity was precisely that behind its modern facade, something very sentimental was often lurking (287). For all *Variety*'s modern technical virtuosity, the film is not merely sentimental, but very conservative in its critique of aspects of modernity. It participates in the cynical strategy of dressing its conservative message in the most modern of forms—given its commercial success, one might say that it is one of the most successful examples of the strategy. For the evil that destroys the good-natured family man, Boss, is clearly connected to his desire to be a star of the trapeze again—to be at the center of the spotlight of mass entertainment, the beneficiary of the appetite of the modern masses for spectacle and distraction. His seduction by Berta-Marie is what motivates him to strive again for success in the world of the carnival, and it is Berta-Marie who then pushes Boss to accept Artinelli's offer to move up from the carnival to the classier world of the variety show.

The film's cynical ambivalence about its own project creates a distance between narrative and spectacle that is reflexive. Its technical virtuosity is typical of the New Objective fetishization of technology, and its use of a lurid, sensational melodramatic plot mirrors the move in New Objectivity toward more accessible narratives and toward an apparent embrace of mass culture.[32] The film's most famous cinematic techniques involve the use of mobile camera from subjective points of view, most impressively in the dizzying shots of the acrobats high above the audience in the Wintergarten, and these techniques tend to foreground themselves through a virtuosity in excess of the needs of the plot. In addition, the film's own constructions of looking are foregrounded, thematized quite explicitly— even melodramatically—in a collage of eyes that is intercut with shots of Boss on the trapeze at his most conflicted moment, as he is indeed being watched by everyone in the huge hall. It can be argued that even the melodramatic narrative itself reflects on the institution of the cinema (although perhaps unintentionally so): the protagonist's precipitous rise from his origins as a "vulgar" carnival performer to a performer in a glamorous hall in which the upper classes ogle him is a trajectory that parallels the rise of cinema itself from despised lower-class entertainment to a more bourgeois one. But the comment on cinema is in that case quite negative, for it becomes a part of a topsy-turvy world of glittering mass celebrity that is marked as clearly dangerous and destabilizing.

GENDER, SPECTACLE, AND SPECULARITY

Also reflexive is the film's thematization of its own specular relations, which in turn is closely linked not just to spectacle in the film but also gender. The basic plot of the film is very similar to what Kracauer considers the standard story of the "street film" genre in Weimar cinema: the hero leaves the boring safety of domestic life, lured by a woman of "the streets" into that dangerous but exciting realm, only to meet betrayal at her hands (with help from her criminal accomplices).[33] But *Variety* varies this basic plot in some interesting ways: the shift to the carnival milieu turns the domesticity that Boss flees into a shabby, almost lumpen variety—as is his occupation as barker for and manager of a tired and worn-out troupe of exotic dancers. (Predictably the American version eliminates this initial social degradation, making Boss start already as a star of the carnival, about to move even higher, into the world of variety shows.)

And while the urban streets of modernity are actually documented here in a more straightforward way than in many "street films,"[34] the chaos of modernity is embodied more compellingly in the milieu of mass entertainment—and not so much in its least glamorous depths, where we first encounter Boss, as in its loftier realms. For what is demonized in the film is clearly the glamorous celebrity and dizzying upward mobility that this subset of modernity offers, whereas the shabby life at the bottom that Boss deserts actually becomes recuperated by the film's narrative frame as the domesticity that in the end "saves" him. The petition for clemency sent to the prison director originates with Boss's wife and son in Hamburg, and it is to this refuge of domesticity that he is allowed to return.[35] When the gates of the prison open before us at the end of the film revealing a gloriously sun-lit view of wind-blown trees (in what is apparently the film's first exterior shot in daylight that depicts non-urban reality), it is as if Boss's return to his family is "bourgeoisified" with all the glories of nature that middle-class ideology ascribes to the family. The conservative message here seems as much a demonization of upward mobility—that is, of not knowing one's place—as of adultery: both are symptoms and causes of the moral chaos modernity brings through its destabilization of the social and sexual order.

And both—unseemly social ambition as well as sexual lust—are connected to the figure of the vamp. Berta-Marie is, certainly in the German version, an archetypal femme fatale, a nameless woman of uncertain identity and mysterious origins. Indeed, in Ufa's program for the film's premiere at the Ufa-Palast am Zoo on November 16, 1925, Lya de Putti's character is not listed as Berta-Marie, but rather as "A Strange [or "Foreign"] Girl" ("Ein fremdes Mädchen"). Her real name is never mentioned; the ship's captain who brings the young stowaway to the carnival in Hamburg's harbor district tells Boss that her name is so exotic (so "crazy," or "verrückt" according to the German titles) that the shipmates have named her after their ship, the Berta-Marie.

Thus named for a ship that plies international trade routes, Berta-Marie is no mere woman of the streets, she is truly a foreign element immediately disruptive of the status quo in Boss's life. Her exotic belly dance quickly eclipses the tired troupe of dancers Boss manages, and her solo performance before a leering male audience is so seductive that one man (played by Kurt Gerron) comes onto the stage.[36] Enraged, Boss closes the show, which nearly causes a riot; he decides to run away with her to Berlin. Berta-Marie is explicitly called a "vampire" in the film's screenplay for the way she controls Boss with her sexuality.[37] But Boss runs away with her not just out of sexual desire, but also out of his longing for stardom: he wants to use her disruptive beauty to ornament his own return to the world of the spectacle on the trapeze. And then he is able to "control" neither Berta-Marie's sexuality nor the ambitious drive to stardom that she motivates and later comes to embody.

Certainly Berta-Marie herself enters Artinelli's room in the first place primarily out of her own ambitions, interested to hear about the offer from America he has received in a telegram. How much she initially desires Artinelli is also unclear, since in the original version of the film, his "seduction" of her appears to be a rape (certainly to our sensibilities today—see Figure 4.1). This is an interesting scene, because it gives the viewer a rare insight into Berta-Marie's perspective, something the film otherwise neglects, for her function in the plot is limited almost entirely to the role of catalyst in Boss's story of male crisis. Not only are the origins of this exotic young woman shrouded in mystery, so too is her fate at the end of the film. Horrified at Boss's murder of Artinelli, she attempts to stop him as he lumbers down the corridor of the hotel; grabbing his arm, she fails to stop him and falls down the stairs as he continues on, driven to give himself up to the police. We see Berta-Marie for the last time in the background of this shot, collapsed on the stairs; what becomes of her the film never discloses. She is no longer of interest in Boss's narrative.[38]

As is typical of a story of male humiliation, the protagonist is "feminized"—that is, the film frustrates his attempt to achieve the power, control and autonomy that match the ideal of masculinity in Western patriarchal ideologies. But the film seems to be making the point that Boss is susceptible to Berta-Marie because he is *already* "feminized." Boss's nurturing, indeed motherly qualities are visible from the very beginning of the film, notably in his concern for his infant son, whose diaper he changes very

Figure 4.1   The brutal 'seduction' of Berta-Marie (Lya de Putti) by Artinelli (Warwick Ward) in Dupont's *Variety* (1925). Photo courtesy of Bundesarchiv-Filmarchiv, Berlin.

cheerfully (see Figure 4.2). Later, sharing a wagon with Berta-Marie at the carnival in Berlin, he not only nurtures her but darns the hole in her stocking. And while it might be suggested that Boss is here being idealized as a paragon of a new "sensitive" masculinity meant to appeal to women longing for more "companionate" heterosexual relationships,[39] this behavior is highlighted right at the moment of the first covert exchange of glances between Berta-Marie and Artinelli—right at the fateful moment, that is, when the end of Boss's happiness can first be anticipated. The film thus depicts his "sensitive" deviation from more rigid gender roles as a threatening destabilization—a threat to male dominance, a "feminization."

But it is not only Boss who is depicted as "feminized." So too is his rival Artinelli, albeit in a different fashion, for what is depicted in his case is an "effeminate" sophistication. This is made even more explicit through the way he is filmed putting on his make-up, filmed from Boss's perspective after he has learned of Artinelli's betrayal of his friendship. Artinelli is depicted negatively here both as "effeminate" and as duplicitous (a combination that one will find in Nazi cinema's anti-French and anti-Semitic caricatures).[40]

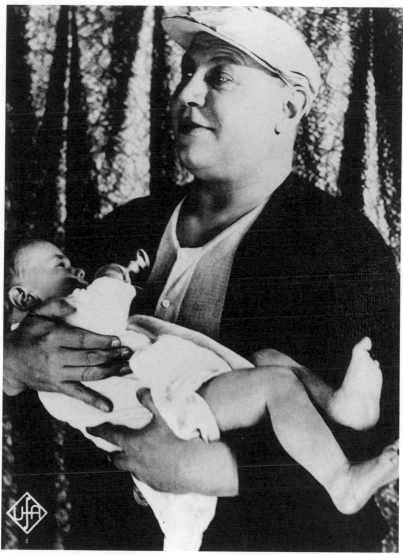

Figure 4.2 Boss Huller (Emil Jannings) as nurturing parent in Dupont's *Variety* (1925). Photo courtesy of Bundesarchiv-Filmarchiv, Berlin.

The film's destabilization of gender roles is fairly complex. Not only are both male rivals represented as in different ways "feminized," the depiction of women in the film also has some deeper implications.[41] In the German version, the two main female characters obviously represent the two poles of the clichéd Madonna/whore dichotomy; nonetheless, both sides of the dichotomy, Boss's shabby wife and the evil Berta-Marie, are discredited to such a great extent that the film's misogyny seems much more powerful—and destabilizing of monogamy—than the somewhat unlikely recuperation of the family at the end of the film would imply. This is perhaps the most subversive aspect of the film's depiction of gender—but this destabilization is clearly demonized throughout the film.

The dynamics of gender in this film are also related to spectacle and specularity in the film and to the film's thematization of its own specular relations. The affair between Artinelli and Berta-Marie is anticipated by a covert exchange of glances between the two; later the audience is continually made aware of their duplicity in manipulating Boss through the film's emphasis on similar exchanges of glances that Boss never notices. Boss himself exhibits the cold, instinctual gaze of murderous jealousy twice in the film—first when the sight of Berta-Marie dancing before the crowd in his tent at the Hamburg carnival incites a riot, and later, after Boss becomes aware that Artinelli and Berta-Marie have betrayed him. But Boss's instinctual nature also arguably "feminizes" him: in spite of the power of his gaze in these two scenes, it is not the rational gaze of control so important to the male observer in New Objectivity. Rather Boss's instinctual nature is evidence that he is merely one of the dumb herd, the kind of "creature" ("Kreatur") that Helmut Lethen has written about as the counterpart to the "cold persona" of Weimar culture. This "cold persona," in turn, is the mask of cold impenetrability behind which, according to Lethen, Weimar's male intellectual concealed his own emotions and fears. The "creature," as a member of the urban masses, was precisely what Weimar's "cold persona" feared and despised most. And of course, intellectuals feared and despised the urban masses in no small part because they perceived them as "feminized," as both Klaus Theweleit and Andreas Huyssen[42] have argued. The masses were "feminized" both in the sense of representing a threatening Other as well as representing "downward mobility," that is, the disempowered status into which male intellectuals and artists feared that modern society, with its disregard of their traditional status, was pushing them.

The shifty-eyed, clever Artinelli is in some ways the kind of cynically manipulative "cold persona" behind a mask of smooth sophistication that was the ideal of the mindset Lethen describes. Artinelli, however, is also depicted as "feminized," and in one sense, this happens in a way that is *exactly* similar to the situation of gullible, instinctual Boss. For all their differences, both men are portrayed in the film as longing to be "on the right side" of the curtain, to be the stars of mass spectacle. And to be object instead of the subject of the gaze—to be looked at, as opposed to being the one who looks—is to be "feminized," especially in New Objectivity, as Lethen has argued.[43] The male intellectuals and artists Lethen describes attempted to retain mastery amidst the chaos of modernity by wielding a cold, controlling gaze on its excesses and its masses. To be exposed to the gaze of others—especially that of the leering, vulgar and/or decadent masses[44]—is clearly to lose power (and thus to become "feminized").

In keeping with the basic conservativism of German art cinema, "Americanist" modernity in this film becomes a world of mass spectacle (and upward mobility) that is clearly marked as negative in the film, a world of faithless tramps, effeminate cosmopolitans, and sensation-hungry spectators. The negative depiction of the leering spectators is nowhere better epitomized than in one striking visual image that consists of a collage of eyes, one that through intercutting appears to be focused on Boss as he sits on the trapeze high above the audience (see Figure 4.3). This occurs at the tense

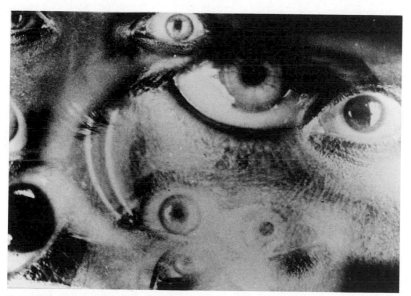

Figure 4.3   Collage of eyes from Dupont's *Variety* (1925), which is very similar to the collage of eyes in Lang's *Metropolis* (1927). Photo courtesy of Bundesarchiv-Filmarchiv, Berlin.

moment in the narrative when Boss hesitates and wipes his brow, afraid that he will kill his rival by not catching him, just as he had earlier envisioned taking revenge upon him. But Boss is too honest to kill his rival in this way, and he seems also to want to resist turning his private act of vengeance into a part of the spectacle that the eyes below would greedily devour.

This is a moment of self-reflexivity typical of Weimar art cinema, very ambivalent about mass spectacle and the cinema itself, but also about modernity; again, it is ultimately a very conservative, undemocratic ambivalence. For the Wintergarten variety palace—and in effect the cinema itself—is depicted as a site of degenerate and sexually ambiguous voyeurism in which boundaries between the classes, too, are transgressed. It is this "evil" public sphere that Boss flees by committing his private act of murder offstage, which leads to his being locked away safely in prison. At the end of the film he is returned to the bosom of his family, blessed by a benevolent authority figure, a prison official with white hair and a beard—a character whom Lotte Eisner described aptly as "a cross between Father Christmas and God the Father" (278).

The narrative closure here is the best evidence of the political bent of the film, and while in some films narrative closure seems inadequate to the task of undoing potential subversive elements in the rest of the film, in *Variety* I would assert that there is no significant political difference between the clear demonization of the sensationalized transgressions throughout the film and what the ending posits. Although my emphasis here on reactionary, anti-democratic attitudes in the film would seem to align my reading with Kracauer's overall verdict on Weimar cinema, I would like to stress where I differ with him: Kracauer (at least in his famous postwar book *From Caligari to Hitler*) has more or less the same take on "male retrogression"/"decadence"/"degeneracy" as the right wing in the Weimar Republic did, namely, that it is bad, one of the serious flaws in Weimar culture.[45] *Variety* sends a very clear—and anti-modern—message about modernity, democracy, and popular culture; linked to these targets is also another target: the emerging fluidity of gendered and sexual identities that many of us celebrate now (and rightfully so). *Variety* is in tune with elite opinion in Weimar when it demonizes that fluidity as "degenerate." But perhaps this film's fascinated obsession with that fluidity is ultimately of more interest than the strident attempt to make its disapproval clear.[46]

Impotence and Therapy, Excess and Containment

"Curing" Male Crisis in G.W. Pabst's Film Secrets of a Soul
(Geheimnisse einer Seele, *1926)*

To the husbands—who especially in this respect have to be the leaders
[*Führer*] of their spouses—because frequently things fail not merely because
of inadequate leadership qualities but rather because they even lack the qualities of a good partner.
They have no clue as to their inadequacies.

—Th. H. van de Velde, *The Perfect Marriage*
(*Die vollkommene* Ehe), 8–9⁴⁷

Secrets of a Soul, released in 1926, demonstrates like *Variety* a joyful "excess"
in its display of cinematic technology. But this technical excess, which is
typical of much cinematic New Objectivity, is not merely a formal or stylistic matter. Its deployment is often intricately related to the anxieties about
gender and sexuality relating to modernity that are foregrounded in this
book. The quote above is taken from the section titled "The Husband as
Leader" ("Der Gatte als Führer") in the best-selling 1926 marriage manual,
The Perfect Marriage (*Die vollkommene Ehe*) by the Dutch physician Dr. Th.
H. van de Velde, which was in its eleventh German edition by 1927. In
New Objectivity—as in many other eras of the modern age—the project
of stabilizing modernity tends to be equated with stabilizing threats to
male subjectivity. This often involves close attention to women—in the
interest of "controlling" any new behaviors that threaten male dominance
(or national interests in trying to raise the birthrate)—but male anxieties
also are examined, as we have seen, often in very explicit ways. This is quite
clearly the case in *Secrets of a Soul,* which attempts to "cure" such anxieties
on the part of men—and it does so in the interest both of increasing the
birthrate and stabilizing the German family.

In contrast to *Variety,* which visualizes the sensational public spectacle
performed by carnival performers, *Secrets of a Soul* represents the fantastic
inner world of the psyche, all the while containing the fantastic within a
realist narrative in the service of a "scientific" project: the cure of male
neurosis and impotence, no less, through the wonders of psychology. And,
contrary to the practice in films of the Expressionist period, the intent here
is to portray the fantastic "realistically." Indeed, according to contemporary
critics, this was one of the reasons for the film's success.⁴⁸ A film like *Secrets
of a Soul,* a "Kulturfilm" (a "cultural film," that is, an educational film) by no
means intended as "low" entertainment, is thus especially emblematic, as an

"educational" attempt to contain sexual and social anxieties through "science"—and not just through the technological apparatus of the cinema. Medical science was also involved—not the physiological/sexological approach exemplified by van de Velde, but rather the new "science" of psychoanalysis.

SECRETS OF A SOUL: *BACKGROUND AND SYNOPSIS*

According to Atwell (37), the original idea for the film belonged to Hans Neumann, a producer at Ufa's unit for *Kulturfilm*-production.[49] Friedberg, however, notes that others have claimed that Ernö Metzner, who would design the sets for the film, first suggested it to Neumann (n. 6, 245). It was Neumann who then approached Karl Abraham, head of the Berlin Psychoanalytic Society, about the project; Abraham and Hanns Sachs, both members of Freud's inner circle of disciples, would serve as advisors to the film.[50] The script itself was written by Neumann and Colin Ross; finally, Pabst, who had just completed *Joyless Street* (*Freudlose Gasse,* 1925), was chosen as director (Friedberg, 45).[51]

Like *Variety,* this film was a big-budget "art" film. Indeed, it was considered an "educational" film, given its production by Ufa's "Kulturfilm" department, and it was rated by the censors as "volksbildend"—which did not prevent them from making cuts (Zglinicki, 581). The film was a critical and popular success, praised for its use of "everyday" reality and its basis in a supposedly real case, for its technical virtuosity in depicting private anxieties and the dream state, for its accessible introduction to the science of psychoanalysis, and for its explication of disturbing but common human fantasies.[52]

The hero of the film is a scientist himself, a chemist—played by none other than Werner Krauss, who had portrayed Dr. Caligari in 1919.[53] The protagonist he portrays has his ordered bourgeois existence disturbed by various anxieties, which are most memorably depicted in a dream sequence that is the technical highlight of the film. According to Atwell, six weeks were devoted entirely to producing the dream sequence (42). Its impressive effects were due primarily to the virtuoso work done on the film by the pioneering German cinematographer Guido Seeber, who was assisted by the other cinematographers Kurt Oertel and Robert Lach and also by the set designer Ernö Metzner.[54]

The film begins with the main character's reaction to certain unrelated incidents one day. A woman's cry for help interrupts him as he attempts to trim the back of his wife's hair, which causes him inadvertently to give her a slight cut with the razor. They learn soon afterwards that a woman has been murdered in the neighborhood—and, as the husband later hears, she has been murdered by a man (perhaps her husband) using a razor. Then, at in his laboratory at work, he gives candy to a small child visiting with her mother. This obviously gives him pleasure, but suddenly he becomes disturbed. Later it is revealed that he feels unhappy (and insecure) about the childlessness of his own marriage. This feeling is amplified by his notice of an exchange of glances between his female lab assistant and the young mother of the child. Later in the film it becomes clear that he interprets these glances as ridiculing ones. The same day, a letter arrives announcing the return of a male cousin, a childhood friend of both the hero and his wife. The cousin has been travelling in Southeast Asia, and his letter includes pictures of himself in a prominent—and very phallic—pith helmet. He also has sent ahead some exotic gifts: the figurine of a fertility goddess and a ceremonial sword.

In a disturbing dream that night, these events are combined in somewhat bizarre ways with other impressions of the day. The dream itself consists of four longer scenes that are demarcated by interrupting shots of the husband restlessly and anxiously tossing in bed; at one point, his wife is shown waking up and going to the window to watch a storm outside. In the first longer scene of the dream, the cousin, carrying a toy rifle and wearing his phallic pith helmet, appears threateningly in a tree in the back garden of the protagonist's house. Seeing the cousin, the husband tries to fly away but is "shot down" by the cousin's rifle; from the protagonist's point of view high above the house, we experience his plunge back down to the patio below.

The second scene shows him looking at a temple from inside some cave-like enclosure. He moves toward the temple but is stopped by a crossing gate: then distorted images of speeding trains pass by, and the cousin, waving, appears to be riding on one of the trains. The crossing gate then rises, and the protagonist is able to approach the temple, which is a lifesized version of the fertility goddess he and his wife had received that day as a gift from the cousin. At the statue of the goddess he finds a note in his pocket that tells of his cousin's arrival; he tosses it away and it explodes. He flees, and then a (cardboard) Italian village springs up, which apparently had been the location of the hero's honeymoon with his wife. After the village rises, a very phallic bell-tower grows up from the ground. At the top of the tower three bells are ringing, and they transform into the faces of three women laughing at him: his maid, his wife, and his laboratory assistant.[55]

The third scene opens with the man standing outside his house, locked outside the gate, holding onto to its iron bars; he is watching what appears to be a murder taking place behind the shades of one of the windows of the house. Then, with his hands still on the bars of the gate, the iron fence begins to grow skyward, and he is soon high above the house, still hanging onto the fence. Suddenly the bars become prison bars, and he is inside a cell; a trial ensues. Oversized toy drums are superimposed over the trial scene; intercut with the scene are shots of the giant shadows of fingers pointing in accusation. The protagonist is accused by his cousin of murdering his wife, and he is found guilty.

In the final scene of the dream, the protagonist is shown in his lab, peering out a window. He is watching his cousin and his wife, who are outside in a boat floating on what looks like a tropical pool of water. His wife then appears to pull a doll out of the water; she holds it like a baby and offers it to the cousin. Back in the lab, a hallucination of his wife appears before the protagonist, and he stabs at this image with the cousin's ceremonial sword. His furious stabbing motions are aptly described by Friedberg as "rutting gestures" (48; also see Figure 4.4).

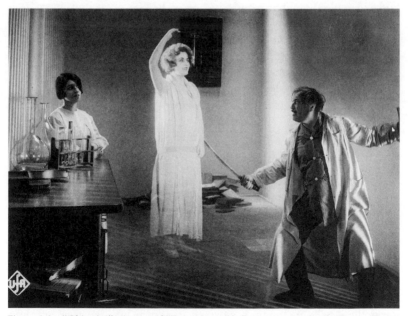

Figure 4.4   "Objective" science and "Expressionist" hallucination: Husband (Werner Krauss) uses sword to attack hallucination of his wife (Ruth Weyher) as his lab assistant looks on, from the dream sequence in Pabst's *Secrets of A Soul* (1926). Photo courtesy of Bundesarchiv-Filmarchiv, Berlin.

Upon waking from the dream, he screams and is comforted by his wife. The second morning of the narrative continues with his attempt to shave: dropping his razor, he finds himself somehow unable to pick it up, and instead he goes to a barber to be shaved. While at work his wife phones to announce that the cousin has arrived; looking overjoyed, he nonetheless drops a test tube accidentally. At dinner that evening with his wife and cousin, he finds that he cannot carve the meat; indeed, he cannot cut the meat on his own plate—or even touch a table knife. Embarrassed by his phobia about knives, he leaves for his club, where he spends the evening. A psychoanalyst there (played by the Russian actor Pavel Pavlov) happens to notice him leave his key on a table as he is leaving the club, and so the analyst follows him into the night. He meets the distraught man at his gate, and the analyst gives him the missing key, remarking that he must have some reason not to want to enter the house. When the protagonist looks surprised at the accuracy of the analyst's remark, the latter says that it is his profession to be able to surmise such unconscious truths.

Inside the house, the man sits down in anguish, only to be joined by his wife, who comes downstairs to try to comfort him. But his knife phobia is combined with a compulsion anxiety about stabbing his own wife: embracing her, he cannot stop looking at the ceremonial sword on the table behind her, and although he fights with the compulsion, his hand starts to reach for the sword (in a scene that anticipates Jack the Ripper's murder of Lulu in Pabst's 1929 film *Pandora's Box*). Distressed, he runs from his house, and he flees to his mother's house; there, with his head in her lap (a common motif in Weimar film that Kracauer emphasizes so much in *From Caligari to Hitler*), his mother asks him if there is anyone who could help him. He has a vision of the analyst from the club—the face of the latter appears over an enlarged image of the key—and the protagonist immediately realizes that here is the "key" to solving his problems. He inquires at the club as to the identity of the psychologist and learns it must be Dr. Orth,[56] whom he then begins to visit. His psychoanalysis with Orth begins.

This silent film then goes on to depict the "talking cure"—successfully, as Friedberg asserts (46). During this section of the film we shift continually from the psychoanalyst's office to depictions of earlier scenes from the film as remembered by the protagonist. These include scenes from the dream, as well as some depictions of childhood memories and of some fantasies: in one the protagonist spies on his cousin in a harem, where his wife begins to make love with the cousin. There are also what Friedberg calls "symbolic representations" (49): for example, when he tells the analyst of the hopes he and his wife had when they first married, one sees an image of the two of them planting a tree against a somewhat unreal white backdrop (with clouds indicated at the top of the image). Many of the remembered scenes are images that have been defamiliarized in a similar fashion by being restaged in front of a white background; some of the more complicated optical effects from the dream are shown again, and they, understandably enough, are not restaged.[57]

All of these disparate and disturbing flashbacks are ultimately connected to a (somewhat unlikely) childhood trauma revealed in a memory that resurfaces in the protagonist's mind. He remembers a quarrel between his future wife and himself from their childhood, with the cousin, at the time also a child, also playing a role. With the trauma remembered and explained by the analyst, the protagonist is cured and can return to his wife. In the film's epilogue we see him fishing in the great outdoors, and then running up to the vacation cottage on the hill to embrace his wife; childless no more, they now have a baby, which he holds up to the sky.

Except for this "happy end," the film is set mostly in interiors: the psychoanalyst's office; the husband's lab, where the film shows two women, his lab assistant and a client, smirking at him (at least they do in the restaged scene that represents his memory of the event); and above all his comfortable bourgeois home, associated with his wife—and the onset of his anxieties about her. The ultimate interior in the film is the mind of the protagonist, of course, the "site" of his terrifying dream, where the camera must penetrate to document his anxieties, just as the psychoanalyst must rationally explain them before we can leave the troubled interior for the virile world of sport and the outdoors.

EXTERIORS VS. INTERIORS, NEW OBJECTIVITY VS. EXPRESSIONISM

The purpose of the penetration of the protagonist's subjectivity is clearly to enable "objective" analysis and control. Eisner maintained that "certain shots" of the dream sequence would not have been possible without Expressionism (31), and this is undoubtedly true, especially for much of the dream's more exotic mise-en-scene. The superimpositions and trick photography, however, that characterize its most impressive effects are primarily Guido Seeber's contribution to the film, and these effects are much more typical of the mid-1920s. Anyone who has seen Seeber's work from this period will note the similarity, especially to the short promotional film "Kipho" for the 1925 cinema and photography exhibition (but also to his montage sequence at the dramatic center of Bruno Rahn's *Tragedy of a Prostitute—[Dirnentragödie]*, 1927). More important, however, is that the "fantastic" is mobilized here with the intention of de-mystifying it, so that it can be integrated into the realist narrative in the same way that the disturbed protagonist will be re-integrated into his marriage as a "potent," virile husband and—finally—a father.

One could maintain that the film's concern with interiority was somewhat out of touch with the emerging New Objectivity, concerned as it was with surface and exteriors, and above all with what Lethen calls the "psychology of the exterior" (*Verhaltenslehren,* 50–52). Indeed, the very attempt to thematize psychoanalysis is suspect in Lethen's construction of New Objectivity precisely because it was a psychology concerned with the interior, with the unconscious, as opposed to behaviorism and other more positivistic schools. While a preference for the latter ways of interpreting human behavior may indeed have been in some ways more amenable to the reigning sensibility of New Objectivity, nonetheless it was precisely in the same decade, the 1920s, that psychoanalysis was finally gaining respectability, especially in Germany (Friedberg, 42). This would explain the mutual attraction of Ufa's "cultural film department" (the *Kulturfilmabteilung,* which was in the business of giving the film industry cultural legitimacy) and the leaders of the psychoanalytic community in Berlin. They collaborated on a film that tried to popularize the theory in accessible, and above all in *visual* terms—a film that would make external a theory about the hidden interior, just as Freud's theory supposedly brought the unconscious into consciousness.

For although Freud himself had doubts about the visual representation of his theory's abstractions,[58] this did not deter Abraham and Sachs, and it was recognized by critics then (see note 48 [194]) as now (Friedberg) that this was indeed one of the major accomplishments of the completed film: it relied primarily on visual means to illustrate the theory. While this resulted in part from the constraints of film technology in the silent era, nonetheless the film used intertitles sparingly. This has also led to criticism: the film has often been criticized for how many of the film's visual images remain uninterpreted. This is, again, because the film's titles do not explain the sexual symbolism of the images, and for this the censors are to blame, or at any rate concern about the censors (see Rentschler, 7–8; Friedberg, 50–51; Zglinicki, 580–81). Nonetheless it is in many ways a strength of the film that the psychoanalysis proceeds almost entirely through images with relatively little text. For this leaves most of the actual analysis to the viewer, as Friedberg asserts (50–51). In any case this valorization of the visual over text and language is fully in accordance with New Objectivity and its fetishization of the surface.

Quotes from contemporary reviewers who praise the film often do so for both its grounding in daily life and its confrontation with "monsters" lurking beneath the surface of everyday life (see, e.g., *Die Filmwoche*). This penetration of the surface—and hence the mask, as it were, of Lethen's "cold persona"—might cause uneasiness (and soon enough a time would come when German films would not thematize such vulnerability, let alone the "Jewish science" of psychoanalysis). But it must be stressed again that the surface is penetrated with "cool" and "objective" ("sachlich") intent. These modifiers are used continually in the history of this film's reception: the reviewer in the newspaper called the *8 Uhr Abendblatt* in 1926 praised the film for taking a pathological case "cleverly and objectively" ("klug und sachlich") out of "real life" and then depicting it (again) in an "objective" ("sachlich") manner. Kracauer wrote in 1947 that the film "maintains the coolness of an expert" (*Caligari,* 172). The 1993 edition of *Reclams Film-Führer* states that psychic distress and confusion, so often the theme of German films in the 1920s, is analyzed in this film "in a cool fashion as a pathological case" ("kühl als Krankheitsfall": Krusche, 218).[59] The purpose of all this "cool objectivity," again, was to tame the "monsters" beneath with the light of reason so that the male persona could once again be made intact and functional.

As much as New Objectivity as a sensibility was concerned only with "facts" and the surface of reality in its deprecation of the "effeminate" and narcissistic cult of "inwardness" associated with Expressionism and neoromanticism, it is quite obvious that the situation was not quite so simple. For one thing, New Objectivity protested its coldness and lack of sentimentality too much. And of course it is impossible to separate any simple dualism like "interior/exterior"; its two terms are always part of the same system. As mentioned above, in 1929 Kracauer wrote that the secret of New Objectivity was that behind its sober facade lurked overwhelming sentimentality (*Die Angestellten,* 287); in 1947 he labeled this concern with the surface a repression based on the "paralysis" of the stabilized era (*Caligari,* 138), when a smiling, Americanized "happy face," as it were, was placed over the underlying tensions of Weimar society.

Martin Lindner goes to great lengths to show that New Objectivity was only a later phase in the long development of what he calls "Lebensideologie" ("vitalist ideology"), which had influenced the German intelligentsia since about 1890 in all its tendential shifts from aestheticism and neoromanticism through vitalism, Expressionism, and New Objectivity to the existentialism of exile (both "internal" and external). New Objectivity and Expressionism are clearly linked to each other by Lindner within this common underlying heritage. Lethen, who distinguishes "cold," mask-like New Objectivity much more radically from the cult of inwardness and authenticity of Expressionism, nonetheless makes it clear that the "cold persona" is merely the other side of the coin from that which the intellectual "cold persona" despises and fears: the feminized "creature" associated with the masses (38).

And indeed that in a sense is what *Secrets of a Soul* is about: a bourgeois professional, indeed a scientist, whose healthy conscious persona cracks, exposing the monstrous fears beneath, reducing him to a feminized, infantilized "creature." As a contemporary reviewer in 1926 ("W.") put it, in this film Werner Krauss persuasively portrays a bourgeois man "who . . . becomes the involuntary slave of his primeval instincts."[60] The loss of will and autonomy, the enslavement to instincts: this was the state to which the male intellectual feared modernity would reduce him. These were the qualities he projected onto those groups he associated with powerlessness—the feminized urban masses, women. The only way to protect oneself was thus to align oneself with the cold, distanced, scientific gaze of modernity, with which one could analyze and control the threatening, "irrational" aspects of modernity. It is this gaze that might be said to motivate most of Pabst's films in the 1920s, a gaze that turns on social unrest (*Joyless Street*, 1925; *The Love of Jeanne Ney*, 1927), female promiscuity (*Pandora's Box*, 1929), and prostitution (*Diary of a Lost Girl*, 1929).[61] In *Secrets of a Soul*, the focus is on the enemy within the male psyche itself, with the goal that the "Kreatur" be tamed and the mask of healthy masculinity—what Theweleit called "armor"—can be restored.[62]

GENDER AND EXCESS

The anxieties lurking beneath that surface—whether called armor or a mask—are depicted very elaborately in the dream sequence of *Secrets of A Soul*. Such fears are explicit references to the so-called crisis of male subjectivity so evident in Weimar cinema and in Weimar culture generally. Indeed, if ever my somewhat hyperbolic term for that crisis, the "discourse of castration," was appropriate, it is with regard to this film, with its knife phobia, its multiple phallic images, its thematization of fears about betrayal, impotence, and childlessness. Also thematized is the rage directed—literally—at a projection of woman: that is, in the dream sequence, when, angry at having seen his wife give his cousin a "baby," the protagonist stabs repeatedly at a ghostly superimposition of his wife, aiming the ceremonial sword low, towards her abdomen, and then swinging it upward in "rutting gestures."

Male crisis is depicted here in order to control and "cure" it, and, as was the case so often in Weimar culture, such depictions displace anxieties about losing (or having lost) autonomy and social status onto the sexual realm. That is, the real issue was power in a broader social context and not merely "potency" in an exclusively sexual sense. Reasons for social and economic anxieties were of course legion in Germany during the 1920s: the overturning of the old social hierarchy, the disappearance of middle class savings in the inflation, the loss of secure middle-class status for the intelligentsia. In Walter Benjamin's *Origin of the German Tragedy* (*Ursprung des Deutschen Trauerspiels,* 1928), he describes Germany in the seventeenth century as a "Katastrophenlandschaft," that is, as a catastrophic landscape, wasted by the Thirty Years' War (56). Lethen maintains that this term resonated with Benjamin's contemporaries because of its applicability to Weimar Germany: another "wasted battlefield" (in the wake of World War I) with social norms in turmoil that again inspired a baroque, Machiavellian/militaristic strategy of masks (*Verhaltenslehren,* 72–73).

Given this perceived need for masks and strong armor, *Secrets of A Soul* is all the more interesting for its focus on the fears beneath the male persona. Above all, there seems to be much more energy devoted to the technically brilliant depiction of the crisis rather than to the crafting of a satisfactory resolution for the film. Kracauer later rebuked Pabst for not fulfilling a "public" responsibility, asserting that Pabst had been more interested in the technical virtuosity of his film than in the resolution of what he felt to be the genuine problem to which it alluded—namely male "retrogression" (*Caligari,* 171–72). For Kracauer, this term apparently meant some combination of emasculation, infantilization, and feminization—in other words, the process of returning to (or remaining in) a state of weakness, of somehow being less than fully masculine.[63]

Thus Kracauer, attacking the film both for its exploitation of popular anxieties and for Pabst's "private" aestheticism, actually argues for a *more* affirmative cinema—a cinema whose public function would be to shore up more effectively the subjectivity of middle-class males. Kracauer's overall point here (and throughout *From Caligari to Hitler*) is that somehow if the Germans—again, meaning primarily the German middle classes—had been "man enough"—that is, had sufficiently "strong," autonomous bourgeois egos—they would have stood up to Hitler and/or resisted "seduction" by him. For Hitler is indeed conceptualized as a "mother" by many male leftists who have written on fascism with some application of psy-choanalytic insights—the Mitscherlich syndrome, one might call it. That this is problematic beyond its psychologizing and allegorizing tendencies ought to be clear to anyone at all conversant with feminism.[64] In demand-ing in retrospect that "Germany" should have acted like a "strong man," Kracauer ignores the fact that this is the very prescription for Germany's ills that the fascists themselves offered: the ideology (if not the "reality") of the strong man.

About one thing Kracauer is however right: the "cure" for male crisis in *Secrets of a Soul* remains in some ways unsatisfactory. First of all, again, there are any number of obvious visual motifs to which the "talking cure" does not refer—especially sexual motifs, including phallic symbols as well as images that allude to the female genitalia. They are not mentioned at all in the intertitles. This omission, due to the censors, is obviously not a failing typical of psychoanalysis. Contemporary critic Axel Eggebrecht complained about this, calling "diabolical nonsense" the fact "that all erotic symbols—the uterus, uterine water at birth, phallic and vaginal images, etc.—are visually displayed in this film, but could not be clearly explained . . ." (ctd. in Zglin-icki, 581).[65]

If one is concerned as Eggebrecht is with the lay public in the audience, this is perhaps a problem, but from the point of view of what we now call a "Brechtian aesthetic," it can be perceived as positive: that is, precisely the fact that not everything is spelled out, but that it is left to the spectator to interpret many visual clues independently. Friedberg writes, "The spectator of *Secrets of a Soul* is positioned as a more astute psychoanalyst than the fic-tional surrogate" (51). What Friedberg calls this "curious excess" of unin-terpreted images (51) is construed by Eric Rentschler as an excess that definitely undermines the happy narrative of resolved male crisis. He cites an image in the film occurring after the successful analysis of the protago-nist, when the latter, now cured, finally returns home. As he enters his house, he finds his wife and takes her hands, but he also finds his cousin there, appearing from behind the scenes. Rentschler notes the implication here that the husband's fantasies about his wife's infidelity may not have been all that "irrational" (7–8).

Above all the epilogue, the happy ending in the great outdoors, seems inadequate to resolving the elaborate anxieties visualized in the film. Rentschler maintains that it too can be read to be a bit more subversive than it initially might seem. When his wife and child wave to him from atop the hill, the man drops his both fishing pole and his bucket of fish, the pole landing on the shore and the bucket falling back into the water. This would seem not only to undermine the sporty, virile image just established, but perhaps also to indicate some lingering anxieties, which the handheld camera that follows his run up the hill to wife and child accentuates. For the same technique was used early in the film as people rushed to the scene of the murder (Rentschler, 7–8).

Even if any irony here is the unintentional effect of a sentimental, obligatory, and formulaic happy ending (relieved by some intentional humor), the fact that the ending is unequal to the anxieties to which the film alludes is certainly significant. There is an excess, an admission of instability, a lack of resolution, for which there would be little if any room in Nazi cinema. Laurence Rickels maintains that the crisis of male identity in the film alludes not just to concerns about male trauma in the aftermath of World War I with regard to impotence and infertility but to fears about latent homosexuality as well.[66] There are certainly moments in the film that might suggest such an interpretation. There is something slightly bizarre in the way the psychoanalyst is portrayed following the protagonist home from the club at night, something vaguely reminiscent of an attempted pick-up. Then, at his reunion with the wife and cousin at the end of the film, the husband hugs his cousin with much more affection than he does his wife, suggesting that the dynamics of the triangle in the film might be different from what has been suggested above.

Such ambiguity in the film about gender and sexual identity is perhaps what makes the film much more interesting than its ostensible project, yet it is another example of unresolved excess in the film. The technical highlights of *Secrets of a Soul* that so exceed its narrative are connected to anxieties about gender and sexuality—anxieties that are in turn clearly linked to underlying issues of social power and status. While cinematic self-reflexivity was a staple of the German art film and often intimately connected to a conservative message about modernity—as in *Variety*—here the excess and reflexivity functions to deconstruct traditional, authoritarian masculinity, rather than to cast modernity (and democracy) in an evil light. In *Variety,* modern mass society—as embodied in mass spectacle—is disavowed as "castrating" and "feminizing"; in *Hinkemann* and in *Secrets of a Soul,* the focus on "castration" and "feminization" is much less implicated in any affirmation of traditional "masculine" authority. In *Hinkemann* it is precisely that tradition that is disavowed, and in *Secrets of a Soul,* traditional masculinity is restored only in a fairly humorous and even somewhat self-ironizing way.

Chapter 5 ⌒

The End of Stability:
"Phallic" New Women and
Male Intellectuals

I had a mother who took a lover whenever she felt like it and it suited her—
then told her husband all about him.

— Maria Riva, about her mother, Marlene Dietrich[1]

"Does your wife have a male harem? My name is Fabian."
. . . . Fabian sat down. Irene Moll slid onto the arm of the chair, caressed
him and said to her husband, "If you don't like him, I'll break our contract."
"But I do like him," the lawyer answered.
"You're speaking about me as if I were a piece of pastry or a toboggan
sled," Fabian protested.
"You are a toboggan sled, my little one!" the woman cried and pressed
his head against her full, black-corsetted bosom.

— Erich Kästner, *Fabian* (1931)[2]

Amoral Modernity as New Woman
Erich Kästner's Novel Fabian *(1931)*

"No," he said, "I'm traveling to my mother's."
"You damned jackass," she whispered in irritation. "Am I supposed to
kneel before you and make a declaration of love? Would you rather have
some silly goose? I've had enough of grabbing after the nearest pair of pants.
I like you. We keep encountering each other. That can't be mere coinci-
dence." She grasped his hand and caressed his fingers. "I'm asking you, please,
come with me." (213)[3]

— Erich Kästner, *Fabian*

The above exchange, near the end of Ernst Kästner's 1931 novel *Fabian,* takes place on a train between Jakob Fabian, the protagonist of the novel, and Irene Moll. Fabian is fleeing Berlin to return to his mother, and Moll, the tall, sexually assertive woman who has been pursuing him since the beginning of the novel, is fleeing Germany, because the Berlin police have found about the "male bordello" she was running. It is clear that Fabian finds the idea of such a bordello, which provided rich women with handsome young men in their twenties, somehow more distasteful than the other, more traditional bordellos he visits over the course of the novel (see 139–41, also, in the dream sequence, 150–51). The above passage is a typical representation of the dynamics of gender and sexuality in the novel: Fabian is leaving the chaotic, amoral decadence of late Weimar Berlin to return to his mother, and Moll turns up yet again to express her desire for him. It might be a bit unfair to suggest that Fabian does indeed want a "silly" (or "dumb") goose ("eine dumme Gans"); he certainly shows nothing but contempt for uneducated women. He does have problems with intelligent ones, however, especially if they are independent and emancipated. Indeed, Irene Moll represents for him everything that is wrong with modern women: sexually aggressive, they betray and exploit men, whose only culpability is their weakness, their inability to control women as they should (cf. Livingstone, xx). For instance, early on Fabian suggests to Moll's husband that he should spank her (23). Indeed, sexually rapacious or "perverted" women seem to represent everything that is wrong with Berlin and by extension the modern world.

Because this is ultimately such a conservative position on modernity, it might appear odd that this novel was attacked so fiercely by the right wing in the early 1930s, while at the same time the Communist newspaper *Die Rote Fahne* (*The Red Banner*) praised it—in spite of its negative portrayal of a Communist character (Livingstone, vii). Upon reflection, however, this is not so surprising: the nationalists could not understand the point of the novel's satire—except when it was directed clearly at them (as at the end of the novel). Nor should one be surprised that they took offense at the mere depiction of sexual license, which so clearly flouted the traditional morality they supported. The Communists had a rather conservative view of sexual morality as well (in spite of their campaign against the prohibition of abortion); for the most part, then, they agreed with the point of the satire, and their praise for the novel is understandable.

The novel is supposed to be a satire, according to Kästner (in his 1950 foreword, 10), and therefore one is leery of becoming what he called a "Sittenrichter," a judge of moral customs (239–41) in one's critique of the novel, especially if one's position today is influenced more by feminist or queer—rather than religious or traditionalist—attitudes toward sexual mores. Yet Kästner also insisted that both his character Fabian and he himself, the author of the novel, were moralists (10, 239–41), and thus the critic is invited to analyze this satire to determine exactly what moral message it might contain.

Fleeing Berlin, Fabian returns to his home town in the provinces, which is not really a small town if Livingstone (viii, xxi) is correct that this town resembles Kästner's own city of origin, Dresden. Fabian refers to this journey literally as a return to his mother, and thus one is unavoidably reminded of the famous cinematic motif noted by Kracauer, of middle-class men with their heads in the laps of mothers, a symbol for Kracauer of male "retrogression" (*Caligari,* 172), an analysis that in turn prompted Peter Gay to warn of "omnipotent mothers" (141–42). Of course, Kästner himself would seem to be alluding to this very motif consciously and with some irony, since this return to the provinces is hardly portrayed as the idyllic return to the bosom of nature one expects in the German cultural texts of the time, especially in texts so critical of metropolitan Berlin.[4]

There is, however, much evidence in the novel that Kästner more or less shares the same somewhat misogynist analysis of Weimar culture as Kracauer et al. It is also well known that Kästner himself was very devoted to his own mother (Last, 11; Wagener, 9), so much so that it has been suggested that it was an obstacle to the forming of lasting relationships with other women (Livingstone, xix). But regardless of any autobiographical parallels between the novel and Kästner's own life, it is worth taking a closer look at the discourse of blaming mothers for their sons' weaknesses. Do "overindulgent" mothers really hold too much power? Certainly in *Fabian* the only mother who comes close to this (very bourgeois) ideal is the mother of the main character, and she is portrayed positively—as Jürgs points out, she is the only truly positive female figure in the book (206).

It is another kind of woman who is portrayed as too powerful and hence pathological, and that is the woman who is "selfishly" devoted to her own pleasure and/or success, the woman who is definitely not selfless in devotion to son or husband. It is the "new woman," the working woman, the emancipated woman, who is really demonized. This woman is more or less epitomized by, and parodied in, Irene Moll, definitely a "phallic" and/or "castrating" woman, and certainly no doting wife or mother. She is at first a bored, wealthy woman subsidized by her husband, a successful lawyer who is cowed by his wife's desires. Later, after the husband's illegal activities are exposed, and he flees the country, she becomes an entrepreneur on her own, making money from a bordello she manages that employs young men to provide sexual services to wealthy women. Thus from a spoiled bourgeois wife she develops into an independently wealthy businesswoman, eventually fleeing the country with her "ill-gotten gains," just as her husband had done.

TRACING MOLL THROUGH THE NARRATIVE

Moll turns up five times in the novel, four times "by chance," although at quite significant moments in the narrative, and the fifth appearance is within Fabian's dream (the fourteenth chapter: 146–54), of obvious symbolic importance. Indeed, using Moll, one can summarize the novel fairly easily. *Fabian* has been criticized for its loose, episodic structure and the dependence of the narrative upon chance, as Last documents in his overview of its reception (34–35), but it is this stylistic characteristic that mimics so well the rapid, distracted tempo of the modern metropolis and makes this moralizing novel nonetheless exemplary of New Objectivity, for which chance and the superficial are much more symptomatic than psychological depth and causality. Jürgs notes that it is the style of the novel that approximates cinema (203), that New Objective fetish that in this book is not at all thematized except in the most negative way.

Fabian opens with the main character, bored after his day at work, as an underpaid, over-qualified writer of advertising copy, sitting in a cafe, seeking distraction. His forays into Berlin's famed nightlife are apparently typical of his day-to-day routine, in the same way that such behavior was the legendary preoccupation of that whole class of white-collar workers so famous in Weimar Berlin. Fabian, who has studied at the university and is the son of a small, independent merchant, is in many ways typical of that segment of the growing white-collar work force that Theodor Geiger analyzed in 1932 as insecure because of its downward mobility. This insecurity manifested itself in "academic arrogance" and an "estate-specific need for validation" (192). Kracauer discussed the importance of distraction for white-collar workers in his famous 1929 study, *Die Angestellten* (282–91).

On the second page of the novel (12), Fabian is solicited by a prostitute on the street, and four pages later, at an exclusive sort of single's club run by Frau Sommer, he is propositioned twice more. The woman who makes the second offer is the one who will take him home, Irene Moll, who first interrupts as he is talking to another woman at the club. She interrupts with a command: "We will dance now" ("Man wird gleich tanzen," 16). They leave the club together in a taxi, where Moll attacks him, biting his lip. Once in her apartment Fabian is surprised to meet Moll's husband, and even more surprised to learn that her husband has a contract with Moll specifying his right to meet all his wife's conquests and to veto the tryst if he does not approve of his wife's choice. He likes Fabian, however, and he is even willing to consider giving Fabian an allowance to keep his wife happy. This offer causes Fabian to flee.

He meets Moll again in the fifth chapter (52–59), at Haupt's, a night club and brothel at which every night is a "beach party," that is, a "party" in which prostitutes parade in bathing suits. He goes to Haupt's with his friend Stephan Labude, who is his guide to Berlin's diverse nightlife. Labude, who like Fabian earned a doctorate in German literature (*Germanistik*), has just finished his postdoctoral thesis (*Habilitationsschrift*) on Lessing. Although they feel out of place at Haupt's, they are approached by two prostitutes. Because these two women are obviously quite hungry, the two men buy them drinks and food. Meanwhile it turns out that Moll is there; she apparently comes to the place frequently, dressed in furs and looking for young men. Here too she scares some young man away. She yells out drunkenly that there should be brothels for women, sings a bawdy song, and recognizes Fabian. With Labude's help, he beats a hasty retreat.

This episode is fairly typical of how Fabian finds distraction with his friend Labude: frequenting brothels and other spots notable for the sexual "decadence" they bemoan yet continue to seek out, in passages that allow Kästner to describe quite accurately Weimar Berlin's famous nightlife.[5] Labude and Fabian go to places like Haupt's precisely because they feel they do not fit in; they are merely voyeurs at Berlin's night clubs—although of course this may have been the role many eager tourists and customers felt they were playing.

Whereas Fabian is the cynical pessimist, Labude is supposedly the idealist of the two, still working hard in the field of literary history Fabian has abandoned. Labude is also active politically, striving to create a kind of "radical bourgeois" movement of idealistic students. The goal of this movement is to counter the corruption and incompetence of the older generation and to join with socialists in a center-left "coalition of reason" in order to save the Republic. In his personal life Labude has very high notions of love and fidelity, and it is a heavy blow when he discovers that his fiancée in Hamburg has been cheating on him (see eighth chapter, 81–86). Yet the upper-class Labude is clearly one of Fabian's main guides to the "seamier" side of Berlin; his high ideals apparently include rather traditional double standards.

The next time Fabian encounters Moll, a number of things have changed in Fabian's life, disrupting his empty routine of boredom at work by day and voyeuristic distraction at night. Accompanying Labude to visit the studio of a lesbian sculptor (Ruth Reiter), he meets Cornelia, who like Fabian is a somewhat disgusted newcomer to Reiter's studio. Cornelia is new to Berlin, and, although no innocent, she still believes in true love. In short order, she and Fabian then fall in love. Just as he has reason to believe in something again—reciprocal love, fidelity, perhaps even marriage—he loses his job due to what now would be called "downsizing." Reeling from this bad news, Fabian then is confronted by his mother, who appears unexpectedly in Berlin to visit him. Fabian pretends to go to work anyway so as not to worry his mother with the news of his unemployment. Wandering about Berlin, he finds himself at one of the most elegant department stores in the fashionable west side of Berlin, the "Department Store of the West End" ("Kaufhaus des Westen," also known by its acronym, "KdW"). By chance he opens the door of an auto for a woman in front of the store, and because she then tips him, he continues to open doors for other women being dropped off in front of the store. It is precisely at this rather humiliating moment for him that Moll appears and offers him money to carry her packages.

Moll tells him that her husband has absconded with some stolen money; she has managed to survive by opening her "Young Men's Un-Christian Association,"[6] which is a brothel of young men who service "ladies of high society" ("Damen der besten Gesellschaft," 139). Doing very well financially, she offers Fabian a job as her secretary. She tells him that, because he is in his early thirties, he is too old to work in her brothel as an escort. She also makes it clear that she still finds him attractive. Fabian's reaction is to leave for fear that he might vomit (140).

Moll's appearance functions as a sort of evil omen at this central point in the novel, a clear contrast to his new love Cornelia and to his dear mother from the provinces, and an indication of how low his economic fortunes have fallen. The sexual objectification of men in Moll's brothel, which makes Fabian want to vomit, reminds him of his own reification in a capitalist society; he too is a commodity whose value is falling.

Soon thereafter, Moll makes an even more symbolic appearance. It occurs in the only dream sequence we find in this "sober," "objective" novel, in its fourteenth chapter (146–54). Here Moll appears eating tiny young men from what appears to be a bag of candy; when she has emptied the bag, she tells Fabian she will eat him next (150–51). She appears in the first scene of the dream, and reification is clearly at issue here, too: children are fed into a machine that produces adults who indulge in orgies; meanwhile, the machine eats its own inventor. In the next scene of the dream, corruption and exploitation are symbolized in a room with a giant staircase on which the entire social hierarchy is arranged, each person stealing from the person immediately above, leaving only the person at the very top depicted as completely innocent—certainly a very non-Marxist model of hierarchy. Labude appears and proclaims a new order of "decency" ("Anständigkeit"); Cornelia also appears, calls Labude a fool, and disappears with a tall, good-looking young man (152). The dream ends with a vision of another world war, with the city laying in ruins, and the survivors in gas masks.

Fabian has this dream, in which Moll appears as one of the chief representatives of a technological order producing degeneracy, exploitation, and destruction, on the night before Cornelia has her interview with the film producer Makart. Fabian knows that the producer wants to discuss the possibility of giving Cornelia a role in a film. Cornelia, who has studied international contract law in relation to the film industry, does indeed become a film star, thus fulfilling the clichéd dream of the popular press of the 1920s with an ironic twist best expressed in a newspaper headline Fabian later reads: "Woman Lawyer Becomes Movie Star" ("Juristin wird Filmstar," 211). Cornelia comes home from the interview, finds Fabian napping, and leaves him a note. He reads it when he wakes up, alone. The note reveals that other clichés about stardom are also true: to become a star, Cornelia will have to sleep with Makart, repulsive as he is. She justifies her determination to withstand this with the following statement: "You only escape from the filth by getting yourself filthy" ("Man kommt nur aus dem Dreck heraus, wenn man sich dreckig macht," 162). This is one of the most significant lines in a passage that Sloterdijk also quotes because he finds it paradigmatic of Weimar sexual cynicism (906, 908).[7] But Cornelia's cynicism and "objectivity" (*Sachlichkeit*) do not exclude love: she makes it clear that she wants to keep her relationship with Fabian intact, albeit on the side. Indeed, in Cornelia's mind, she is doing all of this for him. It is implied that had he not lost his job, she would never have done it.

Nonetheless, as one could guess from his general unwillingness to accept gifts from women,[8] Fabian will not accept such help. Eventually he will flee Berlin, and then meet Moll again on the train. But it is not the loss of his job or Cornelia that finally makes him flee the metropolis; it is the senseless death of Labude. The latter commits suicide because an envious academic functionary lies to him about his *Habilitationschrift*, telling him that it had been rejected by his adviser. Believing the lie, Labude kills himself; learning this, Fabian decides to leave Berlin.

Meeting Fabian on the train, Moll offers to take him with her to Budapest or Paris, but this offer cannot move him. He returns to the provinces, where instead of metropolitan absurdity and "degeneracy" he finds narrow-minded stupidity and reactionary nationalism. Finally, disgusted at his own passivity, he decides to act, to engage himself in life as opposed to just looking on in impotent disillusionment—taking to heart, as it were, the reproach that Moll made to him in his dream, that he acts as though the world were a shop-window display (150).[9] He sees a child fall into a river, and he jumps in to save the child. Unable to swim, however, Fabian drowns, and the child swims to shore. Fabian's decision to act would seem to allude to the "actionist" ideology of the "act" ("Tat"), the transformative deed that was a key concept in the vitalist mindset Lindner calls *Lebensideologie,* which he considers so prevalent in the German intelligentsia after Nietzsche (110–113). Its ironic depiction and tragically absurd outcome here, I would argue, implies not a rejection of that ideology but rather a deep pessimism from within it.

GENDER AND SEXUALITY IN THE NOVEL

Some of the psychological dynamics about gender and sexuality that structure the novel are apparent in this ending, ironic though it may be: only the plight of innocent children stirs Fabian to action. This is demonstrated first at the KdW department store, where he defends an impoverished young girl who has been caught stealing an ashtray for her father's birthday; this child also appears in his dream, one of the few positive figures to appear there. As Lethen asserted already in 1970, behind this "idealization of the child" ("Verhimmelung des Kindes") there seems to be a demand for sexual innocence (145).[10] Among adults there is only sexual corruption, and somehow women are more to blame for this than men.

Among adult women, only his mother seems to be portrayed sympathetically; she is also one of the few women in the text who does not proposition him. She is selflessly devoted to her son, as opposed to Labude's wealthy mother, who spends all of her time far from her son in luxurious exile in Bellinzona, where she learns of her son's suicide. As Fabian puts it: "What a punishment for a bad mother!" (190), a verdict that unavoidably brings to mind Kästner's statement in his 1957 autobiography that his own mother had achieved her sole ambition: to be the perfect mother (ctd. in Wagener, 9).

As for Fabian's beloved Cornelia, she is, as she warns him, no angel (89). She first attracts Fabian's attention by asserting that she is the only "real" female (the only *weibliches Wesen*) at Ruth Reiter's studio (88–89); all the other women are apparently lesbians. Eventually, it is Cornelia who asks him into her apartment (101). Strictly speaking, one cannot call her one of Fabian's "conquests," as Fickert does (52) in order to make the (valid) point that Fabian, like Labude, suffers from his belief in a double standard.

Fabian is too passive, or rather too passive-aggressive, to put anyone in the position of being able to reject him. In discussing the friendship between Labude and Fabian, Fickert (53) cites Istvan Deak, who called close friendships between men among Weimar intellectuals "an exalted form of homosexuality" that had roots in the German youth movement of the early twentieth century. This contextualization implies the possibility of a latent homoerotic attraction between Labude and Fabian, and certainly there is evidence in the novel for that rather common assertion about male friendships in Weimar texts: they go whoring together while dreaming of a pure love for women to which no real women correspond, and, although they both suffer when such ideal love is disappointed, what really hits Fabian the hardest is his friend's death. Indeed, it is perhaps the leading factor that drives Fabian to his own death, also a senseless one, and one that can also be considered suicidal. Labude in turn had committed suicide not because of Leda's betrayal, but because he thought his adviser had rejected his manuscript. What is clear is that homosocial, if not homoerotic, relations between and among men remain the most significant.

Sexual corruption, which bears so much of the brunt of the satirical depiction of Weimar Berlin in this novel, is almost entirely blamed on women, who are aggressive, deceitful, or mercenary about sex. Yet this verdict must be qualified somewhat: Moll is not deceitful, but rather entirely honest about her desires, even to her husband. It is this that makes her the most threatening woman in the book, the one who most symbolizes what is wrong from Fabian's point of view. Deceit is obviously a concession to the old morality and double standard, and this is supposedly horrible, as is clear from Labude's disgust at Leda's brazen lies (and from Fabian's reaction to his recounting of them). But even more horrible to Fabian is Cornelia's honesty in explaining her relation to Makart. Most horrible of all is Moll, who does not see sex as just a mercenary evil but indeed as desirable, something she actively pursues. She does eventually seem to tire of promiscuity, as her final offer to Fabian indicates, but there is no way her character can escape the caricature of a "phallic," "castrating" woman, a "man-eater" who jokes about "slaughtering" Fabian during their first night together (20).

The lesbian bar, "Die Cousine," which Fabian visits the night he meets Cornelia, provides the author with the chance to comment on "abnormal varieties of sexual behavior," as he wrote in an unpublished epilogue to the book (239).[11] In that epilogue he made his famous assertion that he was a "moralist" (as he would continue to do in the postwar era); he also made it clear that he intended to depict sexual "abnormalities" in order to show how bad things were—in order to provide a warning, as he would say explicitly in the 1950 foreword to *Fabian* (9–10). What is interesting about the depiction of lesbian sexuality, besides the expected conservative take, is the explanation offered for this particular form of female desire. Fabian, who appears to be familiar with the lesbian bar, tells the newcomer Cornelia that by no means are all the women in the bar "abnormal" from birth; many of them are simply mad at men (94). While this too smacks of a heterosexist arrogance not unsurprising in Fabian, what is interesting is that here he seems to grant to Cornelia what she had maintained earlier, at Ruth Reiter's, in their long conversation about sexual mores (89–92): that men too are at fault in these sorry times. But this concession is only made in the context of a remark that undermines the autonomy of this form of female desire.

For the autonomous expression of desire (of any orientation) by women is what seems most threatening to Fabian. This is interesting, given his own reluctance to express desire. He picks up "Mucki" in the proletarian Wedding district—on the same night when, as he knows from her letter, Cornelia will be sleeping with Makart. But he only speaks to Mucki with reluctance after she had been repeatedly glancing at him for quite awhile (168–69). In any approach between potential sexual partners, there is of course much more going on than can be summarized by noting who spoke first, an act that is by no means the actual initiation of contact, even though this is the belief that underlies traditional norms requiring that the male play the "active role" in any such interaction. Even this merely formal type of initiation is rare for Fabian, however; here he takes this step clearly because he is "on the rebound," and thus it can be "blamed" first on Cornelia's betrayal and then of course on Mucki's adulterous desire. Fabian seems never to want to take responsibility for what occurs, but rather to be able to experience it as a passive voyeur, as if through a glass window (again, Moll's reproach in his dream). It is as if this attitude toward what he experiences assures him that he has maintained his purity, while only the women make themselves "filthy" in all of this.

When Fabian eventually tries to overcome his passivity by plunging actively into the stream of things, he drowns. Fabian is clearly being criticized for his inability to become involved in anything except something that is obviously foolish—attempting to save someone from drowning without knowing how to swim. Since his passivity is so tied to his sexual voyeurism, and since activity is so tied to women taking sexual initiative in the novel, which in turn is depicted so negatively, one must conclude that the novel's critique of Weimar is a nostalgic one: modernity has turned "natural" gender roles on their heads. Men have become too passive, women too aggressive, and the consequences for "reason" are ominous.

NEW OBJECTIVITY: REASON AND MODERNITY

On the night they first meet, Fabian and Cornelia leave the lesbian bar together, and Fabian walks Cornelia home through the streets of Berlin. Their romance is beginning to blossom. Cornelia remarks, "The moon shines even in this city" (98). Fabian replies, "Isn't it almost like home?" Then he corrects her: "But you're deceiving yourself" (99).[12]

He proceeds to describe what a subtitle for the tenth chapter labels the "topography of immorality" (97) that surrounds them. He goes on to describe bars, cafes, brothels, and hotels in the immediate area in which one can find people from Japan and China, English homosexuals, Hungarian and Russian Jews, and school girls who prostitute themselves to supplement their allowances. At the latter, Fabian relates, an elderly gentleman customer was surprised to find his own daughter in the room he had rented. It is disconcerting to find this barely averted act of incest[13] listed along with hotels and restaurants the main peculiarity of which seems to reside solely in the fact that one finds only Japanese or Russian Jewish customers there. To Fabian, the evils of modern decadence apparently include not merely the sexually but the ethnically "exotic" as well.

At the end of his description of this "immoral" topography, Fabian likens the inhabitants of Berlin to the inmates of an asylum. He concludes with a summary of the entire city: "In the east of the city, there resides crime, in the center swindling, in the north misery, in the west vice, and in all directions of the heavens, ruin" (99).[14] Up to this point in his catalogue of what is wrong with Berlin, there is little to distinguish Fabian's perspective from that of the most right-wing, "anti-modern" critic of the modern, "asphalt" metropolis. But then Cornelia asks him what comes after "ruin" ("Untergang"); he replies, "Stupidity, I'm afraid." Cornelia responds, "In the city where I'm from, stupidity has already arrived" (99).[15]

Stupidity ("Dummheit") is clearly a reference to the right-wing nationalism and bigotry Fabian will find in his own hometown once he flees Berlin at the end of the novel. The basic political position being represented in *Fabian* is a "centrist" one, not unlike the "centrist" defense of reason that motivates Labude's politics: the irrational, absurd excesses of modernity must be curbed by reason, lest modern civilization be overtaken by the irrationalism that motivates the German Right. The "excesses" depicted in the novel are mostly of the sexual kind, but there is also the careerist envy of the academic functionary whose vicious "joke" drives Labude to suicide, as well as the famous explanation of political cynicism offered by the journalist Malmy, who knows he is serving a corrupt system and takes a perverse pride in doing it well (32). The common denominator is the corruption of money, capitalist commodification, combined of course with the lack of will to do anything about it, "lethargy of the heart" ("Trägheit des Herzens"), as Malmy calls it in the novel (37). Kästner writing in 1950 will use the very same term to describe the malaise of the end of the Weimar Republic (10). If the reasonable cannot summon up the will to curb these excesses, then the unreasonable will do it.

The excesses that must be tamed are associated most often with, and most effectively represented by, the overturning of traditional codes of gendered behavior, especially in the sexual autonomy of women. Irene Moll represents all of this; in fact, she embodies all that is negative in the novel (Jürgs, 204). She is an especially apt symbol of modernity out of control, for her husband fails to control her, not merely out of weakness but also apparently because he is too involved in corruption. What is required of men is moral discipline and the will to control women, and if the defenders of reason, like Labude and Fabian, fail miserably, then the job will be done by men who are more brutal, like the reactionary Wenzkat, the former schoolmate of Fabian who likes to beat up prostitutes in Fabian's hometown (227).

In his 1994 study of New Objectivity and the "cold" persona, Lethen finds in *Fabian* an old-fashioned perspective, one still grounded in moralizing, bourgeois "interiority" in its outlook on the "cult of loose morals" ("Lässigkeitskult") of Weimar modernity (*Verhaltenslehren,* 242). This is correct as far as it goes, but in fact there are few examples of New Objectivity that portray the modern world with complete neutrality. There is usually critique, and it is invariably based on a moral perspective grounded in some bourgeois ideology, whether humanism, Marxism, romantic anti-capitalism, or fascism.[16]

More nihilistic depictions of sexual brutality in Dada and the early Brecht (of the kind that Sloterdijk notes) are typical of Lethen's "cold persona." Such nihilism is clearly meant as a provocation to that bourgeois moral order, but in attempting to negate that order such gestures actually prove its hegemony, or so one might argue. In any case, such nihilism is not what one finds in Kästner, to be sure. Let us invoke some of Lethen's categories: the "cult of loose morals" of late Weimar—the "cult" of which according to Lethen Kästner disapproves—involves not the type that is called the "cold persona," but rather the one he calls the "radar type." This is a character type that is much less aggressive, much more "other-directed," and more malleable than the former (235–43). If the radar type is embodied in *Fabian,* however, it is not to be found in Moll, but rather in Fabian himself, whose passivity in the face of events indicates a definite affinity with the "radar type." Fabian does critique this type of behavior, of course, and the novel itself would seem to be an even stronger critique of Fabian's passivity. But it should be stressed again that critique is not atypical of New Objectivity. Certainly most if not all of the New Objectivist paintings of prostitutes and sexual "degeneracy" are social critiques.[17] Particularly in the common association between prostitutes and corrupt bankers (and generals) so typical of the work of Georg Grosz, there is much similarity to the critical portrait Kästner paints of Weimar corruption in *Fabian.*

Kästner himself insisted that his novel was a satire that held up a distorting, or "fun-house" mirror ("Zerrspiegel") to reality (10). Indeed, it has been asserted that critique, distortion, and indeed an "evil gaze" were endemic to New Objectivity (Klotz, 75–77, 81–82). One criticism of Kästner and much New Objectivity is that this critical gaze, which focuses on the real details of modern corruption and alienation in such microscopic intensity, pays too little attention to the larger economic, social, and psychological factors that determine these surface details (Klotz, 74, 89). Beyond such limitations, this "evil gaze" is, paradoxically enough, connected to a perspective that is both moralizing and sentimental.

The novel's (petit-) bourgeois sentimentality is especially clear in its rejection of sexual emancipation and its idealization of sexual innocence. But let me cite Kracauer's insight again, that hidden beneath the surface of New Objectivity's modern facade was overwhelming sentimentality (*Die Angestellten,* 287).[18] Hidden beneath Fabian's passive, voyeuristic gaze, which documents the social and sexual chaos of the modern metropolis in late Weimar in all its fluidity, is of course Kästner's moralizing, sentimental, and nostalgic critique of "cold modernity." Expressionism and New Objectivity emphasized opposing sides of dichotomies such as coldness/sentimentality, exterior/interior, and modern/anti-modern, but they were after all two sides of the same coin.

Certainly *Fabian* is in many ways a superficial, humorous look at Berlin, at the same time that the basically conservative moral thrust of its satire cannot be denied. Part of the problem is one of perspective: most critics—

and I am no exception—tend to equate the character Fabian with the narrative perspective of the novel and both with Kästner. Formally, however, the novel invites precisely this conflation: like much of the prose of New Objectivity, the narrator in the guise of "objectivity" tends to disappear behind the perspective of the main character (Klotz, 80–81). In this novel it is hard to discern any position other than that of Fabian; certainly the narrator gives us little insight into the thoughts of any other characters. There is one example of the reader being provided the thoughts of Cornelia (178), but this is such an exception that one almost has the impression that it is a mistake. The characters one comes to understand best are those most like Fabian, above all Labude, his "idealist" foil. The others are arrayed along a spectrum that spans the distance from Fabian's position—that of a middle-class, Christian (albeit secular and rationalist), and heterosexual male of the younger generation. As one proceeds along the spectrum away from Fabian one finds men (brutal reactionaries like Wenzkat and corrupt and decadent aristocrats like Labude senior), women (especially ones who vary from the traditional bourgeois norm epitomized by his mother), working-class types (see the sixteenth chapter, in which he visits Wedding, a working-class district of Berlin), Jews, foreigners, and other exotics such as lesbians and "perfumed homosexual boys" ("parfümierte homosexuelle Burschen," 99).

Since the novel is in many ways autobiographical (Fickert, 53), the question arises: how similar is this perspective that dominates the novel to that of its author? Obviously it is very similar. And as a satire, the position of the author should be more obvious than in a more classically realist genre. But as a satire, is not the critique directed at the main character Fabian, as well as the society in which he lives? Yes, there is critique of Fabian—even of his double-standard: after berating Cornelia for her illusions about her affair with Makart, for instance, Fabian suddenly remembers that he has just been with Mucki (180). Ultimately, however, the novel criticizes his melancholy passivity, and the futility of his final attempt to overcome it. Fabian fails in his attempt to achieve masculine mastery, and it is mainly this for which the novel criticizes him.

Kästner would seem to be directing this critique at himself and the intelligentsia in general for its apolitical passivity and impotence, a critique he continues, if anything more sharply, in the postwar era. Perhaps this insight can help us to understand the postwar Kracauer better, too—is it ultimately not just "Germany's," but specifically the inability of intellectuals like himself to stop fascism that he rails about in his postwar analysis of "effeminate" passivity in Weimar Germany? If so, it is nonetheless the connection of this concern to stereotypical ideas about gender and masculine "potency" that is most problematic. And this applies to *Fabian* as well—for what the novel criticizes much more harshly than the intellectual Fabian is the modern world around him, which conspires to make "masculine" mastery impossible, a topsy-turvy world epitomized above all by "phallic," "castrating" women like Irene Moll. It would appear to be this melancholic fixation of Fabian—and by extension his creator—on these modern changes in gender and sexual dynamics that keeps him paralyzed in the face of the fascist threat to the Weimar Republic. Indeed, this fixation makes him in some ways complicit with that threat, since the Nazis will indeed take action to address the "threatening" changes that bother him so much.

The Cabaret of Humiliation

Gender, Spectacle, and Spectatorship in *Josef von Sternberg's* The Blue Angel *(1930)*

One of the most famous films produced in Germany during the Weimar Republic was *The Blue Angel* (*Der blaue Engel,* 1930), and it too is a testament to the social and sexual anxieties associated with modernity that typified German culture during this era. But international developments in cinematic aesthetics, technology, and finance were also significant in the production of this film, one of Germany's first major sound films. It was directed by an American, the Austrian-born Josef von Sternberg, who had been hired by one of Germany's most important producers, Erich Pommer. Sternberg was placed at the head of a production team composed of German writers, technicians, set designers, and actors, with the studios of the largest German film company, Ufa, at his disposal.

Such interaction between the German and American film industry was common during the 1920s, especially in the financing of films produced in "stabilized," post-Dawes Plan Germany. There was also considerable movement back and forth across the Atlantic by actors, directors, and producers, as Saunders explores in depth (e.g. 209–211). Pommer had met Sternberg in Hollywood, where the actor Emil Jannings had met him too. Jannings actually worked under Sternberg's direction in the 1928 American film, *The Last Command,* and it was for that role that Jannings won the very first "Oscar" for best actor at the first Academy Awards ceremony.

In Germany, the transition to sound took longer than in the United States, which was one reason that Pommer wanted to bring Sternberg to Germany. Sternberg had already directed his first sound film in Hollywood

(*Thunderbolt,* 1929). *The Blue Angel* would be his second sound film. Produced in Germany, it is a film that cites and pays homage to many of the famous German films of the 1920s. At the same time, the film reproduces some typical sexual discourses of the German cinema, including the trend I have sketched through a number of the most famous films, that is, the shift from depicting feminized monsters (as in *Caligari* and *Nosferatu*) to depictions of "phallic women" (see Chapter 2).

The *Blue Angel* could be said to represent the end point of this progression. Here the figure of the "monster" is a vamp—not a machine as in *Metropolis,* but nonetheless "phallic." Such psycho-sexual connotations are combined with sociological ones as well: the film's vamp, Lola Lola, portrayed by Marlene Dietrich in the role that would make her an international star, is also a working woman, and her marriage to Rath can be seen in reference to Weimar's "crisis of marriage" (Kaes, "Motor," 96). Modern fears about marriage and working women were by no means exclusive to Germany, but in this film they manifest themselves in a very "German" scenario that is an adaptation (albeit a very unfaithful one) of a left-wing German novel from the turn of the century, Heinrich Mann's *Professor Unrat* (1905). The narrative is then visualized in a style that cites many famous German art films, Weimar's "street film" genre, as well as Weimar cabaret.

To come to terms with the film, then, one must understand its implication in this web of cinematic, social, and sexual discourses: this Austrian-American director's homage to German Expressionist film is at the same time a product of New Objective "Americanism," combining elements of Weimar cabaret, sound film technology, and the creation of one of the ultimate cinematic vamps, a figure that evoked modern social anxieties about "New Women." Needless to say, the film also lends itself quite readily to the discussion of issues that have concerned film studies for three decades now: cinematic self-reflexivity, gendered spectatorship and visual objectification, as well as such psychoanalytical topics as sado-masochism, "phallic" women, and "castrated" men who are "feminized" and/or "hysterical."

THE BLUE ANGEL: *MADE IN GERMANY*

In 1929 Sternberg left Hollywood and traveled to Berlin in order to direct a sound film for Ufa. This would be Ufa's first sound film with a large production crew and budget, Germany's "greatest sound film" ("größter Tonfilm"), as the *Film-Kurier* proclaimed on April 2, 1930 ("Erste Ufaton-Großstaffel"). The project that resulted in *The Blue Angel* began with an invitation from Jannings, who asked Sternberg to direct him in his first sound film. Even more significant for the making of the film, however, was Pommer's role, for he was Ufa's most famous producer.

Ufa at this point was owned by Alfred Hugenberg, who had rescued the company from bankruptcy in 1927. The costs of making Fritz Lang's gargantuan *Metropolis* had been a principal cause of the financial woes that had made this rescue necessary. Pommer had produced most of Ufa's most prestigious art films, and he was Lang's producer. In the aftermath of the financial troubles the studio underwent producing *Metropolis,* Pommer left Germany for Hollywood to work there (Saunders, 69, 74, 211). But by 1929 he was back, again in charge of producing art films for the new Ufa under Hugenberg. The latter was a powerful publishing magnate and an ultra-conservative and nationalist, indeed an important ally of the Nazis in the period leading up to 1933, when Hitler became chancellor, and the Weimar Republic ended. In 1933, Pommer, being Jewish, went into exile.[19]

Critics as disparate as Andrew Sarris (in 1966) and Gertrud Koch (in 1986) have asked the question of just how "German" *The Blue Angel* is. Josef von Sternberg was not German. His original name was Jonas Sternberg, and he was born in Vienna to Austrian Jewish parents in 1894. But it is not really accurate to call him an Austrian, as Coates does (55, 72), either. He first came to New York at seven and lived there for three years. Then he and his family returned to Austria, but four years later, at fourteen, he came back to New York. From then on he lived in the United States (Koch, 64; cf. Sternberg, "Fun," 8–15). He got into the film business in New York and became a director in Hollywood.

In his memoirs Sternberg styles himself as an "auteur," a film director who claims total artistic responsibility for the films he directed, including *The Blue Angel.* He was willing to acknowledge few influences on his work, but among those he reveals were the famous German directors of the 1920s. He also admitted to having followed and admired the German cinema during the 1920s before he went to Germany to direct *The Blue Angel* ("Fun," 34–36). Besides providing evidence of this influence on Sternberg's filmmaking, *The Blue Angel* was in many other ways a very German production. Its producer, writers, actors, set designer, lighting crew, and studio technicians belonged to the German film industry. The film was produced in Ufa studios, and it looks like it. The film's designer, Otto Hunte, had often worked with Fritz Lang, and he was responsible for the "Ufa look" of many German films of the 1920s (Wegner, 4). Moreover, the film was much more successful in Germany than in the United States, where it was held for release until after the success of *Morocco* (1930), Sternberg's first American film with Dietrich (Koch, 70).

The Blue Angel transformed Heinrich Mann's novel *Professor Unrat* from a political critique of German society into a sex story "à la *Human Bondage*," as Sternberg himself put it ("Fun," 11). Sternberg, typically, maintains that he was the dominant influence on the screenplay. Regardless of the accuracy of this claim, a depoliticized approach was typical of Sternberg; he would treat Dreiser's *American Tragedy* similarly.[20] Kracauer's postwar critique of the film accused it of a proto-fascist anti-intellectualism and sadism (*Caligari*, 215–18); in response, Sternberg confessed in his 1965 autobiography that he was always naively unaware of political conditions, including the rise of the Nazis, which he ignored during the filming of *The Blue Angel* and even later when returning to Germany ("Fun," 49–51, 241–42). Despite Sternberg's awareness or his intentions, however, a drastic alteration of the novel had definite benefits for the German film industry, given the political turbulence at the end of 1929. Heinrich Mann was hated by the far-right wing (and by Hugenberg); any too faithful adaptation of one of his novels might easily have endangered distribution.[21]

Above all, *The Blue Angel* can be read as a German film because it cites so many of the elements typical of Weimar cinema, including what I have called its "discourse of castration," but which could also be called "male hysteria," defined by Penley and Willis as "men in trouble over masculinity" (xii). It is a typical vamp story, and a film that is also typical of the so-called "street film" genre of Weimar cinema (Schulte-Sasse). The stuffy, bourgeois Professor Rath (played by Emil Jannings) ventures into the disreputable world of the Blue Angel, a bar with entertainment consisting primarily of "girls" singing risqué songs—a "Tingeltangel," not really an example of the more intellectual/bohemian cabaret (Jelavich, 1, 21). In this establishment he meets the seductive performer Lola Lola (Marlene Dietrich). He falls in love with her, causing a scandal that costs him his job and social position. He marries her and leaves town with the troupe of performers. Eventually he has to earn his keep by peddling pictures of his wife and by appearing as a clown onstage in the act of magician, Kiepert (played by Kurt Gerron), the troupe's leader. When forced to play the clown at the Blue Angel, in front of a mostly hostile audience in his former hometown, he sees Lola kissing another man offstage, and he loses his mind. He tries to kill her but is restrained. While she sings onstage looking more glamorous than ever, he sneaks off to die in his former classroom.

The Blue Angel makes direct allusions to the German art cinema of the 1920s, creating a world borrowed from that source rather than contemporary social reality.[22] In its original version, the film opens to music, and the German credits appear in white letters on a black background, ending with the Ufa insignia. Then the first shots are shown: the rooftops of the town, women milling about in the street below, and the rising of a metal blind to reveal a shop-window with a poster depicting Lola.[23] The window to which the poster appears to be attached (from the inside) is then washed by a woman who suddenly notices the image on the poster and then attempts to imitate Lola's stance.[24] The film's first images thus are gothic rooftops like those seen in both *Caligari* (1920) and *Nosferatu* (1922); the next shot of a lower-class street milieu, made up entirely of women, evokes the tenements of *The Last Laugh* (1924). The street itself is filmed a bit later in a way that evokes other street films, especially Bruno Rahn's *Tragedy of the Prostitute* (*Dirnentragödie*, 1927).[25] Heading for the Blue Angel the first time, Professor Rath makes his way down a street that is portrayed ominously as a realm of shadows, an eroticized lower-class milieu in which a prostitute briefly appears (one who indeed resembles the character played by Asta Nielsen in *Tragedy of the Prostitute*).

The end of the film is a direct citation of a scene in F.W. Murnau's *The Last Laugh*, another tragic story of male anxiety and humiliation featuring Jannings. The flashlight of a nightwatchman is used in both films to seek out a ruined man in the depths of darkness: in *The Last Laugh*, it is the demoted doorman collapsed on a chair in the men's room of the hotel; in the *The Blue Angel*, it is the deceased Rath, clutching his desk in the classroom he once dominated. This use of the flashlight's beam is arguably a cinematically "self-reflexive" moment of foregrounded looking, reminiscent of Rotwang's beam in *Metropolis* (1927), which pursues and traps Maria in the dark caverns below the city. At the same time it bears a relation to the "cold," "surgical" gaze so often mentioned in accounts of Weimar society and New Objectivity by recent scholars: Theweleit (222–23), Sloterdijk (817), and Lethen (*Verhaltenslehren*, 187–89), among others.

THE "COLD" BLUE ANGEL: WEIMAR MODERNITY AND NEW OBJECTIVITY

Beyond film-historical evidence with regard to influences acknowledged by the director, the film's production history, and its citations of Weimar cinema, *The Blue Angel* can be read as a German film because of its implication within a much broader social-historical context, namely the crisis of modernity specific to Weimar and the thematization of modernity at the heart of the New Objectivity.

Given the film's obvious citation of earlier German "art films" of the 1920s, it would seem to align itself with, or at least to be in homage to

German Expressionism. What then is its relation to New Objectivity, other than its being produced in 1929–1930? Of course, the very fact of citation indicates a distance from the original that is being cited. At the time the film appeared, it must have been fairly clear that the citation was being made, because few other German films made around 1930 used this style of the early 1920s. The film creates a pastiche of stylistic and thematic motifs of a number of famous German films of the 1920s, but its tone is different. Its use of eroticism is much more frank, perhaps even cynical, and certainly less moralistic—in fact it is much more ambiguous, even "perverse" and/or sado-masochistic.

Unlike the earlier films, it is of course a sound film, and as with so many early German sound films, the use of music is central to it. Indeed *The Blue Angel* could be considered Pommer's first step in his development of the German musical or operetta films, which was the major achievement of what Saunders call his "second career" (248–49): that is, his career after his return from Hollywood in the late 1920s, when he produced German sound films until fleeing Germany in 1933.[26] Also made explicit through the film's use of music is its connection to the world of cabaret and the revue, popular forms of metropolitan night life especially in Berlin—forms of entertainment that were a significant feature of Weimar modernity with very little relation to German Expressionism of the stage or the film. A number of people involved in making the film were also active in that other world of the Weimar cabaret and revues. Friedrich Holländer, who composed the film's music, was one of the most successful composers of music for Weimar revues; in 1931 he founded his own cabaret in Berlin, and he named it the "Tingel-Tangel." The best German jazz band, the Weintraub Syncopators, performed Holländer's music in most of the latter's revue productions in Berlin; the Syncopators also appear in *The Blue Angel* as the band that plays in the title nightclub (Jelavich, 190–91, 207). Also associated with the Berlin cabaret and revue scene were the performers Kurt Gerron and Rosa Valetti, who played the magician Kiepert and his wife Guste in the film.[27] Sternberg first saw Marlene Dietrich (and decided to cast her in the film) while watching a Berlin revue entitled "Two Bow-Ties" ("Zwei Krawatten"), in which Dietrich appeared with Valetti and Hans Albers, who both had already been cast in the film.[28] (Albers would portray the strongman Mazeppa.)

In discussing the film's relationship to Expressionism, one is again confronted by the dilemma of specifying what Expressionism in the German cinema actually involved. *Caligari* certainly attempted to be Expressionist, and most critics would also be willing to categorize *Nosferatu* as Expressionist as well, although even Eisner goes to great lengths discussing how different its style is (99–105), and she is the writer perhaps most responsible for the blanket categorization of all the best Weimar art films up until 1933 as "Expressionist." But beyond those two famous films, and a few others made in the same period, it is debatable what else can be so considered. Even *Caligari* could be considered merely a citation of theatrical Expressionism. In Lang's *Dr. Mabuse* (1922), Expressionism is already cited with an obvious distance, functioning primarily as a trendy decor associated mainly with negative (decadent) characters (and with the villainy of the title character). *The Last Laugh* is definitely a film that heralds a transition to a very different kind of filmmaking.[29]

The Blue Angel also cites the so-called genre of the "street film," which is a genre that was not necessarily "Expressionist" at all, one that in any case represented a type of urban realism in German cinema, albeit a sensationalized one. Because of its frequent thematization of prostitution, it can be considered one of the successor genres to the racy *Aufklärungsfilme* of the first days of Weimar film, before the reimposition of censorship (Murray, 36).[30] Above all the street film represents a (usually ambivalent) attempt to confront the modern metropolis. Schulte-Sasse writes that the ideology of the street film is usually conservative, and this is also true of *The Blue Angel,* at least on the surface. Its narrative follows the basic plot of the street film: a respectable bourgeois is lured from the path of respectability into the shady, modern underworld, where he is ruined.

While this narrative similarity exists, there is an important difference: as in *Variety,* the underworld here is not strictly speaking the milieu of the streets, but rather the milieu of modern entertainment. Jelavich calls the Blue Angel a "sailors' dive" (191) and classifies it as a "Tingeltangel," a bar presenting "a third-rate variety show that was a direct precursor of cabaret" (1). As he explains, the much more big-budget Weimar stage revue and the more intellectual cabaret were also offshoots of the late nineteenth-century variety show. Not just "the street," of course, but also the variety show, as well as the carnival and the amusement park, were often used to symbolize the chaos of modernity. The latter two forms were thematized as such in *Caligari,* depicting the topsy-turvy world out of which its villain emerges. But much more characteristic of Weimar culture than the nineteenth-century carnival in *Caligari* were the revue, the cabaret, and their sleazier imitations in nightclubs like the Blue Angel. And it is this world that is depicted in *The Blue Angel,* a world with a more anarchistic style of performance that might indeed subvert the "conservative" narrative that contains the film.

Of course the film bears an obvious relation to another major discourse of New Objectivity: Americanism. It is true that this relation is most evident at the levels of production and reception: the importation of Sternberg, the urgent need to catch up with American sound-film technology, and then the eager headline in the *Film-Kurier* in August 1930 announcing the American film industry's response to the film: "Hollywood in Awe of the Technique of *The Blue Angel*."[31] In the German reception there are also assertions about the content of the film itself: that Marlene Dietrich, for instance, had not only managed to produce the "sex appeal" (the English term is used) that Americans believed they had invented, but also to raise it to an art in a way that had not been equaled ("R.P.").

Related to the erotic appeal of the film are the coldness and indifference often ascribed to Dietrich's performance. These qualities can be connected to phenomena within Weimar culture such as the sexual cynicism Sloterdijk discusses (see also Brockmann, "Weimar Sexual Cynicism") as well as Lethen's "cold persona" (*Verhaltenslehren*). Lethen emphasizes the importance of the mask to this persona; beneath it, no "authentic" reality but only strategic calculation hides. This concept of the mask, which for Lethen is an almost exclusively male phenomenon, is in some ways oddly similar to Joan Riviere's 1929 article on "Womanliness as a Masquerade." While in Riviere there is lurking beneath the masquerade of femininity nothing but an anxiety that a woman's transgressive "masculinity" might be discovered, in Lethen the mask conceals an anxiety that the scared, vulnerable "creature" might be exposed—a fear of exposure and objectification that is clearly a fear of being "feminized," as well of the "femininity" of that hidden creature. Both in Lethen's notion and in Riviere's, there would seem to be a similar anxiety on the part of the bearer of the mask/player in the masquerade about transgressing some rigidly defined notions of gendered behavior. For its part, *The Blue Angel* places great stress on costume and masquerade as well, but in a very self-conscious way that exposes the game, as it were. This is especially the case with Dietrich's costumes, which so obviously parody femininity in both exhibitionistic and androgynous ways—the skirts that expose her undergarments in front and the white top hat, for instance.[32]

Coldness and indifference in Dietrich's film persona can also be explained biographically, of course: Sternberg noted these two qualities in Dietrich the first time he saw her perform, and they played a role in his decision to select her for the part of Lola ("Fun," 231). The masks and masquerades might also be understood in relation to Sternberg's own personal quirks, such as his reputed fetishism and sado-masochism, as Koch suggests

(63, 65–68), yet this explanation does not explain the resonance these elements in the film found within Weimar Germany, where the film became such an overwhelming hit. In turn that success was greatest in Germany's big cities (Wendtland, 56), where Americanism and urbane cynicism were so popular.

Americanism also included the idea of sexual emancipation and working women, and of course here too the film is exemplary in its thematization of such problems, and as Kaes asserts, the "crisis of marriage" as well ("Motor," 96). This "crisis" was perceived above all by those sexual reformers who were concerned about the birth rate and therefore attempted to control women's sexual (and economic) autonomy by advocating traditional marriage. One of the favored methods was the use of sexual education in order to shore up marriage (by making it less boring), as was propagated in books like Van de Velde's 1926 best-seller *The Perfect Marriage* (*Die vollkommene Ehe*).[33] The campaign to control—and rationalize—women's new autonomy embodied in the sex reform movement alludes to perceived "threats" that were of course psychological as well as social. It is now time to consider the psychosexual dynamics within the text of the film itself, a subject relevant both to critical debates today as well as to the social-historical context of the Weimar Republic.

REFLEXIVITY AND THE CONSTRUCTION OF THE VAMP

As mentioned above, beams of light are foregrounded at certain moments in *The Blue Angel,* such as the night watchman's flashlight on Rath at the end of the film, as well as Lola's "entrapment" of Rath within her spotlight during his first visit to the night club. These scenes allude to similar uses of light in *Metropolis* and *The Last Laugh,* and through such scenes the film thematizes its own specular relations as those earlier films do.

The film also echoes another type of cinematic self-reflexivity found in an even earlier film, Robert Wiene's *Caligari.* In the latter film, the top-hatted carnival magician Caligari first shows his audience Cesare in a two-dimensional illustration. Cesare later "comes to life" as a creature who moves at Caligari's command. This can be read as an allusion to the cinema itself, originally a form of entertainment associated with fairs and carnivals in Germany. The cinema's primary illusionistic trick—turning static two-dimensional images into apparently mobile, three-dimensional ones—was performed mostly in tent-cinemas in Germany before about 1905 (Kaes, "Motor," 47).[34] The creation of *Caligari's* most important illusion, Cesare, takes place after Caligari, holding the sketch of Cesare, beckons to the public to enter his tent. Once inside the tent, he opens the standing coffin to reveal a static Cesare who soon opens his eyes and then begins to move.

This process is paralleled in *The Blue Angel* with the creation of its most important illusion: Lola. She is first glimpsed as an illustration on a poster, then as a photographic image on the postcards at which first the school-boys, and later Professor Rath, leer; they blow on the three-dimensional feathers on one postcard image in order to reveal what lies at the top of the famous legs. Finally there is the cut to Lola herself on the stage in the Blue Angel, first in a medium shot from the waist up, and then from the waist down. The *femme fatale* Lola will become, however, is not completely cre-ated with her appearance "in the flesh" on the stage of the cabaret. She is still more or less the equal of the other women onstage, with whom she shares beer while waiting her turn to perform again, wiping her mouth with no concern for how others might perceive her in a cabaret whose delightful chaos Mayne so aptly calls "carnivalesque" (34; see Figure 2.2 on p. 31, which depicts the first shot of Lola onstage in the cabaret).[35]

In narrative terms it is Rath's desire for Lola that seems necessary for her transformation into the image the film wants to create for her—an image Sternberg claims "some of the responsibility" for creating ("Fun," 226–27). What is interesting is how the film thematizes that very transformation, that very construction of an image of woman that feminist critics have called a "domina" and a "phallic mother" (Koch, 68) or the "ultimate fetish" (Mul-vey, 22).[36]

In the film, this transformation depends not only on Rath's desire but on a relationship between the image of Lola and a specific male spectator. Rath is shown being "trapped" as spectator—by a beam of light. As in *Metropolis,* a beam of light is used to catch someone, but not as spectacle, as Maria will become in that film. Rath is instead trapped in the role of spec-tator (at least at this point—later he too will be onstage). Lola, the woman associated with the spectacle, is responsible for his entrapment; it is she who directs the spotlight at Rath in the audience when he first wanders into the Blue Angel.[37] Also playing a significant role is Kiepert, the top-hatted magician and director of the troupe, who ultimately pushes Rath up into the balcony, positioning him so that Lola can sing "Falling in Love Again" directly to him (see Figure 5.1) and not to the lower-class, multi-racial audi-ence on whom the professor looks down. Is the magician another reference to Caligari, the carnival trickster who manipulates the cinematic illusion (and a reference to Sternberg himself)? The magician Kiepert is not only the director of the troupe of performers, but a sort of "pimp" who controls the troupe's women.

Figure 5.1   Another top-hatted musician, Kiepert (Kurt Gerron) makes sure his spectator, Rath (Emil Jannings) can watch Lola perform in Sternberg's *The Blue Angel* (1930). (Compare the top-hatted Dr. Caligari in Figure 2.1 on page 26). Photo courtesy of Film Museum Berlin.

By the end of the film, with Rath's elimination, no more spectators are shown. Lola is alone onstage and alone in the frame of the image, looking now more glamorous—and much more the hard-hearted vamp—than earlier in the film. She sings "Falling in Love Again," but more harshly this time; she wears black, and sits with legs wide open, straddling the back of the chair. (See cover art.)[38] The low-life audience of the "sailors' dive" is no longer shown. Obliquely addressing the cinema audience, she is no longer a theatrical phenomenon, but rather truly a "cinematic" illusion in the classical sense: an illusion of reality unburdened by any evidence of its construction or the existence of the audience that watches it.[39]

SPECTATORSHIP, "PERVERSITY," AND RESISTANCE

As a cinematic illusion in the classical sense, the threat Lola represents to masculinity is supposedly contained. Such a containment of woman's resistance or threat is in line what feminist film theory has defined as a main goal of "classical" narrative cinema—as consolidated in Hollywood. For such a reading, Sternberg's most significant achievement in making *The*

Blue Angel would perhaps be an "American" appropriation of the German discourses cited in the film, such that Weimar's sexual anxieties are mobilized but tamed, used for comedy, and then sentimentalized—thus creating a more consumable (and less threatening) fantasy for the commercial cinema.[40] After *The Blue Angel,* of course, Dietrich followed Sternberg back to Hollywood, the most powerful commercial film industry, where she would continue to be marketed—and to market herself—as a *femme fatale.*

It is easy to read the film in the psychoanalytical terms of much film theory of the last three decades. Castration anxiety operates on many levels in *The Blue Angel.*[41] It is also not difficult to connect this psychological anxiety to men's social and political anxieties in Weimar society (also evident in many of the older Weimar films it cites). The film, after all, shows a man of secure bourgeois status transformed into a made-up clown and a cuckold because of an erotic involvement with an "amoral" vamp, someone in turn connected to rootless, cosmopolitan types who entertain the "uneducated rabble" (as Rath himself calls them).

Such a reading, however, implies that the film intends Rath to be a sympathetic figure and the entertainers in the Blue Angel to be unsympathetic. If Rath is not sympathetic, then his "fall" will not provoke anxiety but instead seem ridiculous. In fact it can easily be argued that the professor is indeed a figure of ridicule, the character toward whom almost all the laughs in the film are directed: he represents precisely the stuffy, pompous bourgeois type so often ridiculed in the world of Weimar variety and cabaret that the film obviously cites. And if one focuses more on Lola's story, and not Rath's, as Mayne has suggested, one begins to see the film quite differently. Sternberg himself observed that Lola was "the most important component of the film," writing also: "Without the electricity of a new and exciting female, the film would have been no more than an essay reflecting on the stupidity of a school tyrant" ("Fun," 232).

As Mayne also observes, however, Rath comes to exercise "supreme narrative authority" over the course of the film (35); the film becomes Rath's "tragedy," and Lola, in spite of her initial belonging to a very non-hierarchical, "carnivalesque" anarchy, becomes the tragedy's catalyst—and a fetishized "star." For the end of the film to be effective, then, the sympathies of the audience must have been transferred to the humbled professor and turned against the cynicism of the nightclub entertainers—above all Lola, whose role has been reduced to a cliché: playing the hard-hearted vamp to the sentimental old man she has seduced.

But *is* the end of the film effective? Have viewers' sympathies been redirected toward Rath? Some of the film's very first reviews suggested that the end is not effective because it is a reversion to the conventional and the sentimental (for example Henseleit and Ihering).[42] Mayne's reading of the film sets the "carnivalesque" anarchy of the beginning of the film against the hierarchical performance style of Lola the star/vamp at the end. This is significant for the interpretation of the film: it makes a difference if the end of the film does not tame that earlier anarchy and effectively transform the film into a male tragedy caused by a stereotypical vamp. No less an aesthetic and cultural critic than Theodor Adorno faulted the film precisely for its too sympathetic treatment of Lola (656–57).

This certainly complicates any reading of the film solely focused on the dominant discourses of castration anxiety and male crisis. As mentioned in Chapter 2, Mulvey may have been right to call Sternberg's version of Lola Lola the "ultimate fetish" in patriarchal cinema, but other dynamics were involved as well, given the extreme popularity of *The Blue Angel* in Berlin's lesbian subculture during the early 1930s.[43] This particular appreciation for the film and its female star has of course continued. Julia Lesage has written: "Dietrich fascinates women as a lesbian figure with whom they can identify" (ctd. in Studlar, 49). Offscreen, of course, it was an open secret that Dietrich herself was bisexual.[44] Gaylyn Studlar makes the point that the androgynous appeal of Dietrich's onscreen image is not only noted by lesbians: "Her overt eroticism seems to elicit sexual feelings from straight and lesbian women, gay and straight males" (49). This appeal is thus not just lesbian, but indeed "queer," as Doty defines the term (xvii–xviii).[45]

Thus in *The Blue Angel* Lola can be seen not (just) as a masochistic patriarchal fantasy but (also) as a woman with a top hat and an androgynous aura who seems bored by men, if occasionally amused by them. In considering other narratives besides the one built around Rath's rather trite tragedy, in considering other aspects to Lola's appeal besides the clichéd version Rath constructs, in considering other spectators open to those aspects and less willing to be satisfied with Rath's version, the possibility of other readings of this film becomes clear. A "dominant" reading—one determined by the perspectives that dominate a society—cannot not preclude other, more emancipatory interpretations that might resist dominant meanings. But the existence of such subversive or resistant perspectives on a text cannot totally undo the power of what is socially "dominant." As Mayne emphasizes, Dietrich's resistance to stereotypes of the vamp is deployed in *The Blue Angel,* along with the entire "carnivalesque" milieu of the cabaret, only to be "contained" at the end of the film by her transformation into something much less ambiguous, the hard-hearted vamp within the clichéd male fantasy Rath constructs (42).[46]

But again: how well the "containment" of Lola works is a question of how well narrative closure works in this film. How much overall importance should be ascribed to the narrative in this film anyway, given that it was made by a director whose work was cited by Laura Mulvey in her most famous essay as an example of a type of film in which erotic spectacle continually interrupts and hinders narrative? According to Studlar, the fetishism that Mulvey claims is so typical of Sternberg is essentially masochistic and thus pre-Oedipal— not related, therefore, to the castration complex at all. The consequences, then, of emphasizing a masochistic spectacle would undermine any narrative based on castration.

Even within the terms of such a narrative as it has been understood in much psychoanalytical film theory since Mulvey, that is, with regard to castration anxiety and the male gaze, there are some interesting quirks here. As noted, the specular relations within the film are foregrounded, but it is Lola who places the spotlight on Rath. Rath's ultimate humiliation occurs in a clown suit while being abused by Kiepert on the stage of the Blue Angel—that is, it is Rath who becomes the center of the spectacle at the climactic moment of the film. Within the very terms of Rath's narrative, then, it is the visual objectification of the *male* that is thematized at this crucial moment, with an emphasis on the staging of male humiliation (see Figure 5.2). There are various ways to categorize this humiliation: castration, masochism, hysteria, or feminization. It can also be described using the terms Lethen has used to describe Weimar culture (in *Verhaltenslehren*): what is shown is the ripping away of the mask of the proud, masculine/ bourgeois persona and the exposure of the feminized "creature" beneath, a creature that indeed has been reduced not just to a clown but to an animal, a crazed rooster who crows in disturbed anguish.[47]

This masochistic staging of humiliation may proceed in the service of being "contained," yet it is both provocative and telling. Clearly, such displays of male weakness would soon vanish from the German cinema: the Nazis hated *The Blue Angel*—and any such wallowing in humiliation.[48] The anxieties in the film are not exclusively psychic, of course; they are a part of larger fears triggered by modernity and its destabilization of traditional gender roles (and other identities). Is the mobilization of such anxieties in *The Blue Angel* so destabilizing as to be culpable in the oncoming repression? Brockmann suggests this in his discussion of sexual cynicism in a number of Weimar texts.

But I would disagree. There is rather something emancipatory in the power and the sexual ambiguity of Dietrich's Lola, as well as in the film's exposition of anxieties about traditional masculinity. As Silverman writes

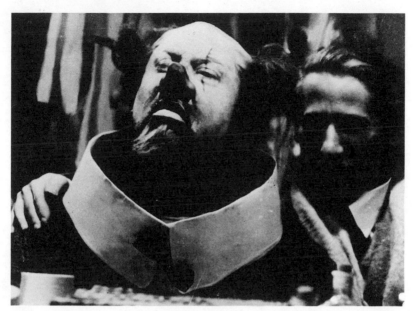

Figure 5.2   The mask of humiliation: production still from *The Blue Angel* (1930) showing Emil Jannings as Rath in his clown make-up, with director Josef von Sternberg looking on with approval. Photo courtesy of Bundesarchiv-Filmarchiv, Berlin.

(54), these anxieties are most often repressed in patriarchal cultures. Perhaps this is a utopian moment when "masculinity makes a humorous, self-questioning spectacle of itself in unsettling ways" (Penley and Willis, xix). And what is being questioned (or parodied) in *The Blue Angel* is the whole system of gender roles—or personae: "masculinity" as well as "femininity," for men as well as for women.

Chapter 6 ∽

Girls in Crisis:
Women's Perspectives in Late Weimar

At home, you know, they are always talking about the time that is coming
when we shall need soldiers again, and mothers of soldiers.

—Christa Winsloe, *Girls in Uniform* (1930)[1]

Mass Culture, Downward Mobility,
and Female Resistance

Irmgard Keun's Novel The Artificial Silk Girl *(1932)*

And so I was exactly what you call faithful. But then he had his Ph.D. and
was finished studying—physics and all that. And went to Munich, where his
parents live, he wanted to get married there—someone from his social background and a daughter of a professor—very famous, but not like Einstein,
whose photograph you see in an awful lot of newspapers and you still don't
get a good idea of. And I always think, whenever I see his picture with the
cheerful eyes and the featherduster hair, that if I would see him in a cafe and
happened to be wearing my coat with the fox collar and drop-dead elegant
from top to bottom, then even he might tell me that he was in the movies
and had unbelievable connections. And I would toss back at him, perfectly
cool: H_2O is water—I learned that from Hubert and it would amaze him.[2]

—Irmgard Keun, The Artificial Silk Girl

D oris, the title character of Irmgard Keun's 1932 novel *The Artificial
Silk Girl* (*Das Kunsteidene Mädchen*), ends this digression about
Einstein in her diary with the next sentence, "But I was talking

about Hubert" ("Aber ich war bei Hubert," 13), and continues the story of her relationship with him, the young man who was her first love. Just as this conversational device is typical of the way Keun has her fictional diary writer end a digression, so the passage as a whole contains a number of thematic elements and stylistic traits characteristic of the novel as a whole. In terms of style, one notes here an approximation of the digressive logic both of free association and filmic montage as well as a hint of the restless tempo of Doris's stream of consciousness, which is in tune with the surface dynamism of the metropolitan culture of distraction so typical of the Weimar Republic. One also can appreciate the humor so typical of the novel, both in Doris's own consciously flippant, matter-of-fact style, as well as in the naiveté her remarks reveal, which demonstrates the limitations of her class and educational background.[3] The fact that in Doris we have an example of Weimar's New Woman, and that we learn about this New Woman from her own viewpoint—indeed, as Kerstin Barndt stresses, through what is represented as her own attempt to write about and make sense of her experiences—makes this novel a very significant one for those who study Weimar culture.

One finds as well in the passage above that preoccupation with superficial celebrity so prevalent in the illustrated press, especially as it addressed women readers. The passage also contains one of the explicit references to film on which critics like Lensing have focused. But it is mistaken to look at this passage as only revealing Doris's naiveté and her unwitting reflection of the metropolitan mass culture that seems to define her. Lensing especially seems to look at Doris with almost complete condescension, all the while arguing that this is the point of Keun's novel, which he praises as a detailed critique of the type of working woman caught up in consumerist and cinematic fantasies that Kracauer ridiculed so famously in his essay "The Little Shopgirls Go to the Movies" ("Die kleinen Ladenmädchen gehen ins Kino").[4] Yet this is precisely the type Keun claimed that she wanted to *counter* with her protagonist (qtd. in Kreis, 91). Lensing sees in the above passage nothing but a fantasy Doris has passively absorbed from *The Blue Angel:* an attractive young woman bowls over a repressed intellectual of a higher class (130). A closer look at the above passage, however, indicates that Doris is demonstrating much more skepticism about both men and cinematic fantasies. She speculates that the famous Einstein might indeed turn out to be like so many other men: finding her attractive, even he might use what is one of the most common lines used by the men she knows to impress women, that he has connections in the film industry (cf. 11). This is indeed what Marlene Dietrich represented in German popular culture in the wake of the success of *Der blaue Engel*: the dream of being discovered, becoming a movie star, and going to Hollywood.[5] Instead of falling for a line about a chance to break into the movies, Doris will impress him with her knowledge of the chemical composition of water. She seems less interested in seducing him à la Lola Lola (using her "sex appeal") than to stun him with her (comically limited) scientific knowledge.

Whereas Lensing sees in Doris the sentimental shop girl, Lethen writes that Keun's novels are notable for their development of female versions of a new personality type in modernity, not what he calls the "cold persona," but what he labels the "radar type."[6] This type is not at all bound to bourgeois sentimentality and inwardness (*Innerlichkeit*), but rather totally oriented toward—and guided by—external social forces (*Verhaltenslehren*, 242–43). Whether embodying cheap sentimentality or a combination of emancipated pragmatism, narcissism, and conformism, Keun's protagonist is evaluated as superficial by both critics. Lethen understands a point made earlier by Livia Wittmann, that there is something especially provocative about these new types being embodied by a female character, and about using a female perspective as the viewpoint on the chaos of modernity. Nonetheless, he seems to downplay the complexity as well as the agency of this female type, even though agency is crucial to his very explanation of them as "Simultanspielerinnen," women who can play many games at once (games of chess or any other games demanding careful and clever planned moves toward a goal), women whose skillful mimicry of various social roles and expectations he defines as a *weapon*.

For as von Ankum notes, Doris is quite aware of her status as a commodity and indeed tries to use it to her advantage ("'Ich liebe Berlin,'" 377), yet precisely therein she demonstrates how little room to maneuver she has: for the most part she reinforces the very trap that has confined her. Nonetheless, there is in her agency a vitality that is empowering (cf. Rosenstein, 281); and, as Shafi stresses, Doris, always a skeptic about society, over the course of the novel begins to see through a number of her illusions (324). Her options remain very limited, but she does come to realize this—as she has indeed demonstrated in her reflexive inscription of her experiences in writing for the reader.[7] While she is "both commodity and consumer," as Gleber puts it, she also exposes those identities to a critical gaze that she herself wields (*The Art of Taking a Walk*, 204).

Rather than comparing Doris's story to the narrative of the one film Doris watches at the cinema in the course of the novel, the film *Mädchen in Uniform*, as Lensing does, I would like to compare her story to that of a woman in another film, without denying the significance of Keun's direct reference to Sagan's 1931 film. Doris's story is that of a woman who consciously uses her sexuality in a bid to achieve both autonomy and upward mobility, yet she discovers that it is a commodity in a market over which she ultimately has little control, and as a commodity she loses value with almost every exchange, ending up homeless and with almost no alternative to prostitution in its clearest and least attractive form. Put this way, the parallel to the story of Lulu in G.W. Pabst's *Pandora's Box* (*Büchse der Pandora,* 1929) is obvious. The similarities and contrasts between the two narratives about female commodification are instructive in their illumination of the common topic—and the two very different perspectives on it. After comparing the trajectories of Doris and Lulu, I shall return to the question of the text in its relation to New Objective discourses on emancipation, sentimentality, and modernity. Finally, I will consider the text's ending to determine whether Doris's trajectory represents only defeat and regression, and what relation it bears to the options open to women at the end of the Weimar Republic, as the economy was collapsing.

DORIS VS. LULU: PERSPECTIVES ON SEXUAL COMMODIFICATION

Pabst's 1929 film adaptation changed Lulu, the central character of Frank Wedekind's two dramas, *Earth Spirit* (*Erdgeist,* 1895) and its continuation *Pandora's Box* (*Büchse der Pandora,* 1902), in some significant ways. He transformed Wedekind's turn-of-the-century "demonic woman" (*dämonisches Weib*) into a "New Woman" of the 1920s. While the film like the Wedekind original is in many ways an imaginary narrative, a very male fantasy about a mythical Woman, the reshaping of Lulu into what is very much a contemporary woman of the Weimar Republic by a film director noted for his realism makes it appropriate to examine this imaginary construction for its implicit commentary on contemporary women. Although Pabst's Lulu remains an ideal creature of male fantasy who incites desire and possessiveness in almost every male with whom she comes into contact (as well as in the lesbian character, Countess Geschwitz), she also is a commodity in circulation among men, a commodity that loses value with each exchange. Beginning as a wealthy man's mistress who inhabits a very luxurious, modern apartment, she ends the film reduced to the status of a prostitute on the streets of London (a fate she resists, but in that very resistance she meets her end as a victim of Jack the Ripper). Film scholars like Thomas Elsaesser and Mary Ann Doane have tended to read Pabst's Lulu in terms of recent film theory as "pure image," a pure object of the filmic "gaze" (Elsaesser, "Lulu," 50–52; Doane, "The Erotic Barter," 67). Not only does such an interpretation ignore the moments of resistance and agency that the film does allow the character, it also misses the historical specificity of the image embodied by Lulu. To the extent she appears to be pure image, a mirror that reflects back the desire of the onlooker, she represents the New Objective fixation with pure surface and its denial of interiority. At the same time she exposes the ideal of pure surface as a myth, because that surface is itself a mask behind which there is a clever but anxious agency, certainly not an autonomous subject, but an individual will trying strategically to take advantage of commodified beauty while resisting—in vain—the downward trajectory toward which the total commodification of the female tends in a male-dominated sexual economy. And to the extent that "emancipated" sexuality in Weimar was merely a sexual cynicism that permitted transgression of many traditional taboos but ultimately accepted the status quo of power relations between the sexes (Doane, "The Erotic Barter," 63), that commodification was all the more total.[8]

Lulu's tragic journey of downward mobility bears some significant similarities—and contrasts—with the adventures of Doris in *The Artificial Silk Girl*. Starting out as a typical "New Woman" of the office work force, Doris exploits her desirability to keep her job but balks at actually submitting to the sexual favors her very undesirable boss thinks of as his due. Instead, she flees the drudgery of office work for a job as an extra in the theater. When her ambitions in the theater also bring her trouble, she flees her provincial city for Berlin, where she pursues her dream of becoming a "Glanz," the shimmering image of a beautiful woman propagated in late Weimar culture by its advertising and consumer culture, its fashion industry, as well as the star system of both the German film industry and of Hollywood. Doris in many senses wants to become the pure image Lulu seems to embody, and at one point in her Berlin adventures she does indeed briefly become the kept mistress of a wealthy man. Doris is hindered like Lulu by an insistence on the autonomy of her own desire, and she is just as fearful of being reduced to the cheapest commodity, the streetwalker, for which she is occasionally mistaken.

Doris's trajectory is much less linear than Lulu's: it has many ups and downs, and it does not have the pathos of such a tragic end. It is far less mythologized, and it documents much more accurately not just the plight of women in Weimar Germany, but the bitter reality of downward mobility in a severe economic depression (something no one would have guessed in early February 1929 at the premiere of Pabst's film). Keun's novel also tells the story from the perspective of an erstwhile New Woman herself: Doris narrates in the first person. One consequence is that the reader has no trouble glimpsing behind the image(s) Doris tries so hard to create. There is clearly distance between Keun and her protagonist—indeed, there is a critique in the novel of many ideals that Doris holds. But perhaps what is most subversive here is the unsentimental exposé of Weimar sexual cynicism from a female point of view. I shall attempt to elaborate this comparison of these two works, the male film director's mythic version of the New Woman, and the female novelist's critical depiction of the same myths and the realities behind them through her frank, funny—and sympathetic—main character.

While Doris is the narrator in Keun's novel, in Pabst's film the narrative perspective is distanced from Lulu, and if it can be identified with any characters at all, it would be with the male ones, as Elsaesser has demonstrated. Pabst's Lulu is an object of fascination for a number of male characters, as well as for the camera. Her own subjectivity is not completely denied (pace Elsaesser and Doane),[9] but it remains for the most part the fascinating enigma that "torments" her many admirers (including Geschwitz). Doris's subjectivity, on the other hand—which as I have noted can just as easily be relegated to pure "surface" by critics, as has been done to Lulu—is very clearly present from the first word of the text to the last, and the same holds true for its positioning with regard to gender. There is obviously much more to the fascination that Keun's book holds beyond the mere fact of gender—both of the eighteen-year old protagonist and the author, who was twenty-seven in 1932[10]—yet that shift in position alone cannot be minimized. For here the commodified object of desire speaks, and here her own perspective on the shift from lover to lover is provided.

Doris's perspective is not merely a female one, of course; it is very concrete in terms of its class, educational, and religious background, just as the trajectory of Doris's narrative is much less mythical, and much more realistic in its socio-economic specificity, than Lulu, who so obviously originates in Wedekind's fin-du-siecle "Erdgeist," an earth spirit representing some primordial female principle, at least in the fantasy of intellectual males.[11] Keun's greater social-historical specificity in crafting the origin and fate of her heroine can in part be explained by socio-economic changes that had occurred between early 1929 and 1932—in the third year of the world depression, it was harder to depict economic decline in anything but the most real terms, as opposed to Lulu's soft-focus end in a far-off London that seems still to be the Victorian city Wedekind had used for his play.

Yet at the same time, Pabst's film is otherwise completely updated to the 1920s. This is especially true of the film's first part, set in Germany: notable are the fashionably Bauhaus/deco apartment in which Schoen keeps his mistress Lulu and the theatrical revue his son Alwa directs and in which Lulu stars.[12] Above all Pabst's Lulu is a completely "Americanized" New Woman, portrayed of course by the American Louise Brooks. Recent critics like Coates (55) and Elsaesser ("Lulu," 56) interpret the film as placing German expressive "inwardness" in conflict with the shimmering surfaces of an Americanized modernity that they see embodied in Brooks's Lulu. But Brook's performance is one of the reasons German critics in 1929 rejected the film, in part because they wanted a more "faithful" adaptation of Wedekind's original. They found Brooks too harmless, not "demonic" enough. Kracauer found the experiment of adapting the depths of Wedekind's play to the surfaces captured by film bold but largely unsuccessful. He praised Fritz Kortner's brooding performance as Schoen but saw in Louise Brooks too much the "Girl" ("Lulu").[13]

Doris, too, is in many ways a stereotypical New Woman: she is a sexually emancipated young woman who actually works as a typist in an office before running off to Berlin, where she—briefly—is kept by a wealthy man. Doris's origins are specified in detail, whereas Lulu's are much more shrouded in mist, except for Geschwitz's speech to the state prosecutor that implies that she had grown up in cafes and cabarets. But that was more or less the same milieu that Doris's mother had occupied until she became pregnant with Doris and married to give her a home; the identity of Doris's father cannot be ascertained, as her mother had apparently had a number of lovers (59).[14]

More significantly, both characters insist on their sexual autonomy, even though they are dependent on men, and both resist being reduced to the lot of a common prostitute, yet each is nonetheless forced into becoming, or nearly becoming one, and the reader/viewer is confronted with the dilemma of determining whether this actually occurs. As von Ankum notes, this can be seen as an allusion to the modern difficulty of discerning "streetwalkers" (the "oldest profession") from the ever-increasing numbers of women entering public space because of other (newer) types of employment outside the private sphere. How one ascertains who and what a prostitute is becomes an increasingly difficult task in urban modernity, even for the police (372–74).[15]

TRAJECTORIES OF DECLINING VALUE:
COMPARING THE NARRATIVES

These and other points of similarity and contrast will be facilitated by short synopses of the two narratives. *Das Kunsteidene Mädchen* is told in three parts, the first titled "End of summer and the medium-sized city" ("Ende des Sommers und die mittlere Stadt," 5), the second "Late autumn—and the big city" ("Später Herbst—und die große Stadt," 43), and the third, "Lots of winter and a waiting room" ("Sehr viel Winter und ein Warte-saal," 91). Both the second and the third part take place in Berlin; the more medium-sized city in which the novel begins is more like Keun's own hometown, Cologne.[16] It is there that Doris begins the diary entries that make up the book: nine in Part 1, twenty-eight in Part 2, and forty-six in Part 3.[17] When she begins the diary, she is living at home with her mother and her stepfather, who is unemployed and depends on the money Doris gives him for room and board, which she earns as a typist. Doris has trouble with punctuation, especially with commas, and can only keep her job, she feels, by giving suggestive looks to her boss, seeming to indicate her interest in him. She realizes that eventually he will act on his misunder-standing that she is attracted to him, but she hopes to delay this as long as she can. When it eventually occurs, she quits rather than to have to gratify him sexually, at the same time asking him how he, an educated lawyer, could really believe that a young woman would be attracted to him:

> I kick him in the shin to get him to take his hands off me and ask: "Now tell me, you idiotic lawyer, what are you thinking about, really? How can some-one who's gone to college like you be so stupid and think that a young pretty girl was crazy about him. Haven't you ever looked in the mirror? I'm just asking you, what kind of charms do you think you have?" (17)[18]

Her mother, who works checking coats and hats at a theater, manages to get Doris a job as an extra in a production of Schiller's *Wallenstein*. Some-what amazed by the snobbery of the other extras, most of whom are from acting school, she manages to impress them by inventing an affair with the managing director of the theater, and then to take a comical revenge against one young actress who is the most arrogant to her. By locking the young woman in a lavatory, Doris causes the young woman to lose her sin-gle line—which is then awarded to Doris. After the opening night, how-ever, it appears that her deceptions have been found out and her brief career is over. Meanwhile her first love, Hubert, a student who had left her to marry in his own class, has arranged to see her again. She steals a fur coat hanging in the coat check room to impress him, but at their rendezvous it turns out that Hubert's marriage and career have fallen through, and he is hoping that she will support him. She is willing to help him, but his obvious disappointment at the news that she seems to have no lucrative future in the theater makes her realize that there is really nothing between them anymore.

She leaves Hubert, and with the stolen fur coat she heads for the big city. Part 2 begins with her arrival in Berlin, where she hopes to fulfill the dream she first articulated while working in the theater in the medium-sized city (cf. 29–31); that is, to become a "Glanz," a shimmering beauty or "luster," as Gleber translates it (*The Art of Taking a Walk,* 196). To Doris, this term appears to mean the kind of elegant, modern, fashionable, beautiful, wealthy, and (relatively) independent woman that is her ideal—not necessarily a movie star, by the way, but definitely a type she sees in Berlin.[19] She plans to achieve this status is by using her attractiveness to men, yet none of the men she meets advance her very far. This is in large part because she insists on following her own desires rather than cold calculation, sleeping in one instance with a man she desires instead of her wealthy employer, for whose children she is supposed to be a nanny. Thus, she loses the nanny position. Reflecting on this episode, she comments bitterly on the salient difference between what is considered a good German wife and a "whore":

> If a young woman with money marries an old man for his money and nothing else and sleeps with him for hours and looks pious, then she's a German mother with children and a decent woman. If a young woman without any money sleeps with someone without any money because he has smooth skin and she likes him, then she's a whore and a swine. (55)[20]

Socially sanctioned sex for money and without desire is thus rewarded, while desired but unsanctioned sex meets with scorn. Doris's next sexual involvement is with a blind man named Brenner, whom she tells of her adventures on the streets of Berlin. Brenner is by no means a handsome young man, but her affection for him is genuine. Neither wealthy nor powerful, Brenner is also about to be placed by his wife in a home for the blind—he is thus not the wisest choice of man for a would-be "shimmering beauty" or "Glanz."

Doris finally achieves the status of a "Glanz," but only briefly. She is kept by a rich businessman in an apartment, but all too soon he is arrested for shady business dealings. Returning to her friend Tilli's apartment causes a strain because the latter's husband is now unemployed, bored, and interested in Doris; meanwhile she ponders the fate of Hulla, a prostitute in Tilli's building who commits suicide to escape the wrath of her pimp boyfriend. At first, Doris had had no understanding for Hulla, but now she can identify with her only too well. Leaving Tilli's to save the friendship, she lives with a journalist for awhile, but she leaves him and becomes homeless on Christmas Eve rather than to put up with his shabby treatment of her.

Part 3 begins on Christmas day, with Doris staying in the waiting room at the downtown train station near the Berlin Zoo. Homeless, but still with her fur, she meets Karl, an unemployed worker willing to let her work and live with him out in the garden colony where he now scrapes by. She still has too much ambition for that, yet is afraid that she will become a prostitute, for which she is constantly being mistaken. On New Year's Eve, she is so hungry that she agrees to go with a man who speaks to her on the street; this is Ernst, who takes her to his apartment and lets her stay, without asking for sex in return. Thus he "saves" her from prostitution at the moment she had decided to try it just once out of desperation. Ernst is an illustrator who works in advertising and has an ultramodern apartment. He is also lonely and heartbroken, because his wife has left him: once a dancer herself, she has fallen in love with a male dancer and run off with him.

Ernst takes care of Doris, and regaining her health, she starts to take care of him: she shops and cleans for him. Becoming the perfect housewife for him, she also begins to fall in love with him. Still obsessed with his wife, Ernst is hard to seduce, but Doris manages it, only to realize that she will not be able to make him forget his wife. She leaves him only to persuade his wife to return to him, and then she returns again to the waiting room at the train station. The ending of the novel is somewhat open, but Doris seems to decide to accept Karl's offer to live in the garden colony, as long as he will leave her alone sexually. The last sentence of the novel implies that she has revised her goal: "It doesn't really matter so terribly much about being a 'Glanz,' maybe" ("Auf den Glanz kommt es nämlich vielleicht gar nicht so furchtbar an," 140).

Lulu in *Pandora's Box,* in contrast, begins the film secure in her status as what Doris would call a "Glanz": kept in a stylish modern apartment (far more expensive than what Ernst could offer Doris), she does not seem bothered that Schoen, the man who is keeping her, will marry another. Indeed it would seem that she keeps the apartment anyway, with Schoen's newspaper meanwhile guaranteeing her success as the main spectacle of the revue being directed by his son Alwa. At the beginning of the story, therefore, Lulu appears to have everything that Doris wants. In a fit of pique, Lulu manages to cause Schoen to lose his respectable fiancée and to marry her instead. But marriage to Lulu, as Schoen had predicted, leads to his death. Loving, and especially wanting to possess Lulu, is portrayed as extremely dangerous, not out of any malicious intent on the latter's part, but out of her strange, almost innocent indifference to the demands of the men around her.

At this level, she is of course primarily a male fantasy, a beautiful, narcissistic woman kind to almost any man but capable of no deep attachments. Yet it is clear that Lulu does have her own will and her own desires; if there is anything that she wants, it is the autonomy to be able to love whomever she chooses. And it is this autonomy that she insists upon even as her value as a commodity begins its long decline. Fleeing Berlin with Alwa after being convicted of manslaughter for Schoen's murder, Lulu ends up in France as a commodity unknowingly exploited by the evil Count Casti-Piani, who extorts money from Alwa with the threat of notifying the German police. When Alwa has no more money, Casti-Piani wants to sell her into (supposedly "high-class") prostitution in Egypt, and only at this point does Lulu understand the role Casti-Piani has been playing. Desperate to avoid this fate, she flees again with Alwa and Schigolch to London, where she winds up in the slums of London. Impoverished, she is apparently a prostitute, although when she goes down to the street, Alwa seems very upset, as though he still cannot accept the idea. But Lulu's old crony Schigolch holds him back. Lulu then unknowingly meets Jack the Ripper on the street, and it is at this point that her autonomy is her undoing: although Jack has no money, she takes him upstairs anyway because she likes him. Her kindness does disarm him—literally: he throws away his knife before going upstairs with her. But while embracing her he sees another knife gleaming on the table, and overcome, he murders her.

Lulu's trajectory of decline is thus much more direct than Doris's: in the beginning she has a status that Doris never really attains, and from that high point in Berlin there is only decline, first to the still somewhat glamorous underworld milieu of the gambling casino in the ship off France, and then to the slums of London.[21] Doris's trajectory leads her neither quite so high nor quite so low, and there are many more ups and downs, beginning with a mundane, low-paid office job, moving up to her brief stint as an extra in the theater, then "fleeing the law" (like Lulu, although in a much more comical and less melodramatic fashion), only to scrape by from man to man in Berlin. She briefly becomes the mistress of a wealthy man only to plunge further, all the way to complete homelessness and hunger, then to be "saved," on the brink of prostitution, by Ernst, for whom she becomes an ersatz-housewife, and finally to leave him and confront the option again of homelessness, prostitution, or the retreat to the garden-colony in working-class solidarity with Karl—an end at once more open and much less melodramatic than that of Lulu.

Another obvious contrast has to do with the streets: whereas Doris hits the streets of Berlin—and is mistaken for a prostitute—as soon as she reaches Berlin, Lulu never appears on the streets until the very end of the film. Indeed, Lulu is seen almost entirely in more or less "private" spaces throughout the film, with only two exceptions. The first consists of a few moments of well-orchestrated public spectacle onstage during the revue, but even then we see her mostly backstage during the theater revue, and that of course is where the key action is, above all in the private confrontation with Schoen. The second exception is the courtroom scene, and here too she does not speak but is indeed the object of orations with conflicting interpretations of her life. Doris's plight is quite different: she continually faces homelessness in Berlin, having no secure private refuge at all for very long.[22]

Lulu in this sense is much less a "modern" or "new" woman than Doris, given the former's primarily private existence, as well as the fact that she flees the metropolis of Berlin for the hidden underworld of the French casino, ending up in a still somewhat Victorian-looking London, where she makes the briefest appearance on the street. Doris meanwhile identifies with Berlin so intensely that she implies that in having sex with the blind Brenner, she is giving him Berlin: "I bring him Berlin, which lies in my lap," (65).[23] While this might imply a very cliched equation of illicit female sexuality with the metropolis (such as the Whore of Babylon to which Döblin refers in *Berlin Alexanderplatz*), this is subverted by a much more original inversion of gender cliches: in her relationship with Brenner, Doris becomes his eyes—she becomes the "flaneur's" gaze upon the modern metropolis, as Gleber argues so persuasively (*The Art of Taking a Walk*, 200–04), a gaze that is so often considered exclusively male.

Identifying thus not just with the metropolis but with the modern specularity associated with the modern city, Doris resists as long as she can the idea of moving out of Berlin to its fringes, to Karl's hut in the garden colony, which is why von Ankum implies that this would mean regression and defeat for her (384). On the other hand her quest for the status of "Glanz," which in her mind of course consists of a very public glamour, leads her at best to much more private types of existence protected by men, as a kept woman (like Lulu) or as a would-be housewife, and at worst to more public states like prostitution and homelessness. Her disenchantment with that quest must also be seen as proof of her ability to learn—another ability Lulu in her "natural innocence" does not appear to possess.

Lulu has been interpreted by Elsaesser ("Lulu," 55–56) and Coates (55, 59) as a symbol of Americanist modernity, and one that is sexually ambiguous as well. Both critics see her as therefore also representing the cinematic apparatus itself. But as Doane points out (71), and Elsaesser admits as well ("Lulu," 56), androgyny is clearly aligned with femininity here, and it is femininity as sexual fluidity that appears so threatening, especially to a masculinity conceived as the longing for solidity, stability, and clearly defined boundaries. And for all the play with androgyny and bisexuality in the desirable figure of Lulu, the film's position on these issues seems less than emancipatory: the portrayal of Geschwitz as a lesbian is, although mainly sympathetic, nonetheless stereotypically "masculine."

In any case, Lulu's autonomy, combined with the freedom and sexual fluidity (and ambiguity) that she embodies, brings only disaster—not just to the men who desire her, and to Geschwitz, but to Lulu herself as well. Because of her threat to the more traditional status quo, in the film represented by a brooding, anxious, possessive bourgeois masculinity, the latter seems compelled to control and destroy her. Pabst's film does not really blame Lulu, indeed if anything it sympathizes with her against a masculinity that appears pathological. But the film also seems to portray the destruction of Lulu as inevitable, for she represents a freedom too threatening to exist. The implicit comment about the supposedly destabilizing autonomy of the New Woman is clear, although Lulu's explicit function in the narrative would seem to be as a catalyst of male crisis, not really to address the situation of women in modernity.[24]

Doris's story does much more clearly address that situation, and it much more explicitly exposes the trap inherent in modern mass-cultural fantasies about the "power" women wield as desirable sexual commodities.[25] In many ways Doris's story is just as pessimistic with regard to certain myths about female sexual emancipation in Weimar modernity as is Pabst's film. Does Keun's novel end, indeed, with only resignation and defeat for Doris?

DORIS AND NEW OBJECTIVITY: SURFACE / SENTIMENTALITY / AGENCY?

The language with which the fictional protagonist Doris supposedly tells her story in *The Artificial Silk Girl* provides some classic—and often quite humorous—examples of an "objective" ("sachlich"), desentimentalized prose, some of which I have quoted above. Lethen, who calls Keun's hero-ines "players of many games at once—without luck" ("Simultanspielerin-nen ohne Fortune") asserts that their jargon demonstrates the "emphatic quality" ("Forciertheit") that must be produced in order not to collapse into sentimentality (242). As he implies, the seemingly tough exterior that Doris maintains through her wisecracking is in part a defensive posture, a mask that protects her vulnerable emotions.

Nonetheless, it is mistaken to frame the tension in this text (or in New Objectivity in general, I would argue) as merely the contrast between the clever, tough, cold pragmatism so beloved by the male avant-garde and the fatuous bourgeois sentimentalism it loved to deride—a derision that, as we have seen, reveals how much projection was involved in creating this dichotomy in the first place.[26] Doris is neither as cold and cynical as the avant-garde liked to style itself, nor should her underlying capacity for friendship, love, and solidarity be suspected of being merely sentimental or even reactionary as that avant-garde in its own projections might have assumed. While Doris is very skilled at seeing through and making frank remarks about bourgeois male hypocrisy and sexual double standards, she is not nearly as calculating or as cold as she would need to be to succeed truly as a "Glanz," let alone as a female equivalent of Brecht's Baal or one of Walter Serner's "con men" ("Hochstapler")—these being two primary examples of what Lethen calls the cold persona. In fact Doris is constantly giving of herself—to "Garage-Frank" ("Garagen-Franz"), to Brenner—and she continually sacrifices her own happiness and/or comfort for the sake of others: she leaves Tilli's apartment in order to avoid coming between Tilli and her husband, and she leaves Ernst because she realizes he will always love the wife who deserted him. In both of these instances her sacrifice entails becoming homeless.

Doris's "emancipation" is not the coldness to which the male avant-garde aspired and which they projected onto the vamps they found so fas-cinating. Doris is heartless in her verdict on bourgeois male-morality, and she indeed indicts the coldness of the women who in conforming to it secure their own social and economic well-being—the "decent" German mothers who marry rich old men they do not love (55). For Doris is not as calculating as they: although she realizes that love and desire are dangerous to her aspirations, in the end her sexual relationships are almost always motivated by love, desire, or affection.

Her skepticism about sexual double standards are as much rooted in her experience of class as of gender injustice. It is this skepticism that informs her own both amazed and mocking perspective on Ernst's melancholy cult of love, based as it is on bourgeois notions of deep interiority, of high culture, and an unacknowledged level of material comfort. This is clear in Doris's reactions to Ernst's pronouncements about the beloved wife who has deserted him:

> "My wife could sing so very high and clearly."
> I sing—"That's the love of the sailors"—most wonderful song there is.
> "Schubert," he says. How is that? "She sang like Schubert composed."
> "That's the love of the sailors"—it's maybe garbage, a song like that, is it?
> What is Schubert, what does he mean? "That's the love—that's taken from real life, like my mother says about good movies. (109)[27]

> I buzz around with the vacuum cleaner—sssssss—I'm a thunderstorm. By accident I break the picture of his wife. They had so many words in common, he says—and there are such small, tender memories, completely inconsequential on their own. I say, "She's gone, and you have to direct your mind to other things."
> He says, "Nothing gives me joy anymore, for whom do I live, for whom do I work?"
> "Nothing's ever really gone wrong for you, has it?"
> "No, it has too." Well, I want to ask what he means by going wrong. There are people who shed tears for themselves out of self-pity if they still haven't had anything warm to eat by three in the afternoon." (110)[28]

> "You look really beat," I tell him. "Today bedtime will be at ten."
> "Oh, I don't sleep anyway," he sighs.
> Makes me furious. "Don't make up any such nonsense, what a bunch of lies, can't sleep at night because of sorrow and all that, when I hear you clearly every night, snoring in the next room" (112).[29]

Causing damage to his idolatrous cult of love as she zooms about with the vacuum cleaner, Doris is sensitive both to his economic privilege and his snobbery. She is defensive about her affinity for the popular culture "taken from real life" ("aus dem Leben gegriffen") and she is unwilling to put up with his refined melancholy (here one is unavoidably reminded of Kästner's Fabian). Yet in the end she decides to respect his love, as pretentious as it seems to her, leaving him and trying—successfully—to manipulate his wife into returning to him.[30] At the same time she notes the open cynicism that the wife confesses to Doris about her motives for returning to Ernst (136–37).

Besides identifying herself with a commodity—her *Feh,* the beloved fur coat she stole before fleeing to Berlin—Doris engages in a kind of objective "reification" of the people around her, humorously naming them in her diary in association with some object or concept, be it a possession, an unavoidable association, or simply a descriptive metaphor—that is, in a fashion sometimes metonymical, sometimes metaphorical: black rayon (*schwarzer Rayon*), big industry (*Großindustrie*), blond movie (*blondes Kino*),[31] red moon (*roter Mond*), pink sphere (*rosaroter Kugel,* green moss (*grünes Moos*), cork rug (*Korkteppich*), cardboard box (*Pappkarton*). This is a kind of reified shorthand in keeping with the book's modernist "telegram style," which imitates the rapid tempo of the metropolis and film montage (Kaes, *Kino-Debatte,* 4–9; von Ankum, "Ich liebe Berlin," 376).[32] But it is also a trait that characterizes Doris herself as much as the people she seemingly instrumentalizes by means of this shorthand; I would argue that its satiric humor, like Doris herself, is ultimately humane and self-critical, not really dehumanizing.[33] In the end Doris is much too humane to be very effective at instrumentalizing people, regardless of her wisecracking nicknames for them.

The same can be said about her identification with film and with popular culture—damned by Lensing as superficial or praised as modern and "externally directed" ("außengelenkt") by Lethen (*Verhaltenslehren,* 242–43). Lethen does not consider Doris a "cold persona," but rather the even more modern, other-directed "radar-type" who is no baroque masked type but rather a modern consumer guided by external forces and social pressures (above all the media). But Doris is neither merely a passive object resulting from modern reification nor simply a passive receiver of ideological messages beamed at her from the outside. She actively works within the limitations of modern consumer society and within older patriarchal constraints to create a sort of identity for herself; in this sense, she is more the "cold persona," or at any rate a woman who definitely practices a kind of "feminine masquerade." Her options are limited by the class and gender hierarchies of German society, and she cannot transcend these limitations; indeed she demonstrates the force of their power all the more clearly as her negotiations continue—but this is a process by which she too becomes aware of the limits of her dreams, as she states at the end of the novel (140). Furthermore, as Barndt stresses, it is a process that is represented as Doris's inscription of her experiences as writing, a writing that engages readers interested in negotiating their own identities (192–93).

Von Ankum interprets developments in the last part of the book as a "regression" from autonomy to the refuge of marriage, or its equivalent, first with Ernst, and then with the much poorer Karl—a regression that also means a flight from the metropolis, especially if she does indeed join

Karl in the garden colonies on the edge of Berlin ("'Ich liebe Berlin,'" 384). Perhaps it is instead both a rejection of the mass cultural/consumerist dreams of gaining female autonomy as a glamorous sexual commodity and at the same time a harshly accurate measure of shrinking possibilities, especially for women, as the Weimar economy collapsed.[34] Might not her implied choice of living with Karl in a sexless relationship[35] mean that she is choosing a class-conscious solidarity, as indicated in her final dialogue with the boy she calls "cardboard box" at the train station (138–39)? This interpretation might seem to imply the leftist idealism of the films *Mother Krause's Journey to Happiness* (*Mutter Krausens Fahrt ins Glück*, 1929) and *Kuhle Wampe* (1932), in which the female protagonists find love and happiness in working-class struggle,[36] yet at the same time it reflects a political attitude on the left at the time with which Keun seems to have sympathized. But the end of her novel can hardly be compared to the paternalistic enlightenment the young heroine of *Mother Krause* comes to accept. Nor for that matter is it mere socialist dogma about the value of "productive" labor—Doris still has no interest in going back into the work force (140)! In a time of severe worldwide economic depression, solidarity and collective action must have seemed much more reliable solutions than the consumerist/individualist dreams of upward mobility of the stabilized period. Doris has also learned solidarity with other women (with whom as a potential "Glanz" she had tried to compete); at the end of the novel she mentions again with affection and empathy even the battered prostitute Hulla (140).[37] The end of the novel implies the same awareness of the need for a "collective solidarity" ("solidarisches Miteinander") Rosenstein sees at the end of Keun's first novel *Gilgi—One of us* (*Gilgi—eine von uns,* 1931), as opposed to the competitive ambitions of atomized individuals (280).

Keun's novel is best understood as a materialist and realistic appraisal of women's situation in a time of general downward mobility, an appraisal that debunks both traditional and modern bourgeois notions of individual autonomy. And it is empowering because it shows the perspective of, and gives a voice to, the "new" type of woman constructed so often in the culture, giving that woman agency, wit, desire, skepticism, and the capacity to expose, to understand, and even to revise in some ways the limitations of the mass-cultural dreams (and other dominant social discourses) that have shaped her. Keun's novel provides this perspective in a way that thematizes a process of identity construction through writing that is at the same time a critical appropriation of an otherwise male "gaze" upon the modern metropolis and its chaos, dynamism, and fluidity. Doris is both commodity

and consumer, diary-writer and camera-eye, object and subject of the flaneur's gaze, embodiment of mass-cultural fantasies and a critical but accessible voice in a debate waged in popular culture in the early 1930s about
women's identities.[38]

Coming Out of the Uniform

Political and Sexual Emancipation in Leontine Sagan's Film Mädchen in Uniform *(1931)*

We sat together at the movies, it was a film about girls in uniform. They were
high-class girls, but it was the same for them as for me. You care for someone, and what you get sometimes is tears and a red nose. You care for someone—it can't be understood at all, it makes no lousy difference whether it's a
man or a woman or dear God almighty.[39]

—Irmgard Keun, *The Artificial Silk Girl*

There have been many women filmmakers to emerge from Germany and
Austria, especially since the late 1960s, but, unfortunately, the most well
known German woman to direct films remains Leni Riefenstahl, whose
work was primarily in the Third Reich. But before her famous propaganda
film for the Nazis, *Triumph of the Will* (1935), and even before her director-
ial debut with the "mountain film" *The Blue Light* (1932), there was another
film made by a woman, one that was not only a national but an international success, and one with very different politics. Given all the books and
films by men in the Weimar Republic that thematized new models of gender and sexual behavior, depicting them usually in a negative light, it is
important to discuss this film, the most famous film made by a woman during the Weimar Republic, especially because it celebrated an almost unspoken form of sexuality that threatened the status quo.

This 1931 film was called *Mädchen in Uniform* (or *Girls in Uniform*), and
it was not only directed by a woman, Leontine Sagan, it was adapted from a
popular stage drama written by a woman (Christa Winsloe), and acted by
an all-female cast. It was a popular and entertaining film that nonetheless
took a clear position in favor of Weimar's most democratic and emancipatory tendencies and in opposition to the authoritarian and repressive forces
mobilizing to destroy the Republic in the crisis years of the early 1930s.
For within a year and a half of the film's release, in January, 1933, Hitler
came to power, a political event that put an end to the relative tolerance for

the blurring and transgression of traditional gender and sexual boundaries that had characterized popular culture in Germany's first democracy, the Weimar Republic (1918–1933).

Mädchen in Uniform is a film that is implicated within a number of progressive and emancipatory discourses of the late Weimar Republic: the movement for homosexual rights and the flourishing of urban, queer subcultures; "New Objectivity" and other avant-garde tendencies in the arts and popular culture; and the intersection of modernity, the movies, and democratic egalitarianism. It is with regard to such discourses about gender and sexuality as well as about aesthetics and politics that I will attempt to contextualize this film.

The film can indeed be read as an anti-fascist film; certainly its representation of authoritarian, militaristic "Prussianism" is clearly negative. While women in the film are by no means portrayed as innocent of Prussianism—the film's "villain" is after all the boarding school's headmistress—the film nonetheless depicts the school's values as patriarchal and anti-democratic. And the greatest threat to such a value system turns out to be emotional attachments that develop between women, which are portrayed as disruptive of the school's rules and hierarchy. The school's authoritarian values are shown in turn to be deadly.

As B. Ruby Rich asserted in her famous essay on the film, over the course of the film's reception, its anti-authoritarian stance was almost always emphasized, while its sexual politics were mostly ignored until the 1970s. This is evident in two of the most canonical verdicts on the film, written years later in exile by German critics who first saw the film in 1931: writing in 1947, Siegfried Kracauer discussed the film exclusively in terms of its anti-authoritarianism, which he found too meek, including it in a chapter on "Timid Heresies" *(Caligari,* 226–29). In *The Haunted Screen* (which originally appeared in French in 1952), Lotte Eisner was much more positive, calling it the "last word" on the repressive practices of the Prussian aristocracy. Eisner's main interest in this film (and all films) was aesthetic, but by implying that its stylistic beauty can be ascribed to Sagan's "feminine reading" of German film traditions, she anticipated some potential for a feminist interpretation. To the extent she dealt with the film's sexual politics, however, her reading was problematic (325–26).

For it is sexuality that has complicated the film's reception from the very beginning. Central to its narrative is a fairly overt homoeroticism. Critics for years tended to downplay the erotic aspect of the schoolgirl Manuela's infatuation for her teacher Fräulein von Bernburg. Kracauer, for instance, in disagreeing with the critical consensus about the extent (and the "bold-ness") of the film's anti-authoritarianism, nonetheless manages to repress almost any allusion to the film's homoeroticism, leading one to suspect that for him Manuela's love for Bernburg was distasteful and a "trivialization" of any political message in the film.[40]

When the film was re-discovered in the 1970s, it became a cult film in the United States, England, and France among feminists. Many lesbians had a special appreciation for the film, considering it an early "coming-out" film that affirmed love between women. The reaction of many German feminists to this reception of the film was that it was too simple, that it ignored the film's politics and its original historical context (Gramann and Schlüpmann; Lenssen). In the early 1980s, Rich wrote a long and persua-sive discussion of the film, with extensive research into its political and his-torical context; she maintained that the film is indeed a lesbian "coming-out" film, but that there is no contradiction between the film's sexual politics and its anti-fascism: in fact they are integrally related. More recently, Richard Dyer has done a thorough analysis of the film's place within gay and lesbian debates on homosexuality in the 1920s (31–60).

There are, however, critics and scholars who question reading the film as either a "coming out" film or as an anti-fascist film. Lisa Ohm has argued that the film is not at all a "coming out" film, and she comes to a much more negative reading of the film's politics with regard to fascism (more or less agreeing with Kracauer). She stresses the dominant influence of the film's producer, Carl Froelich, hardly an anti-fascist, as it would turn out. Froelich had great control over the look of the film and the shape of the narrative, and he created the happy ending of the film, which reversed the ending in Christa Winsloe's original play. Christa Reinig sees this changed ending as completely in contradiction to Winsloe's intentions. Other objections have to do with the issue of motherhood as it is depicted in the film: does Fräulein von Bernburg represent a substitute mother to Manuela, or an object of erotic desire for her—or both? A recent study connects the discourse on motherhood in the film to reactionary social ideologies and forces in the early 1930s.[41] Is the film about lesbianism, mothering, or both, and what difference does this make for the evaluation of the film's politics? Does the film attempt to subvert, or is it too "timid," or even in some sense complicit with the rise of fascism? Not unrelated to such questions is another fundamental one: how is this film relevant to the discussion of New Objectivity and the other discourses of modernity in the Weimar Republic we have been investigating?

FROM STAGE TO SCREEN

The screenplay for *Mädchen in Uniform* was adapted from a play by Christa Winsloe that had gone through two versions. It was produced first in Leipzig as *The Knight Nerestan* (*Ritter Nerestan*) in 1930, directed by Otto Werther and starring Hertha Thiele as Manuela; then it was produced in Berlin as *Yesterday and Today* (*Gestern und Heute*) in 1931, directed by Leontine Sagan, first with Gina Falkenberg as Manuela, and then with Hertha Thiele in the lead role. Both versions were great popular successes, so much so that plans were made to film it. The film was completed later in 1931, and it was produced by Carl Froelich, who was listed in the credits as responsible for "artistic supervision" ("künstlerische Oberleitung"); he also chose the film's title, *Mädchen in Uniform*. With some supervision by Froelich, then, Sagan directed the film.[42] Winsloe co-wrote the screenplay with F.S. Andam, and Thiele played Manuela. The film too became a big hit, both within Germany and internationally, and the critics generally praised it as well: "One spoke of the best film of the year. In the United States, too, the critics were enthusiastic" (Wendtland, *Jahrgang*, 1931, 223).[43]

Like the original play, the film is the story of fourteen-and-a-half-year-old Manuela, whose mother has been dead for some time, and whose father is an officer. Manuela is brought by her aunt to a boarding school for the daughters of Prussian officers and nobility. The school is characterized by the rigid, authoritarian discipline demanded by its headmistress, who is determined to raise obedient "mothers of soldiers." The school also seems to be in rather bad financial straits, feeding and clothing its charges in an extremely stingy manner; the headmistress tries to portray this as a virtue, saying, "We Prussians have starved ourselves to greatness!" ("Wir Preußen haben uns groß gehungert!").

The only sympathetic teacher is Fräulein von Bernburg, who modifies her strictness with a fair amount of open kindness and affection, symbolized best perhaps by her ritual of giving a good-night kiss on the forehead to each one of the girls in her dormitory. Learning that Manuela has lost her mother, Bernburg shows her some special attention, and Manuela responds to this unaccustomed kindness by breaking the unspoken rules of the ritualized good-night kiss on the first night she experiences it. She throws her arms around Bernburg, and Bernburg then kisses her on the lips in one of the most famous close-ups of the film. Manuela becomes so infatuated with Bernburg that she cannot perform well in her class. Bernburg, learning from the staff that Manuela's underclothes are in woeful shape, gives the pupil a chemise to wear from her own underwear drawer.

Manuela gives an outstanding performance in the school play, dressed as a man in the leading role of Schiller's *Don Carlos*. Getting drunk on spiked punch at the party after the play, she tells the other girls of the chemise from Bernburg that she is wearing, and she proclaims her love for the teacher. The headmistress witnesses this proclamation and declares a scandal; she has Manuela isolated from all contact with the other girls (see Figure 6.1)—and she also forbids Bernburg to see her again. Bernburg does talk to Manuela, but only to explain why it is best that they do not see each other anymore. The headmistress berates Bernburg for doing even that much, and this leads to a showdown between the two women. Bernburg defends Manuela's feelings as love, not sin, and she declares that she will resign rather than continue to watch the headmistress turn the girls into scared and timid creatures. Meanwhile those very girls, concerned about Manuela, break the rules and begin to search for her. Bernburg too has a premonition that something is wrong, and she joins them just as they have found Manuela—just as they

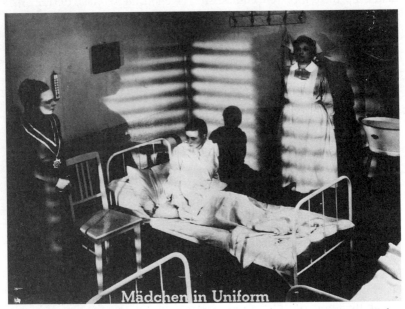

Figure 6.1   Clinical confinement in chiaroscuro: in Leontine Sagan's *Mädchen in Uniform* (1931), Manuela (Hertha Thiele) has been in isolation after her drunken profession of love for Bernburg; to her left, the school's Headmistress (Emilia Unda), admonishes her as a servant stands at attention to the right. Photo courtesy of Bundesarchiv-Filmarchiv, Berlin.

succeed in stopping her at the last minute from jumping to her death from the top of the school's central stairwell. Bernburg confronts the head-mistress with the tragedy that was only barely averted. Stunned and for the first time silenced, the headmistress walks away down the corridor, seem-ingly defeated; meanwhile the military bugles of Potsdam sound outside the school.

Kracauer mentions the bugles at the end of the film to make his point that the revolt at the end of the film was merely a "timid heresy": the authority structure outside the school remains unchanged by anything that had gone on inside it. The only thing that happens inside the school is the victory of Bernburg, who has only attempted to humanize its authoritarian system, something that Kracauer sees as "in the interest of its preservation" (*Caligari*, 228–29). This interpretation, however, overlooks the transforma-tion of Bernburg at the end of the film: as Rich argues, up to this point she has indeed played "good cop" to the headmistress's "bad cop" (68–69), but in her final debate with the headmistress she decides to quit the "system" altogether, now fully aware of the toll it takes on the girls. Upon learning that her complicity with the system has nearly killed Manuela, she only becomes more defiant, not less (Rich, 76–78). As for Kracauer's charge that the "happy" ending of the film ignores larger political forces, the fact is that his point about outside forces is made by the film itself. It relativizes the headmistress's defeat with those very bugles, reminding us of the powerful patriarchal militarism beyond the walls of the school.[44] The ending is more open than he would have it: Manuela survives, but what happens next is unclear.

The political warning in the film about the situation in Germany is actually fairly explicit. Edelgard, the schoolgirl whose pedigree is the most aristocratic of all her classmates, states: "At home, you know, they are always talking about the time that is coming when we shall need soldiers again, and mothers of soldiers."[45] This makes the implications of the head-mistress's views about the purpose of educating her charges very clear in the context of Germany in the early 1930s—and the accuracy of the pre-diction is uncanny. For earlier in the film, the headmistress stressed the goal of creating "mothers of soldiers"—and the film's opposition to all that the headmistress stands for is unmistakable. Also relevant is the fact that most of the important figures who made the film—Winsloe, Sagan, Thiele—went into exile soon after the Nazi seizure of power (*Machtergreifung*) in 1933.

One person who did not go into exile and who played a very important role in making the film was Carl Froelich, who continued his filmmaking career successfully through the Third Reich. After his production of the anti-Prussian *Mädchen in Uniform,* Froelich would go on to direct *The Hymn of Leuthen* (*Der Choral von Leuthen,* 1933), one of the many films (from the 1920s into the 1940s) that catered to nationalist tastes by glorifying Prussian history.[46] According to Herta Thiele in a 1981 interview, Froelich was involved in the decision that banned her from film acting in the Third Reich. She also stated that in making *Madchen in Uniform,* it had been Froelich who tried to mute the play's homoeroticism for commercial reasons (34).

The only person among the people who made the film definitely known to be lesbian was Winsloe, who was actually "coming out" during the very years that the various versions of the story were written (Dyer, 35).[47] But the argument for a lesbian reading of *Mädchen in Uniform* is based on much more than this biographical fact. Thiele explained that in the first production of the play, the Leipzig production, its lesbian aspect had been more or less avoided, but that Leontine Sagan's Berlin production of the play was different:"Sagan had directed the play back then in the theater as purely lesbian."[48] Margarete Melzer played Bernburg in the Berlin play, and Thiele characterized Melzer as "a completely masculine type" ("ein absolut männlicher Typ," 32). One of Froelich's attempts to mute the lesbianism of the Berlin production was thus to replace Melzer with the much more stereotypically "feminine" Dorothea Wieck. As first noted by Gramann and Schlüpmann (30), who interviewed Thiele, one gets the impression from Thiele's comments that there was a split between the makers of the film, Sagan and Winsloe being on one side and Froelich on the other, with Froelich having the advantage of technical knowledge of film production and control of the film crew on his side.[49]

MÄDCHEN *AND NEW OBJECTIVITY?*

Lotte Eisner's only reference to questions of sexual identity in *Mädchen in Uniform* "contrives to make the film sound somewhat anti-lesbian" (Dyer, 32). She asserts that the film touches on a mere adolescent "phase," implying that the school is to blame for misreading an otherwise normal adolescent phase of confusion (326).[50] Eisner ascribes the film's high aesthetic quality to Sagan's "femine reading of the *Kammerspielfilm* [chamber play film] which "led her to turn her back on the 'new objectivity'" (325). There can be no doubt that New Objectivity was in many ways perceived as a very "masculine" sensibility, and that *Mädchen in Uniform* can be read as a very "feminine" film—Dyer especially does a thorough job demonstrating this (38–41). The *Kammerspielfilm* tradition Eisner mentions, however, was arguably a fairly naturalistic form, although in the early 1920s, in a film like Leopold Jessner's *Backstairs* (*Hintertreppe*, 1921), for instance, it was undoubtedly combined with a certain expressionistic exaggeration in acting style and set design. But little of that can be found in *Mädchen in Uniform*.

Beyond such quibbles about genre and style, however, the film can be related to New Objectivity and various discourses associated with it in a number of ways. For a start, of course, one only needs to mention the emancipatory sexual politics in the film that Eisner manages to distort. In addition, the film manifests a number of specific, positive attitudes toward phenomena commonly associated with modernity in Weimar: jazz, the adulation of film stars, "trashy" popular novels, and "sex appeal."[51]

The film sets up a number of clear oppositions both on the narrative and the stylistic level, all of which work to portray the aristocratic "old order" negatively, and a new, emerging "modern" order in positive terms. The hierarchical, militaristic and anti-democratic order that the school upholds is obviously embodied by the headmistress, whose bearing, medallion, gait, and cane are obvious allusions to Frederick the Great of Prussia, as commentators since Eggebrecht (11) in 1931 have noted (cf. Kracauer, *Caligari*, 226) have noted. Next in the hierarchy comes the headmistress's toady, Fräulein von Kesten, and then the intimidated, insecure, competitive staff of teachers. The obvious exception is Bernburg, whose reformist humanism leads her eventually to revolt and side with the pupils, the young girls who best embody an emerging modern, democratic, egalitarian order. It is the world of the girls that provide the strongest contrast to the stifling military discipline, the archaic pomp, and the hypocrisy of the school and all it represents. The girls are characterized by their pranks, their love of modern mass culture, their insouciant rebelliousness (exemplified best by the character Ilse), their enthusiasm and emotion, their crushes on each other, and ultimately their insurrectionary solidarity, which saves Manuela from suicide.

The association of the girls with modernity and mass culture is clear: in the locker room Ilse proudly shows off her hidden collage of photos of the film star Hans Albers, arguing that he has more "sex appeal"—she uses the English term—than the actress Henny Porten, who is apparently the favorite film star of some of the other girls. Meanwhile there is an amusing visual reference to Weimar's obsession with sports and body culture, as two other girls giggle at pin-ups of scantily clad male athletes.[52] Finding the romantic novel Manuela is reading, Ilse grabs it, opens it, and reads a "racy" passage aloud to the girls. The girls are obviously attracted to "trivial" romance novels and other mass cultural pleasures, all of which are forbidden them. At the party after Manuela's bravura performance of Schiller (high culture, but in drag),[53] the girls quickly tire of waltzes and demand jazz from their fellow pupil at the piano. The headmistress and the school are tied to an older high culture, and even that culture appears to be a censored, very narrow, rather uncomprehending version of German classicism. As the headmistress has tea with the aristocratic alumnae, they worry about Schiller writing too "freely."

In stylistic terms, the film—like most German films of the era—is indebted to the chiaroscuro effects created by lighting techniques first developed during Expressionism. Some of the ways in which the film uses lighting do correspond to a dualistic scheme opposing innocence to evil, as exemplified most obviously by the bright close-ups of blond Manuela in contrast to the dark costumes of the headmistress and the staff, and the shadowy, confining spaces of the school, or the looming abyss of the staircase so central to the structure of both the school and the narrative. But even with regard to the filming of the staircase there is ambiguity in the use of shadows, for it is here that Bernburg first sees Manuela, before the latter notices her. As Bernburg looks over the pupil approvingly (indeed, with a mixture of voyeurism and desire), the shadows over the stairwell seem to convey both something ominous as well as an erotic tension.[54] Even more ambiguous, and not at all chiaroscuro, is the muted lighting of the dormitory after Bernburg dims the lights to begin the nightly ritual of the good night kiss: here there is little that is ominous, only the creation of an aura that has something of religious ritual yet also has romantic and erotic undertones.

As in many early German sound films, there is some music and some singing. There is martial music over the opening montage, and it will continue to be associated with those visual images of Prussian order, so that when the bugles are heard at the end of the film, those images will be evoked without being shown. The martial music is undermined from the very beginning of the film, however, by undertones in the music expressing a fanciful lightness that can be associated with the girls who are such unwilling initiates into this militaristic order. This is also emphasized when the girls are shown singing—the beauty of their voices reminds us of the song heard outside the classroom window in *The Blue Angel,* but here we see the girls singing. The patriotism of the lyrics of this song glorifying Prussia is undermined by the close-up of Ilse and the amplification of her voice as she turns praise for Prussia into a complaint about the meager diet at the school. And of course there is jazz, associated with the party when "innocent Manuela" makes her rebellious declaration of love.

It is the style of montage that opens the film, however, that best illustrates how distinct it is from Expressionist style—and how much it, like so many other German films since the mid-1920s, betrays the influence of Soviet filmmaking, which since the success of Eisenstein's *Potemkin* had been as great as the influence of Chaplin and the American cinema. As Rich notes (63, 83), the montage that depicts the authoritarian Prussian grandeur of Potsdam not only provides a dynamic contrast to the more theatrical interior scenes of the film, with its moving camera and quick cutting; it also performs an important narrative function as well. At the very beginning of the film it establishes the oppressive social context of which the school is an integral part, and it is to an economically brief reprise of similar shots of that outside world to which the film returns at two crucial moments in the film: just after the close-up of Bernburg kissing Manuela on the lips, and again after she gives her the chemise. Thus after two of the most important events in the narrative of the love developing between Bernburg and Manuela, the film reminds the viewer of the dominant authoritarian (and patriarchal) order violated by these erotic infractions.

Also significant is the contrast between the visual content of the opening montage and the style with which it is filmed. The neoclassical palaces and statues of Potsdam with their obvious attempt to claim a timeless authority for a relatively young aristocratic order are filmed with a constructivist tension that in effect "deconstructs" their symmetrical harmony and their pompous veneer of high culture. These architectural structures could not be more distinct from favored constructivist (and social realist) subjects: cranes, factories, modern buildings, construction sites (there is such a sequence in Brecht and Dudow's *Kuhle Wampe* of 1932, which also featured Herta Thiele). But while the content of the opening images is neoclassical, the manner in which they are filmed accentuates angles and diagonals in tension. Structures designed to emanate classical harmony are framed so as to make them seem grotesque and asymmetrical, and this technique can also be noted in the shots of the famous stairwell in the school. The building used in the film was Potsdam's Kaiserin-Augusta Stift, the very boarding school Winsloe herself had attended as a child (Thiele, 34).[55] The school's stairwell, like the building itself, was built in a style that emphasized neoclassical grace and harmony, but the stairwell is shot from high above and from such oblique angles that it appears quite ominous, and almost abstract.

There is thus an obvious polarization in the film on both stylistic and narrative levels: between an authoritarian regime garbed in neoclassical grace and a modern dissonant style of camerawork and editing;[56] between that repressive order on the outside of the school and the anti-authoritarian—and sexual—revolt breaking out on the inside of the school; between the Prussian rigidity of the headmistress and the spirited, democratic anarchy of the girls over whom she presides. To this polarization might be added the stylistic contrast between, on the one hand, the film's use of originally Expressionist lighting techniques, and, on the other hand, the film's use of montage and "documentary" footage of Potsdam and the school. In addition, one could mention the use of so many non-actresses to portray the pupils,[57] all of which provide evidence of its connection to trends in New Objective/"realist" filmmaking in Germany in the late 1920s and early 1930s.

Some aspects of all this tension and polarization in the film may reflect the political polarization in the aftermath of the economic depression that began in late 1929: the tension between the Right and Left, between authoritarian and democratic forces. In looking at the politics specifically depicted in the film, one might perhaps concur with Kracauer that the film is too "timid" with regard to the depiction of class in the film: the focus here is on a school for upper-class girls, after all. But the critique of the hierarchical values of the school is fairly clear in the film: the servants in the school are portrayed positively, and, like the girls, are shown to be irreverent about the attitudes of the people who run the school. The cross-cutting after the play which juxtaposes the celebration of the girls with that of the servants aligns those two groups against the staid tea party held by the Headmistress with the aristocratic patronesses of the school.

And this tension between the authoritarian values of the school and the more democratic values of the students and the servants is clearly related to the deep political polarization that had characterized the Weimar Republic from the beginning. It may have eased a bit during the "stabilized" prosperity after 1924, but it had never disappeared, as the crisis after 1929 made quite clear. On the narrative level, at any rate, this is clearly what the film is "about," whether one agrees with Kracauer that it is too timid in its attack on reactionary forces or not. This is also why (pace Freiburg) it is not merely due to hindsight that it is persuasive to read the film as anti-fascist. The tensions within the film articulate political tensions between the Right and the Left that were quite real at the time. These were not new tensions, and they had very much to do with the struggle for power soon to be won by the fascists in Germany.

However, it is also true that the polarization between reactionary evil and emancipated modernity as established in the film may be a bit too simple, indeed suspect, as Kracauer maintained. I would also assert that the polarization in the film can be related to other contentious debates about the film, not just with regard to whether it is truly anti-fascist, but whether its politics on female identity and sexual identity are as progressive as we might like to think.[58]

FEMALE IDENTITY: LESBIANISM AND/OR MOTHERHOOD?

For of course, as mentioned above, it has been asserted that the film is neither anti-fascist nor emancipatory in its sexual politics, in contradiction to Rich and Dyer, who assert that it is both. Again: to what extent, if at all, is the film "lesbian"? As we have seen, the people most responsible for the film were working to some extent at cross purposes: Winsloe and Sagan seem to have been committed to an openly lesbian film, at least from Thiele's characterization of the Berlin production of the play (32), whereas Froelich wanted to make the thematization of lesbian love less overt (34). Perhaps this topic is not completely explicit in the resulting film, yet many early critics acknowledged it, even though they often tried to dismiss it as something harmless, an adolescent phase. Most critics praised the film; in a more negative review, there is perhaps more forthrightness: the conservative *Kinematograph* objected mostly to the satirization of Potsdam (and national values), which it found unnecessary and in bad taste. But its review also contains the somewhat acid remark that viewers who have not been initiated into all "erotic specialties" might not understand what the film is about. Herbert Ihering, however, who was very positive about the film ("One of the best, cleanest, clearest films of the year . . .") was even more forthright, calling it a tragedy with a "slightly lesbian emphasis"(ctd. in Wendtland, *Jahrgang 1931,* 223).[59]

Why was this lesbian aspect to the narrative only *slightly* emphasized? This may have been more the result of the fact that the filmmakers were working at cross-purposes than of anything specific that Froelich did. For some of the changes we know him to have made, in spite of his reputed intention to tone down any overt homoeroticism in the interest of commercial success, do not necessarily have the effect of lessening the lesbian component to the film, as Dyer demonstrates, at least within the context of lesbian and gay debates about homosexuality in the Weimar period. In that context, the replacement of Melzer with Wieck in the role of Bernburg can be seen to signify the replacement of an androgynous, "butch" or *Bubi*-style of lesbianism with a "female-identified" type of lesbianism.

According to Dyer's characterization of that specific historical context in Weimar, there were within both the male and female homosexual communities two main philosophies or discourses of homosexuality, as it were, each opposing the other but both part of the broader community. One was the androgynous, "in-betweenist" model, the "third sex" in Magnus Hirschfeld's famous formulation, including "masculinized" (or "butch") women and "feminized" men; the other was the same-sex identified model, that is, of male-identified ("butch") gay men and female-identified ("femme") lesbians. The advantage of the latter model for lesbians in a homophobic society was greater invisibility, and homophobia was increasing in late Weimar. Beyond this pragmatic consideration, however, the fact that in a film like *Mädchen in Uniform* the central relationship "can be seen as simultaneously a pupil-teacher, mother-daughter, and a lesbian one," is, as Dyer writes, an ambiguity that is "a source of delight" (39).[60] Thus the film appeals both to a general female solidarity and to lesbian sensitivities in such a way as to make it difficult to separate the two—a pleasurable ambiguity that today would be considered queer.

Furthermore, Dyer argues that one cannot avoid the lesbianism of the narrative by stressing motherless Manuela's search for a replacement mother figure. This stress on motherhood was the strategy behind the attempts Thiele describes for muting the film's lesbianism in the Leipzig production, and it remains the interpretive emphasis of a critic such as Ohm, who disputes that the film thematizes lesbianism in an emancipatory way. But Dyer asserts that the "mother-daughter quality" of the relationship between Manuela and Bernburg only makes the film "*more* lesbian, not less"—especially since it is a typical feature of early 20th-century lesbian novels (55).

Nonetheless, the "female-identified" strategy could have negative political consequences for the film. Dyer rather clearly associates the "male-identified" tendency with reactionary tendencies in Weimar, namely a homosocial "masculinism" clearly aligned with the Right, and specifically with the Nazis.[61] But he admits no such problem with regard to the glorification of essential femininity within the "female-identified" tendency. In an era in which a very traditional cult of German womanhood, in combination with the cult of German motherhood, was about to triumph, however, this glorification seems more problematic. Indeed, in the early 1930s a return to traditional femininity was already triumphing over the fashionable trends a few years earlier associated with the "masculinized" New Woman.

On the simplest level: to the extent the lesbianism of the film remains camouflaged, it can be denied. This is what Lotte Eisner does: she compliments the film's "feminine" qualities while making it appear that Manuela's infatuation is merely a "phase" exacerbated in an "unhealthy" way by the school. And to the extent that the lesbianism is denied, the film's radicality fades. This is a dynamic, of course, that is still at work in much more recent films: "The unconscious deployment . . . of a cinematic lesbian continuum organized around the figure of the femme is politically and erotically ambiguous, both presenting and erasing lesbian identities and sexualities" (Holmlund ctd. in Doty, 44).

In the context of Germany in the early 1930s, there is an even more troubling possibility: a much more conservative concept, that of a "separate sphere" for women, might be relevant to the film in a way that undermines its reputed anti-fascism. The concept of a "separate sphere" is what Claudia Koonz found so fundamental to explaining the willingness of women to cooperate with fascists. The attraction to the idea of a "separate sphere" for women was characteristic of many middle-class women, especially women involved in church groups and opposed to (or threatened by) any "emancipation," but also women in the bourgeois women's movement, especially its conservative wing. This attraction was connected to a number of elements: a distaste for the more "masculine" New Woman of the 1920s who worked in the "man's world"; a fear of the loss of middle-class privilege, which having to work often connoted for middle-class women; but also, as Koonz asserts, a somewhat realistic appraisal of how little equality with men had actually been won compared to what the Weimar Constitution had promised women (1–17). Competing with men seemed undesirable and/or futile, and the idea of a return to some mythic past wherein women could achieve some autonomy in their "traditional" sphere of influence seemed positive to such women. Koonz maintains that this attitude helps to explain why so many women put up so little resistance to the victory of such an obviously misogynous movement like the Nazis—and indeed why some women enthusiastically joined the Nazi movement.

If this sort of "separate sphere" were indeed glorified in *Mädchen in Uniform,* it would indeed be troubling, but this is not the case. Such a sphere is arguably thematized in the film, but it is criticized, not valorized. For the boarding school itself serves as—and to some extent represents—such a traditional "female sphere," and it is this aspect against which Manuela and Bernburg rebel: a school which keeps girls separate in order to train them to be obedient wives who will give birth to soldiers—precisely the role for women which National Socialism would soon gloriously proclaim.[62] Here the erotic love of Manuela for Bernburg makes the rebellion all the more radical, for what could be a greater threat to the traditional female role than lesbianism, especially when that traditional role was defined so explicitly (both within the film and in the Weimar Republic in general, at least in its latter years) in terms of motherhood, pro-natalism, and militarism—giving birth to soldiers?

Lesbianism would certainly be a threat to a worldview whose goal for women above all is that they give birth, increase the birth rate. Like most women, most lesbians are of course able to give birth, and there are many lesbians who are mothers, but this fact would probably not comfort the pronatalists, if it in fact occurred at all to them. Nonetheless, it can be argued that the discourse of motherhood pervades *Mädchen in Uniform:* certainly Bernburg describes her more nurturing teaching philosophy as explicitly "maternal," and her decision to stand up for Manuela is not only a courageous "coming out" but also a stand on behalf of all the young women whose spirits are being crushed by the school. Freiburg and Reisdorfer (192–203) both see maternalism as central to the film, with the latter reading it positively in the tradition of German feminism, while Freiburg reads it negatively, connected ultimately to the reactionary gender politics of the Nazis.

The bourgeois ideology of motherhood had been used by feminists since the nineteenth century in Germany and elsewhere as strategy for increasing women's sphere of activity—the concept of "social motherhood," for instance, which justified women's move into professions like teaching, nursing, and social work. This strategy was pragmatic in the nineteenth century and not necessarily reactionary, but it was also not unrelated to more reactionary tendencies, which would indeed lead to the cult of motherhood in fascism. It seems to me, however, that moving from a strict biological/reproductive understanding of motherhood obviously loosens the concept from biologically determinist/essentialist notions of femininity. Arguably, even "social motherhood" already establishes some distance from such notions. Lesbianism, however, when combined with a "maternal" concern for the welfare of younger women, certainly does it much more clearly—and in a way that the fascist cult of motherhood most definitely does *not*. Is not the "mothering" in *Mädchen in Uniform* actually a form of female solidarity that includes a defense of homoerotic love—and a defense that is mounted not only by lesbians?

It is true that—as Rich asserts—so long as Bernburg plays "good cop" by directing all the homoerotic impulses of the girls toward herself, thus making them both harmless and beneficial to the institution with which she is identified, Bernburg is complicit in shoring up the school as a traditionalist "separate sphere." But as soon as Manuela's love transgresses the bounds of what is allowed, Bernburg, after a somewhat craven period of hesitation, defiantly chooses to quit the school and openly to side with Manuela.

Thus, we must return to the question of how much the film mutes the explicitly lesbian nature of Manuela's love for Bernburg. Why does the headmistress scream "Skandal!" when she hears Manuela's speech about the chemise from Bernburg—and about her love for Bernburg? Why does she demand Manuela be isolated and worry about "contagion"? Why does her chief flunky, Fräulein von Kesten, tell Edelgard that she is too young to understand exactly why Manuela must be isolated?[63] Why does the headmistress tell Bernburg that Manuela's attitude is a "sin," and why does Bernburg defiantly reply that what the headmistress calls "sin" is "the great spirit of love which has a thousand forms"? While the film may allow some viewers to ignore or downplay its lesbianism (in harmony with Froelich's commercial motivations and intentions), the narrative really does not make sense without it.

There has nonetheless been some disagreement as to whether the film actually depicts Bernburg's coming out (as opposed to Manuela's). Rich asserts that it is, but Gramann and Schlüpmann are not so sure. The logic of the two famous superimpositions of Manuela's face over Bernburg's face, however, is that they are from Bernburg's perspective, thus indicating that she too is haunted by Manuela and, therefore, that she too is in love. The first of the two superimpositions, it should be added, happens as Manuela begins to recite a psalm from the Songs of Solomon; the passionate words of this song can easily be taken for the expression of secular love as well as of religious devotion.[64] Manuela begins reciting its words as Bernburg watches her from the front of the classroom. It is from a reaction shot of Bernburg that the superimposition of Manuela's image begins.

Another point of controversy has been the film's "happy ending," another mostly commercial choice by Froelich, who thought a suicide at the end of the film would be "grotesque" (Thiele, 35). Does this affirmative ending undermine either the film's lesbianism or its anti-authoritarianism? Whatever Froelich's intentions, the fact that Manuela does not commit suicide is a great improvement on the conventional ending of traditional lesbian novels: "deviance" punished with the suicide of the "deviant."[65]

That the film was both accessible and extremely popular is proof of the fact that popular culture at the end of the Weimar Republic was not invariably reactionary, as so many critics have assumed.[66] The fact that the suicide is averted at the end of the film by the open rebellion and solidarity of the other schoolgirls and Bernburg underscores the anti-authoritarian reading; the revolt against authority is all the more radical when the lesbianism is taken into account.[67] The two discourses—anti-authoritarianism and lesbian rights—are intertwined, and not only within the text of the film. To separate issues of sexual freedom from other political struggles is a mistake, as feminists above all have so long emphasized. Homophobia was a crucial aspect of fascism, and it remains one of the most important weapons of some of the most patriarchal, reactionary, oppressive, and ultimately anti-democratic forces at work today. Its defeat in this film, however momentary, is one that should cheer us all.

Chapter 7 ⟿

Weimar Culture Now: "Americanism" and Post/Modernity

Indeed: Americanism is a new European method. How much this method is influenced by America itself seems to me very unimportant. It is a concrete and energetic method, completely oriented toward intellectual and material reality. Also conforming to it is the new (Americanized) appearance of the European: beardless with a sharp profile, a goal-oriented gaze, a narrow, steeled body; and the new type of woman (which is still not well understood even from a sexological perspective): boyish, linear, dominated by lively movement, by her gait, by her legs.

—Rudolf Kayser, 1925.[1]

From where does this terrible wave come that threatens to wash away everything colorful, everything unique from our lives? Anyone who has been over there knows: from America.

—Stefan Zweig, 1925.[2]

We held on to America. America was a good idea: it was the land of the future. It was at home in this century . . . . For long enough the glorious discipline of technology had been evident here in Germany only in the form of tanks, landmines, the blue cross, only for the purpose of the destruction of human life. In America it stood in the service of human life.

The sympathy that one expressed for the elevator, for the radio tower, for jazz was demonstrative. . . . It was against the cavalry; it was for horsepower. Its doctrines led toward transforming the flamethrower into a vacuum cleaner. . . .

—Hans A. Joachim, 1930.[3]

In 1935 Earl Browder, the general secretary of the American Communist Party, proclaimed Communism "the Americanism of the twentieth century."[4]

I think the label "postmodernism" . . . *is* about how the world dreams itself to be "American" . . .

—Stuart Hall, 1986.[5]

I n juxtaposing the above quotes from the 1920s, 1930s, and 1980s, which contain quite disparate ideas about America and "Americanism," I want to point out how what one sometimes calls "Americanization" has come to be seen as synonymous with the processes of modernization in the twentieth century and—already toward the end of that century, and now, at the beginning of the next—even with the "postmodern" conditions of global consumer capitalism. That many of us feel ambivalent about these developments is also clear. Certainly to the extent that they represent a process of democratization progressive critics consider them positively. This is the understanding of "Americanism" in which the German literary critic Joachim professed his faith, and it is the one to which the American Browder connected Communism—in a move that strikes us today as quite odd, given the fact that the consolidation of Stalinism during the 1930s surely put an end to the last vestiges of any democratic dreams that might still have been contained within Marxist-Leninism.[6]

Other aspects of "modernization" tend to be viewed negatively by many cultural critics—and here there is some agreement on both the Right and the Left, for on both wings one can find "cultural conservatives"—because of the commodification and reification that accompany the triumph of global capitalism. In the longer passage from which I have excerpted Stuart Hall's remarks, he asserts that this "American" conception of postmodernism is also "irrevocably Euro- or western-centric" (132); there can be no doubt that this is also true of most of the forces currently driving globalization.

With regard to the changes wrought by modernization in the realm of gender and sexual relations (and politics), one can sense a similar ambivalence, because there is evidence both of social and political emancipation as well as of social atomization and sexual reification associated with these changes. Already in Germany's Weimar Republic the same ambivalence was evident with regard to modernization, connected as it is both to democratization and to international capitalism, to consumerism and a uniform mass culture but also to political and sexual emancipation and the possibility of a diverse, democratic popular culture.[7] The quotes with which I have opened this chapter demonstrate this ambivalence, as do the texts I have examined in this book.

Toller's *Hinkemann,* for example, is a plea for a new, democratic and humane society that deconstructs traditional masculinity at the same time it projects its anxiety about modernization and reification onto a female sexuality depicted as threatening and aggressive (especially in the dream sequence). Dupont's *Variety* deploys similar anxieties about the modern destabilization of male identity to articulate a culturally conservative message critical both of mass entertainment and the destabilization of social class boundaries—at the same time that it packages this message within a mass spectacle produced with all the technical virtuosity that the modern cinematic apparatus could command. Pabst's *Secrets of a Soul* tries to restore male potency and mastery through the modern "science" of psychoanalysis, but its fantastic depiction of male crisis is more impressive than its half-hearted narrative resolution—and it is this focus on gender and sexual destabilization that is emancipatory, I would argue.

Male crisis is conflated with a critique of modern reification, and both problems are blamed on women and female sexuality in a fairly reactionary fashion in Kästner's *Fabian,* but in Sternberg's *The Blue Angel,* whereas the narrative lends itself to a similar reading, the film as a whole (combined with Dietrich's performance) tends to parody these concerns in its fascinated exploration of how both the cuckold and the vamp are constructed.

Keun's *The Artificial Silk Girl* uses a female perspective to explore the modern reification of the female as well as women's complicity in the phenomenon, critiquing the emptiness of the promises of both traditional and more modern, mass cultural conceptions of women's identities. The book grants its main character an agency that is linked to her development of a critical perspective on the limitations of the choices offered within the class and gender hierarchy—at the same time it addresses a popular audience (especially its women readers) faced with similar problems and choices. Sagan's *Mädchen in Uniform* critiques the traditional conceptions of female identity and sexuality crucial to anti-democratic, authoritarian forces in Weimar Germany with an optimistic narrative about the triumph of a "forbidden" love and of a rebellion in solidarity with that queer love against the forces of authority. The ambivalence here can be noted in the fragility of the film's happy ending: while heartening, this is a rebellion within the walls of one school that is in turn inside of a much larger power structure, one that nearly compelled Bernburg to deny that love—or rather to warp it into something that conforms to, and shores up the status quo.

The overwhelming success of Sagan's film (like that of Keun's novel) with the public, however, proves that accessible popular culture at the end of the Weimar Republic was not inevitably "völkisch," reactionary kitsch.

(POST)MODERNITY, GENDER, AND SEX: REIFICATION VS. EMANCIPATION?

But what if anything does modernity as it can be seen to have configured itself in these texts, and in the culture of the Weimar Republic in general, have to do with "postmodernism" or "postmodernity"? This of course depends on how exactly these very elusive terms have been understood within academic discourse in North America and Europe over the last two decades, and this is a question to which one can only respond with multiple answers, because the postmodern has been understood in a variety of often contradictory ways. Indeed, as a concept the postmodern would seem to be connected to a programmatic aversion to any unitary or "monolithic" definition. It has been asserted that postmodernism as a concept refers precisely to irreconcilable contradictions within the (post)modern world, contradictions that must be held simultaneously rather than seen as canceling each other out according to the dictates of logic. Or rather, as Linda Hutcheon has expressed it, there is a specifically "postmodern" logic that is the logic of "both/and" rather than "either/or" (49).

This is of course one possible response to Stuart Hall. His critique of "postmodernism," parts of which I have excerpted above, is as follows: "[P]ostmodernism, especially in its American appropriation . . . carries two additional charges: it not only points to how things are going in modern culture, but it says, first, that there is nothing else of any significance—no contradictory forces, and no counter-tendencies; and second, that these changes are terrific, and all we have to do is to reconcile ourselves to them" (132).

Those who defend the value of the term "postmodern" could respond to this critique with the argument that what characterizes the "condition" to which the term refers is precisely a number of contradictory forces or tensions—the tension between, say, globalization and regionalisms/local resistances on the economic, political, and cultural fronts; or the tension between the agenda of "universal" human rights and particularist/separatist wars of ethnic/national "liberation"—and/or "cleansing"; or that between enlightened secularism and various religious fundamentalisms. In turn this response itself could be critiqued for its co-optive tendency to subsume the political and cultural struggles of all the peoples on the planet into mere oppositional terms within an overall system that tends usually to valorize the other position, the Western (or "western-centric") one. One can perhaps overcome this bias by describing the conflict as that between global capitalism and anti-modern religious fundamentalism, as in the trendy formulation "Jihad versus McWorld," a pessimistic (and too dualistic/binary) appraisal that nonetheless seems all too apt in the aftermath of the horrific attacks on the World Trade Center and the Pentagon on September 11, 2001.[8] What cannot be disputed is that any analysis of globalization at the beginning of the twenty-first century must take into account international political and economic power differentials that still reflect colonial/imperialist histories and current "post" (or neo-) colonial relations. At the same time anti-modern religious fundamentalism is not only found on the anti-Western side of the current conflict (and indeed such extremist attitudes on both sides tend to reinforce each other).[9]

Problematic as the term "postmodern" surely is, let me sketch briefly what similarities Weimar modernity might be said to share with "postmodern" characteristics that have been defined primarily in terms of the late twentieth century. Weimar culture—and in particular the dynamics in that culture connected to modernization and modernity, as well as the attitudes toward the latter I have grouped under the label "New Objectivity"—can be related to "postmodernity" first with regard to certain economic, social, and cultural developments during the Weimar Republic, primarily the growth of the "new class" of white-collar workforce (in German the employees who were called *die Angestellten*) and the new importance of consumerism and mass culture. In the artistic and cultural life in Germany in the 1920s and early 1930s, one also notes an apparent renunciation of modernist manifestoes by "sober" (or "cynical") artists and intellectuals, as well as an interest in undermining the high culture/mass culture dichotomy. At the very least there was a clear opposition to what one might call the "high modernism" of Expressionism: for, again, what characterized the German avant-garde of the 1920s—from the Bauhaus to Brecht, from Heartfield to Höch—was an enmity to elitist, "auratic" art, as well as the attempt to create an art less separated from modern life, a more democratic art that learned from mass culture. This too is arguably a "postmodernist" development.[10] In addition, one notes in the political sphere in Weimar already the confounding of—if not even the beginning of the collapse of—the traditional Left/Right dichotomy, because on both the Right and the Left there is not just ambivalence about, there is also the embrace of technology and modernization.[11]

I would assert that this ambivalence was quite unavoidable precisely because of the "both/and" nature of modernization as the West has experienced it: both democratization and capitalist commodification, both the destabilization of older (aristocratic-feudal) hierarchies and identities and the development of newer (capitalist-technocratic-bureaucratic) ones. And, just as there was in general political, economic, and social terms a process both of emancipation and reification, so too specifically in the area of gender and sexual relations (and identities). Thus one can speak of both of a cynical, exploitative sexual libertinism that flourished especially in the economic and social chaos of World War I and the most turbulent periods of the Weimar Republic (in its early years and at its end)—but also of an emancipatory period with new opportunities for women and for homosexuals, just as there were new opportunities for others from traditionally oppressed groups, like the Jews and the lower classes. It was furthermore a period that also included concerted political struggle on behalf of women's reproductive rights and the rights of homosexuals.

In the 1980s Sloterdijk stressed cynicism in his discussion of Weimar culture, and in the 1990s Lethen has stressed masks, but both phenomena can only be understood in terms of a related tendency in the culture, namely "Enthüllung," the tendency to "un-mask," to expose the underlying dynamics behind traditional facades, as Karl Mannheim explained already in 1930:"This unmasking sensibility is a basic feature of our time, even if a widespread tendency sees in it the expression of a vulgar attitude, of a lack of respect . . . , one therefore may not forget that an epoch of transformation such as ours, which is breaking with so many facades and forms that have already become unbearable for us, must needs adopt for itself such a sensibility" (17).[12]

As Mary Ann Doane suggested in her reading of *Pandora's Box,* no transgression of traditional sexual norms and taboos is of use to feminist emancipation if it does not also question the status quo in terms of power relations between sexual partners with regard to gender hierarchies—and other hierarchies, such as class and "race." Such a transgression of norms without any questioning of power relations is merely cynical, and indeed it enables an even more exploitative use of sexuality by more socially powerful men in dealings with women (and by upper-class men and women with lower-class men and women, for that matter) than under more traditional patriarchal codes.[13] But the fact is that there *was* a questioning of that sexual and political status quo in Weimar culture, for it like many traditional forms of hierarchy and identity was in crisis. It is the very sense of crisis as perceived by traditionally more powerful groups—men, the upper classes—that is the proof that they felt their privileges under threat.

Crisis and emancipation are inseparable. While a destabilization of the rules governing gender and sexual relations does indeed allow some more powerful groups to exploit others sexually in new ways, the same situation also allows opportunities for greater autonomy to the less powerful. An analogy to the "sexual revolution" of a later decade in the twentieth-century history of the West makes this perhaps clearer: certainly in the 1960s there was much that enabled greater sexual exploitation, especially of women, yet the emancipatory aspects of the period cannot be denied: for one thing, precisely this exploitation was one of the motivating forces that fueled the ascendance of "second-wave" feminism, and furthermore, very few women today, feminist or otherwise, would want to "turn back the clock" to the more cloistered, "chivalrous" mores that were overturned in the 1960s.

I want to assert once again as I have throughout this book that we must not lose sight of the emancipatory aspects of Weimar modernity in particular and of modernization (and "postmodernization") in general. And here I would include some of the attempts made in Weimar culture to create an accessible and democratic popular culture that was neither "high culture" nor "mass culture," but one that attempted to bridge that gulf.[14] I also want to demonstrate how the attempts to demonize emancipatory developments in the undoing of traditional gender and sexual identities have continued through the century. Here the specific example of Germany is instructive, for in that nation the Nazis came to power to do battle with what they perceived as degenerate challenges to traditional identities they considered "natural" and "biological." Later, after the Nazis had been defeated, elite groups in Germany (who had mostly collaborated with the former) discredited fascism itself as an example of the very "degeneracy" the Nazis had campaigned against. This elite strategy left "traditional identities" and values intact and conflated challenges to those values with totalitarian threats associated with fascism and communism.

THE DEMONIZATION OF GENDER AND SEXUAL EMANCIPATION: HISTORICAL CONTINUITIES FROM WEIMAR TO NOW

The tracing of historical continuities within German history since the end of the Weimar Republic is a project that has relevance for more than just Germany, especially if one focuses on the issues of changing conceptions of traditional gender and sexual identities—and the interpretation of those changes as "decadence" or "degeneracy." In a cursory overview of subsequent German history with this focus in mind, I shall attempt to demonstrate how this might be relevant to broader discussions of modernization and postmodernity.

As I have asserted, in New Objectivity and in much of Weimar culture one notes a public fascination with the instability of traditional, fixed gender and sexual identities in modernization together with attempts to "control" them—attempts that seem to be related to tendencies toward homogenization and control in popular culture in general. In contrast to New Objectivity, National Socialism proclaimed much more definitive "answers" to the modern destabilization of traditional identity categories (including gender and sex, but also class, and, most famously of all, "race" and nationality). There would be little tolerance for destabilization of any kind, as well as for any divisive elements in mass culture and any other doubts about national resolve. As a "reactionary modernism," fascism was an emphatic disavowal not so much of modernity as of heterogeneity in modernity; along with many others, the new managerial class whose fate was tied to modernization acquiesced in this disavowal for the sake of a strong, "masculine" and homogenous national identity. This disavowal had disastrous effects, among them a new, mechanized world war much more barbarous than World War I, as well as an even more barbarous program of genocide waged against the Jews and other minority groups—the "gypsies" (Roma and Sinti peoples) and male homosexuals—carried out across Europe. This barbarism was executed with all the "rationalized" efficiency a modern industrial society could muster.

After World War II, there was not much of an attempt to return Germany to the raucous politics and culture of its last democracy, the Weimar Republic. Indeed, dominant voices were now raised in support of yet another attempt to restore a homogenous and stable national identity and culture as a bulwark against what was perceived as the dangerous instability and "decadence" of both Weimar and the Third Reich. In West Germany, or the "Federal Republic of Germany," as the postwar German state in the West was named, one can detect an interesting discursive phenomenon connected to this new attempt to create a new national identity (not unrelated to developments elsewhere in Europe): the Nazis themselves, while sometimes considered "anti-modern," at the same time became marked as a decadent modern perversion of an otherwise classical, enlightened German culture[15]—that is, they became associated with the very same things against which they had campaigned in the Weimar Republic.

There was a certain rehabilitation of the classic bourgeois sphere in West Germany, a state that did grant a certain autonomy—via repressive tolerance?—to dissident literati such as those in "Group 47" ("Gruppe, 47"). But of course mass culture and consumerism played a greater role than ever in the West German "economic miracle" of the 1950s. The postwar German film industry in the West, although decentralized, nonetheless changed very little from its pre-1945 identity in terms of personnel and the type of entertainment films produced. Above all, tremendous commercial success was achieved by the "Heimat films" of the early and mid-1950s, Technicolor romances set in rural landscapes of great beauty where neither troubling urban modernity nor postwar rubble was anywhere to be seen.

The same cultural and political continuity was evident in West German society with regard to gender relations and sexuality: in political discourse (from politicians and church officials) and in literary and cinematic representation, Germany's postwar problems were blamed on women who had become too independent and were not sufficiently supportive of the embattled German male after the lost war. The emphasis on the perspective of the traumatized male veterans of the defeated German army can be noted in the most famous play to be written after the war in the part of Germany occupied by the Western Allies, Wolfgang Borchert's *The Man Outside* (*Draußen vor der Tür*, 1947), and in the very first postwar German film, Wolfgang Staudte's *The Murderers Are Among Us* (*Die Mörder sind unter uns*, 1946), produced in the Soviet zone of Berlin. Rather than the radical questioning of masculinity in Toller's *Hinkemann,* one finds in these post-World-War II works the implied conclusion that male subjectivity must be shored up and restored (especially in Staudte's film).[16] The postwar discourse about independent German women of "loose morals" is nowhere better exemplified than in Willi Forst's film *The Sinful Woman* (*Die Sünderin,* 1950) and the controversy that it provoked in West Germany, as Heidi Fehrenbach has demonstrated.[17]

Without the ideological trappings of fascism, but instead with recourse both to "Christian values" and "value-free" market imperatives, one notes another attempt to restore a stable national identity through the re-establishment of traditional gender roles. Again: just as the Nazis had once labeled the Weimar Republic as decadent and inimical to traditional values, now they themselves were marked as decadent. Indeed, they often became inscribed in popular culture as "perverse," and even—ironically enough for such a homophobic movement—homosexual.[18]

The blend of rampant development of the consumer economy with "stable," "traditional" gender roles was typical of the 1950s, and not just in West Germany; one notes the same tendencies in the United States and throughout Western Europe. While this "idyllic" stabilization was neither idyllic nor even very stable for very long, it became the postwar ideal of the "good old days" as well as of a Cold War identity meant to be clearly distinct from what a different managerial elite was putting into place in East Germany, or what was called the "GDR," the "German Democratic Republic."

Given the technocratic, masculinist self-image of the GDR, it is somewhat ironic that after its collapse in 1989–1990 it was so often gendered "feminine" in discourse, but of course in patriarchal cultures that is how the loser tends to be gendered.[19] One of the more common tropes in the public discourse around the trauma of reunification in the early 1990s was a concern about the "emasculation" of the men of the ex-GDR. Such discourse of course ignores the plight of women in the ex-GDR, which was—and is—arguably much worse.[20] Meanwhile, the first decade of a united German state has been characterized by disturbing acts of violence against many of the minorities considered "foreigners" by Germany's less than progressive citizenship laws (based primarily on bloodlines), which tacitly reinforce xenophobia by their denial of citizenship to these "foreigners," many of whom were born in Germany and have lived their whole lives there.[21]

All of these examples of the treatment of "others"—East German men and women, and of course even worse, "foreigners" and others of different ethnic heritage—might be considered to present disturbing parallels with the late Weimar Republic. But the relevance of the Weimar Republic today is not to be found in any too specific construction of historical parallels, but rather, I would suggest, in its formative role as a site where the "stabilization" of identity in a modern state with an emergent consumer economy was in flux and openly thematized. As long as this "stabilization" remained incomplete, the illusion of a homogenous identity was also impossible: a field of competing "publics" and multiple identities was possible.

Weimar culture, in spite of the predominantly masculinist, misogynist intentions of many of its leading figures, provided a space (if only for exploitative, sensational reasons) in which anxieties about gender and sexual difference were more or less openly conceded, and thus its spectators were addressed in a sort of public debate. In contrast to the Weimar Republic, Germany's Third Reich demonstrated the danger of shutting down that debate in the interest of mythic, essentializing constructions of homogenous public, ethnic, or national identities. And such constructions of identity, and of "threats" to such identities, are still with us. Indeed they are all too prevalent, both in united Germany, plagued as it is by lingering East-West distrust and by ugly racism and xenophobia; as well as in the

United States, with its long history of racism by no means completely overcome, with virulent homophobia on the extreme Right, and with many of its "liberals" only too willing to blame social and cultural disarray on "single mothers," "welfare," and "foreigners" and/or undocumented immigrants (especially in the early 1990s—and perhaps again soon in the aftermath of the destruction of the World Trade Center). Indeed, these constructions of identity and otherness are all too prevalent throughout the planet, in this "new world order" of globalization, economic dislocation, and ethnic and religious violence. The investigation of such cultural phenomena in (post)modernity is essential, and for such a project Weimar culture remains a crucial site.

"QUEERNESS" AND RADICAL DEMOCRACY

In the continued demonization of emancipatory developments in sex and gender relations over the course of the century that I have sketched above, one of its more fascinating aspects has been, not the way in which elite groups and "mainstream" commentators have participated in the process (that would seem only to be expected), but rather the way critical thinkers on the Left have done so as well. From Kracauer to the Mitscherlichs to the discourse of "homo-fascism" Hewitt analyzes in the writings of Adorno, there is a tradition of blaming fascism on some of the very groups fascism itself came to power demonizing: "strong" women, effeminate sons, and any disruptive influences on the patriarchal family. As Hewitt demonstrates so persuasively, this tradition locates the problem in anything that hinders the development of strong, distinct bourgeois egos, for which the strong, father-dominated family is supposedly essential, in order that more malleable "narcissistic" types will not develop who would be susceptible to seduction by (pick the threat:) homosexuality, fascism, mass culture, "Americanism," consumerism, Communism (in the Cold War version of this fantasy)—and "postmodernism," for that matter.

Let me once again dispute this argument, which of course I have represented here in an intentionally polemical caricature. While there is much ideological manipulation to which the (post)modern subject is susceptible, there is no reason to blame this on democratic and emancipatory impulses in modern culture, nor is it clear that a return to more authoritarian, patriarchal models of the family would have a beneficial effect—certainly not if what is at stake is a democratic ideal of society and culture, in which all hierarchies of identity and culture are contested and open to debate. The encouragement of critical thinking about such issues is not "narcissistic," and it does not work to the advantage of global consumer capitalism, either. While consumerism depends on an instrumentalization of desire, and while denial, the traditional ascetic response to desire in culture by Leftist rationalism, clearly doesn't work, the critical interrogation of desire *is* a promising strategy. Nor can we withdraw to some safe realm of "high culture," closing ourselves off from the ambiguities of popular culture.[22] In investigating the dynamics of desire, culture, and politics, the insights of feminist and queer theory have been invaluable. In the end, no true democratic project can coexist with misogyny or homophobia—in contrast to authoritarian (and fundamentalist) politics and regimes, which so often make use of precisely these sentiments.

As the feminist writer and activist Meredith Tax has written, in her attempt to encourage the American Left not to concede the "culture wars" to the Right: "None of our movements will get very far unless we recognize the centrality of struggles around culture. As we can see from the former Yugoslavia, culture wars around questions such as national identity, women's roles and minority rights have a way of turning into wars of blood. The way we frame our issues now will resonate for generations. Unity in the U.S. progressive movement—not to mention survival, and our ability to defeat . . . antidemocratic, atavistic forces . . . depends on solidarity with all those attacked by racists, zealots, and thugs, at home and abroad . . ." (28).

Those attacks, Tax, summarizes, have to do both with racism and with the attempt to quash any threats to patriarchal control over sexuality and reproduction. Which brings us back to Weimar. Again: it was Weimar's "queerness" that was emancipatory, precisely in its interrogation of tradition, hierarchy, identity, desire, and culture. This was an interrogation that was often anxious, sensationalized, and certainly ambivalent; and ultimately it was overpowered by other forces much more averse to democratic debate and cultural heterogeneity. But it is this legacy that must be championed today, as a crucial part of any campaign for a just, humane, pluralistic, and democratic world order in the new millennium—an order that is under attack by anti-modern, fundamentalist extremists associated with factions within many faiths—not just Islam.

Notes ⌒

Chapter One

1. On "Americanism," see, for example, Lüdtke, Marßolek, and von Saldern, eds., *Amerikanisierung*. See also Saunders: the movement of influence between America and Germany in the 1920s and early 1930s did not occur on a one-way street; it involved—certainly in the dealings of the American and German film industries that Saunders studied—a great deal of complex interaction between forces in both countries.

2. On the widespread opposition to "Americanism" among groups who shaped public opinion in Weimar (such as politicians), see von Saldern. She presents a very differentiated view of this opposition, which could be found among Social Democrats (at least with regard to some issues, such as the valorization of German "high culture" over Americanized "mass culture") as well as liberal, conservative, and nationalist politicians. She also asserts that right-wing opposition to Americanism was not completely "anti-modern," but rather in favor of a restrained, "German" version of the modern, as opposed to an excessive, "Americanized" or internationalist modernization. In this regard her analysis complements Herf's ideas about "reactionary modernism" in Germany.

3. See, for example, the 1925 book of the same name by Giese; see also Hake, "Girls and Crisis"; Grossmann, "*Girlkultur*"; Frame, "Gretchen, Girl, Garçonne?"; and Barndt, "Sentiment und Sachlichkeit," esp. 110–26.

4. Alice Kuzniar's chapter on Weimar cross-dressing films is a must for scholars of Weimar film; it is the first chapter in her impressive new book on "queer German cinema," The Queer German Cinema. As for my use of the term "emancipatory" here and elsewhere in this book, it can, I suppose, be considered "dated," but I would disagree. Why would anyone give up the goal of political and social emancipation—which includes the emancipation from hierarchical ideas about political power belonging to social elites based on

"noble birth," socio-economic class, "race," and gender (the latter clearly connected to oppressive constructions of gender and sexual norms)? Certainly any radical democratic politics depends on a belief in emancipation.

5. Petro's *Joyless Streets* (1989) was the first major book to analyze Weimar film and culture from a feminist perspective; in it Petro, a film scholar, focuses on the female spectator addressed both in the illustrated press as well as the cinema of the Weimar Republic. Even earlier, the volume *When Biology Became Destiny* (1984), edited by feminist historians Renate Bridenthal, Atina Grossmann, and Marion Kaplan, made an invaluable contribution to the feminist analysis of Weimar and Nazi culture. Important feminist work from the 1990s is anthologized in *Women in the Metropolis* (1997), edited by Katharina von Ankum; Anke Gleber's *The Art of Taking a Walk* (1999) and Janet Ward's *Weimar Surfaces* (2001) are other important new books exploring Weimar culture. Among many other works, note Kerstin Barndt's dissertation, "Sentiment und Sachlichkeit" (1999) and Vibeke Petersen's *Women and Modernity in Weimar Germany.*

6. With regard to Kracauer, one has to distinguish the postwar from the prewar critic, of course. It is also impossible to avoid a reconsideration of Kracauer's position on decadence in the light of what is now known about his own sexuality: Miriam Hansen, an expert on the Frankfurt School, has recently mentioned "Kracauer's own gay sensibility" ("America, Paris . . . ," 173). Why the postwar Kracauer espoused such a conservative position on decadence and "male retrogression" deserves study.

7. In Hewitt's *Political Inversions,* see the introductory chapter as well as the second chapter dealing specifically with the Frankfurt School.

8. It could be argued that Linda Mizejewski's *Divine Decadence* is a feminist attack on decadence, but this would be a misreading: in studying the evolution of the fictional character Sally Bowles, what Mizejewski critiques is the male appropriation and trivialization, beginning with Isherwood, of the figure of the emancipated woman in Weimar Germany. In the end this trivialization contributed not only to a misogynistic but ultimately homophobic reading of emancipatory trends in Weimar culture.

   It is true that libertinism in societies characterized by class exploitation can involve a crude sexual commodification of both women and men from the poorer classes, and there were distressing examples of this in certain types of prostitution in late Wilhelminian times and during Weimar—especially during periods of crisis like the war, the inflation, and the Depression. But this was due to social exploitation, not sexual emancipation. That these two phenomena were conflated by the Nazis and used by them to demonize the Weimar Republic is also true—and it is another example of their demagoguery and their skill at manipulating popular prejudices.

9. Butler, *Gender Trouble,* 141. On connections between masks, masquerade, and gender/sex performativity, see also Butler, *Bodies That Matter,* 13, 230–33.

10. See, for example, Becker and Weiss, Lethen, Lindner, Barndt, and Ward.

11. As Thomas Elsaesser writes at the very beginning of his new book on Weimar cinema, "The German cinema of the Weimar Republic is often, but wrongly identified with Expressionism" (*Weimar Cinema and After,* 3).

12. Huyssen—following Peter Bürger—stresses the opposition of the avant-garde beginning with Dadaism to modernism, and this is important for his understanding of "postmodernism" as well (see "Mapping the Postmodern").

13. See Rosenhaft's discussion of the value of Petro's work for historians who want to bring the role of women into history, "Women, Gender," 172–73. The valorization of the role and agency implicit in the concept of the female spectator as developed by Petro must be distinguished from other work (some of it feminist) that tends to see the role of the spectator, reader, or other recipient of modern popular culture as entirely shaped by a (usually monolithic) culture industry.

14. My translation of the original: "Ich lag im Bett—eigentlich hatte ich mir noch die Füsse waschen wollen, aber ich war zu müde wegen dem Abend vorher, und ich hatte doch gleich zu Therese gesagt: 'Es kommt nichts bei raus, sich auf der Strasse ansprechen zu lassen, und man muss immerhin auf sich halten.'" All subsequent translations are mine unless otherwise noted.

15. This short film is famous in large part because of its production crew: it was directed by Robert Siodmak and Edgar Ulmer, with a screenplay by Billy Wilder and Curt Siodmak, and cinematography by Eugen Schüfftan and Fred Zinnemann. All six of these young film artists would end up in Hollywood within a few years.

16. Russell Berman (*Cultural Studies,* 16) writes that an "oscillation between close reading and contextualization" is characteristic of the Frankfurt School's method, one that obviously has had a strong influence on German studies. But this is also characteristic of much feminist work, I would insist—indeed, as de Lauretis asserts, it is at the core of the feminist project.

17. My own approach to film is unthinkable without the influence of feminist work on the analysis of film texts that attempts to make connections between formal systems and the social and psychic construction of gender in specific historical cultures. German studies is enormously indebted to feminist and gender studies, and this is true of the field of cultural studies in general, as historian Geoff Eley stresses in his essay on "Cultural History" (in the same special issue of *New German Critique,* 25–26).

18. Although it is apparently no longer in print, *The Artificial Silk Girl* was translated into English in the early 1930s.

19. In this I follow Butler (for example, *Bodies That Matter,* 21, 227, 229) and Eve Kosofsky Sedgwick (e.g., *Tendencies,* 5–9). I am indebted to critics like Butler, Sedgwick, Doty, Hewitt, and Kuzniar for their discussions of "queerness."

Chapter Two

1. An earlier version of this chapter appeared as "From *Caligari* to Dietrich: Sexual, Social, and Cinematic Discourses in Weimar Film" in *SIGNS* 18.3 (1993): 640–68. That article in turn was a revised version of a paper first presented at the conference "New Historicism as Cultural Critique: Perspectives from German Studies" at Brown University, Providence, Rhode Island, March 16–17, 1990.

2. Orig. from *Berliner Lokalanzeiger*, 26–28 August 1928; cited in Peter Sloterdijk, *Kritik der zynischen Vernunft*, 806. My translation. See also Sloterdijk, *Critique of Cynical Reason*, trans. Michael Eldred, 453.

3. Cf. Lethen, *Verhaltenslehren der Kälte*, 133–34, on the dichotomy between fusion and *Trennung* (separation) in Weimar culture, and the attraction of the right wing for the former.

4. See Theweleit, *Männerfantasien*, vol. 1, Chapter 2, "Fluten Körper Geschichte" ("Floods Bodies History"), 235–456, among other sections especially the ones entitled "Was da fließt" ("All that Flows"), 256–97, and "Brei" ("Mush," or as in the Stephen Conway translation, "Pulp"), 410. See also Theweleit, *Male Fantasies,* vol. 1, trans. Stephen Conway, 249–88, 394.

5. See especially Rich.

6. For example: Petro, Clover, Doane, Silverman, Williams, Linville, and Staiger.

7. It will become clear that I am no orthodox Lacanian. I tend to find such an approach to gender and sexuality (and language and meaning) much too "binary," and thus I would align myself more with what Judith Mayne called the shift away from Lacan and back toward the more "bisexual" Freud ("Feminist Film Theory," 16). Nonetheless I do find Lacanian analyses useful, and they have influenced me. Kaja Silverman, for instance, uses Lacanian insights to very original ends and productive analyses, and feminist film theory has profited from her doing so.

8. Even the "realist" Pabst, famous for his skill at "invisible" continuity editing, was no classical realist. See for example Elsaesser, "Lulu and the Meter Man," 52.

9. On the importance of context, see Staiger, who now sees context as in many ways more important than text.

10. On the situation with regard to the cinema before the 1920s and the role of women as an audience to which early films were addressed, see Hansen, "Early Silent Cinema," and Schlüpmann.

11. This image has a historical meaning within Germany that exceeds its relation to the prevailing international stereotype of the vamp—that is, the mysterious and seductive temptress who would lead men to their ruin, an important staple of the international cinema in the 1910s and 1920s. For a short history of the concept of the vamp beginning with the literature of the nineteenth century, see, for example, LaSalle, 36–40.

12. Patrice Petro in her book on Weimar cinema and photojournalism criticizes the discourse of "male subjectivity in crisis" (*Joyless Streets,* 13) that dominates so many discussions of Weimar. She points out its bias and its limits as a narrative explaining an era notable precisely for an unprecedented public presence and activity by women. My use of the term is not meant to efface that aspect of the era; I agree with her that much of the "crisis" can be explained precisely as a reaction to (and as a demonization of) that new public presence of women.

    For the discussion of a similar "crisis of male subjectivity" in a different historical context—the United States in the mid-1940s—see the second chapter in Silverman's *Male Subjectivity at the Margins.* Her book as a whole is a fascinating discussion of this "crisis" as the basis for a feminist rethinking of the relationship between psychoanalytical theory and ideology.

13. Cf. Bridenthal et al., *When Biology Became Destiny,* 5, 21–22. Grossmann points out that women actually posed little real threat to men in the job market ("*Girlkultur,*" 66).

14. See Peukert, Ch. 1 on the actual relationship between the fairly spontaneous workers' uprisings of 1918 and the less-than-successful attempts by the Spartakus/Communist faction to lead them. On the November revolution, see also, e.g., Hermand and Trommler, 14–19.

15. In German this attempted coup led by Hitler was named in a much more glorified fashion: "Der Marsch auf die Feldherrnhalle," or the "March on the Field Commander's Hall."

16. It should also be noted that Toller's play does not necessarily thematize male anxieties in an uncritical way. See Cafferty and also Chapter 3 of this book. There is also a purely literary discourse of literal castration that goes back to Lenz's *Hofmeister*—there it represents the self-imposed servility of the German bourgeoisie. Another Weimar text that thematizes castration is Brecht's *Mann ist Mann,* in which it represents the attempt of the old soldier class to eliminate any desires that might conflict with military discipline.

17. Tatar discusses the novel in her sixth chapter (132–52). See also Hake, "Urban Paranoia."

18. See Chapter 5 of this book for a detailed discussion of *Fabian.*

19. On the representation of hyperbolic masculinity on the Left as symptomatic of the destabilization of traditional class and gender identities, see Rosenhaft, "Lesewut," 133, 141; on the representation of maternal, proletarian femininity on the Left, see Petro, *Joyless* Streets, 95–103, 110.

20. Cf. von Ankum, "Ich liebe Berlin," 370.

21. This "New Woman" was not just a discursive figure or a male projection, and she was not just a consumer, either (Grossmann, "*Girlkultur,*" 64).

22. On feminists (especially bourgeois feminists) and the New Woman, see Bridenthal et al., 11–12, 17–20. See also Bridenthal and Koonz and note 32 below. On attitudes of the left with regard to the New Woman, as well as

the discourse about the New Woman as developed in fashion and photo-journalism, in advertising and political campaigns, see Petro, *Joyless Streets*, 79–139. See also Grossmann, "*Girlkultur.*"

23. The concept of a "phallic" woman has its origin in the psychoanalytical theory that at one stage a little boy believes that his mother has a penis. Because the penis becomes associated with male power (in patriarchy, anyway), the boy's fantasy of the "phallic mother" becomes associated with any powerful women who induce "castration anxiety" in men (a rather stereotypical sexist put-down of independent women, seen from another perspective).

24. Jonathan and Nina are the names used in the American version of the film and derive from the Stoker novel. In the original German version Jonathan was called Thomas and his wife Nina was called Ellen (in part to distance the film from the literary original).

25. Cf. Coates, 95–96; he also notes the similarity between the association of Nosferatu with rats and the juxtaposition two decades later of Jews with rats in the infamous anti-Semitic film *The Eternal Jew* (*Der ewige Jude,* 1940).

26. Indeed, it has been suggested that Nina herself is coded visually as Jewish.

27. Mayne notes the logic of the eyeline matches between Nina in her bed and Nosferatu as he turns away, interrupted, from his attack on Jonathan ("Dracula," 29). She cites Robin Wood's description of the cross-cutting later in the film between Nina at the seashore and the shots of Nosferatu's ship and of Jonathan on horseback ("Dracula," 30).

28. Actually in the original German version of the film there is a double triangle—first there is the Jannings character, his wife, and Berta-Marie, who lures him away from his wife, and then there is Jannings, his mistress Berta-Marie, and Artinelli. It is only in the cut American version of the film that there is a simple triangle (in which Berta-Marie appears to be Jannings's wife). See Chapter 3 for more discussion of the two versions of this film.

29. For a very different reading of the "false" Maria, see Lungstrum, "*Metropolis.*"

30. Because of such self-reflexivity Elsaesser labels Weimar cinema as primarily an "art cinema" ("Film History," 65). Petro challenges this assertion, rejecting the (gendered) high art/popular culture dichotomy she sees underlying such an argument (*Joyless Streets,* 14–17). She emphasizes the melodramatic aspect of much Weimar cinema and its popular appeal—especially to women. While Petro is right about the melodramatic nature of much Weimar film, *including* Expressionist films, there was indeed a special sector of Weimar film production that does deserve the label "art cinema," as opposed to the overwhelming bulk of film production, devoted to entertainment films. While the privileged and well-funded art film sector did produce films that were melodramatic, it also produced films that are arguably self-reflexive—many art films would seem to be both. As Elsaesser makes clear in *Weimar Cinema and After,* however, the art film sector was no

counter-cinema, but rather an industrial strategy—and product—of the German studio system. This strategy was very much based on exploiting the high/low culture split for the purpose of legitimizing the film industry—indicating, again, a rather conservative ambivalence about modernity. See also Kaes, "Motor der Moderne," and Schlüpmann.

31. In this it seems to comment—openly, if perhaps a bit cynically—on the construction of the vamp as a male projection—as does *Metropolis*. This is in contrast to a conception of the vamp as some kind of fact of nature, which would seem to be the case in *Variety*. For a more detailed discussion of *The Blue Angel*, see Chapter 5. Another important Weimar art film focused on a vamp or "femme fatale" is G.W. Pabst's *Pandora's Box*, which I discuss in Chapter 6, in the section on Irmgard Keun's novel *The Artificial Silk Girl*.

32. In a 1981 essay, Mulvey herself attempted to deal with this problem. See "Afterthoughts."

33. Mulvey's writings of the mid- and late 1980s also critique the binarism of her earlier essays. See especially "Changes." Paul Coates speaks of the "fundamental ambisexuality" of the modern cinematic apparatus (64). (Mayne's essay on "Marlene Dietrich" also appears in her book *Framed* (2000).

34. Coates reads the vampire as anti-Semitic (95–96) but also notes the "implicit bisexuality" of the vampire (94). He sees this as part of the uncanny horror of the figure. Obviously, the two discourses can be seen in conjunction—the "feminized" or bisexual and "Semitic" monster, a figure in which homophobia, misogyny, and anti-Semitism are combined. This combination would not make for a positive, emancipatory type of "queer" reading, but the situation is further complicated by what Coates sees as the film's sympathetic fascination with the monster (96).

35. Hertha Thiele, who played Manuela in *Mädchen in Uniform*, makes this assertion about the popularity of the two films (40). *Mädchen in Uniform* is the story of Manuela, a schoolgirl who causes a stir in an oppressive Prussian boarding school for girls by openly declaring her love for her teacher, Fräulein von Bernburg; for a discussion of the film, see Chapter 5.

36. Cf. Mulvey, "Changes"; for a newer and more radical formulation of the importance of the actual social context of reception as against any ideological intentions of the film text, see Staiger's *Perverse Spectators*.

37. Mary Ann Doane, in her response to an earlier version of this chapter (see note 1, p. 178). It might also be asserted that the modern image of the vamp includes some of the (demonized) power associated with much older, archaic patriarchal images of "evil" female sexuality. Like the robot Maria in *Metropolis*, vamps also seem to possess a disruptive agency that exceeds commodification and is difficult for social forces to contain—for a more positive reading of this agency, not associated with the archaic but rather with technological modernity, see Janet Lungstrom's original reading of the robot in *Metropolis* (Lungstrom now writes under the name of Janet Ward). Jan

Wager also focuses on the agency of vamps and on its appeal to the desires of female spectators in her readings of such female characters in Weimar cinema and American film noir.

38. See also Barndt, who focuses on the reception of the "New Woman" among many other topics in her impressive dissertation.

39. See also Bridenthal and Koonz, "Beyond *Kinder, Küche, Kirche*," in Bridenthal et al., 41; Koonz, *Mothers in the Fatherland;* and Hausen's "Mother's Day in the Weimar Republic," in Bridenthal et al., 131–52.

40. On "separate spheres" and the delusions of conservative women about Nazism, see in Bridenthal et al., 17–20, and Bridenthal and Koonz, 41. See Koonz, *Mothers in the Fatherland,* for an in-depth study of these and other related issues.

41. On the history of the League of Jewish Women (*Der Jüdische Frauenbund*) within the larger bourgeois feminist organization, the League of German Women (*Bund Deutscher Frauen*), see Kaplan.

42. Angelika Rauch has suggested that even the image of the prostitute in Weimar modernism can be seen positively because of its power to deconstruct the aura of bourgeois femininity (86–87; I should stress that Rauch means the image and not the reality of the prostitute).

Chapter Three

1. "Was würde ein Chirurg taugen, dem vor Mitleid die Hand zittert? Ein gefühlvoller Arzt ist ein schlechter Arzt. Gott sei Dank sind Sie ja meist nur am Biertisch so zum Kotzen sentimental, Breslauer. Genau wie Ihr Kollege, dieser Chirurg—wie heißt er? . . . . Tüchtiger Mann. Kalt und nüchtern wie ein moderner Kühlschrank." Irmgard Keun, *Nach Mitternacht,* 83.

2. See Gleber, *The Art of Taking a Walk,* 31–35, on the illumination of urban streets and the relationship of this technical innovation to the increasing emphasis on the visual and the specular in modernity. Cf. Munby's remarks in his discussion of America in the 1920s, "Screening Crime," 19, and von Ankum, "Ich liebe Berlin," 377. See also Ward on the surfaces of Weimar urban culture, and how they were affected by electrification, advertising, design, and of course modern architecture, of which there were striking examples in Berlin, which had more than just shabby old facades. Indeed, there had already been removal of kitschy, late-nineteenth-century ornamentation from some of those old facades.

3. *Berlin, Symphony of a City* and *Asphalt* were only two of the most famous films that showed traffic and the daily rhythms of city in excess of its architectural facade, as well as nightlife—the former via documentary footage, the latter mostly in studio reconstruction of the street. See Erich Kettelhut, "Bauten für Joe Mays 'Asphalt'" ctd. in Bock and Töteberg, 249; see also Ward, 156–59.

4. On the "surgical gaze" in Ernst Jünger, see Lethen, *Verhaltenslehren* 187–89; cf. Theweleit, 222–23 and Sloterdijk, 817. For a more ironic take on "surgical objectivity," see the quote from Keun's *Nach Mitternacht* at the beginning of this chapter.

5. See, for example, Joan Landes, Nancy Fraser, Mary Ryan, and Geoff Eley, for their demonstration of the implicit role of gender in the original formation of the bourgeois public sphere. As many of these "revisionists" have asserted (e.g., Fraser, 112–18), access to that public sphere has always been limited, in spite (or because) of its universalist rhetoric, by the effective exclusion of the interests of those marginalized because of gender, class, ethnic, and sexual identities.

6. Like most terms used to characterize a cultural sensibility that is supposed to typify a wide variety of social, political, and artistic attitudes and endeavors during a particular era, there has been a good deal of debate on what if anything the term can justifiably be used to cover. See Lethen, *Neue Sachlichkeit* (1970), but cf. Lethen, *Verhaltenslehren* (1994); Willett, *Art and Politics* (1978); Petersen (1982); Lindner (1994); Becker (1995); Barndt (1999); and Ward (2001).

7. Lethen made the point that the construction of a democratic identity for West Germany in the 1950s was achieved by means of a selective identification with the Weimar Republic, especially with an idealized version of the stabilized period (*Neue Sachlichkeit*, 1). Certain typical attitudes of the post-World War II era (not just in West Germany, by the way)—the proclaimed "end of ideology" and the valorization of a "neutral," "value-free" technocracy—had definite parallels in the "New Objectivity" of the Weimar Republic.

The identification of the Federal Republic of the 1950s with the Stresemann era was made quite explicit by a 1957 West German film titled *Stresemann* (directed by Alfred Braun), seen at the time as an all too obvious glorification of Adenauer.

8. Postmodern because of this left/right confusion, because of its relation to consumer capitalism, because of its apparent (or temporary) renunciation of modernist manifestoes, and because of its proclaimed interest in undermining the high culture/mass culture dichotomy. Eric Rentschler has recently argued that there is much in the Third Reich's emphasis on entertainment and consumer culture that reminds one of conditions more recently labeled "postmodern" (*Ministry of Illusion*, 22–24); I would agree and point out that in this respect, the Third Reich was fostering some developments in consumer and mass culture that had become dominant in the 1920s.

9. Uncritical affirmation of New Objectivity—which would perhaps most clearly match a centrist "Fordism"—is very difficult to find. See Petersen, 472–74 and Roth. On the latter, note also Becker's assertion that Roth's "Schluß mit der Neuen Sachlichkeit" has been misinterpreted as signifying

the end of New Objectivity, when in fact the tendency continued, especially in literature (17).

10. See also von Saldern, 238–40 on a "German modernity" that cultural conservatives in Weimar opposed to Americanism and internationalist trends, and Sloterdijk on the "Fascist way into modernity" (English version, 453, German volume 2, 805).

11. According to Lindner, the common denominator for all these intellectuals was the influence of "Lebensphilosophie," or rather their grounding in the larger ideological tradition he calls "Lebensideologie"; for a discussion of the latter, see below.

12. See Lethen, 10–11; Schmied, "Neue Sachlichkeit and German Realism," 8–10; see also Schmied, Neue Sachlichkeit und Magischer Realismus.

13. On "free-floating intellectuals," ("freischwebende Intellektuellen"), see Lindner, 150; also Lindner, 50, for a discussion of Karl Mannheim's 1929 coinage of the term "freischwebende Intelligenz."

14. On Höch's use of photomontage—which had its origins not just in her engagement with Dada but also with the paid work she did on illustrated publications for the Ullstein Press—see Makholm, Makela, and Lavin.

15. This is not to say that their concept of a "proletarian" counter-public sphere is itself unproblematic; see Hansen, "Early Silent Cinema," 157 n. 22, 159. For a more in-depth (and more recent) evaluation, see Hansen's Foreword to the English translation of Negt and Kluge.

16. See Hake, "Chaplin Reception" on the reaction to Chaplin in Germany, which included Walter Benjamin's essay, "Rückblick auf Chaplin" (1929).

17. Cf. Kracauer's famous 1927 essay, "Ornament der Masse," ("Mass Ornament") and his later 1931 "Girls und Krise" ("Girls and Crisis").

18. Bathrick (130–36) provides an incisive analysis of Brecht's obsession with boxing, which is the conclusion to his article on boxing as icon in Weimar culture. Note also Brecht's "Elephantenkalb: Ein Zwischenspiel für das Foyer," written in connection with his 1925 play Mann ist Mann, in which smoking by the audience is encouraged (87) and boxing is recommended as the solution to the unsatisfactory ending of the short play (99).

19. In the cinema there was of course the famous genre of "mountain films"; see Rentschler, "Mountains and Modernity," for a differentiated discussion of the ideological implications of the genre—at least in the beginning it was not as unambiguously "anti-modern" or even right wing as has often been asserted (most notably by the postwar Kracauer of From Caligari to Hitler).

20. "700 Intellektuelle beten einen Öltank an." Gesammelte Werke (Frankfurt: Suhrkamp, 1967), v. 8, 316; also cited in Lethen, Neue Sachlichkeit, 59–60.

21. The news of Hiroshima led Brecht to revise his play Galileo as part of a general re-evaluation of the role of modern science.

22. One can of course relativize this verdict simply by emphasizing the Tiller Girls, who were so prominent a symbol of the era, especially for Kracauer.

See his "Ornament" and "Girls." And of course, the Tiller Girls were a fairly athletic act and a relatively de-eroticized spectacle on the Weimar stage (certainly compared to the static nude tableaux), as Jelavich points out (175–86).

23. See Willett, *The Weimar Years,* 30, 53, and compare Walter Gropius's 1926 design for the Törten housing project to Erich Mendelsohn's 1920 "Einstein Tower" in Potsdam. The latter is indeed "phallic," but in an obvious "organic" way that rectilinear designs—even for skyscrapers—disavow (as representations of male power with no concessions to "soft" organic reality).

24. Lethen's idea that the seventeenth-century "cold" masquerade needed the corrective of eighteenth-century humanism, involving the French stipulation that rationality be "moralized" by taking into account the "feminine" (e.g., Lethen *Verhaltenslehren,* 14) seems woefully inadequate, in addition to being an intellectual-historian's conceit completely uninformed by feminism. More productively Lethen points out that there was something like a "feminine masquerade" as well in New Objectivity, one that provocatively undermined the masculine confidence about fixed gender roles (242).

25. A literal translation of "Lebensideologie" would be "life-ideology," which is not especially evocative. "Vitalist ideology" is better, because vitalism was a part of the larger system Lindner discusses, but only a part: vitalism along with "Lebensphilosophie" ("life-philosophy") make up only two small parts of a much larger whole (cf. Lindner, 121–22).

26. Cf. Peukert's definition of the term "klassische Moderne" (11–12).

27. Lindner asserts that it was primarily in literary and literary-critical writing, and not in systematic philosophical writing, that the amorphous "Lebensideologie" is developed (1), and this in my opinion he demonstrates persuasively. Yet his approach remains primarily that of an intellectual historian, and he develops a very systematic analysis of the ideology in question that is perhaps too neat. He also constructs this ideological field as an almost exclusively German one, which given all the international cross-influences on European intellectuals seems somewhat unlikely.

28. Cf. Lindner, 129–44, 152; also Bathrick, 123.

29. As Lindner (152) remarks, the generation whose battle cry had been "youth," or "Jugend"—and many of whose members had belonged to the so-called youth movement of the first two decades of the twentieth century—was now no longer so young, and thus it is not surprising that there was now a reevaluation of youth as a transitional stage in the process of maturation. On the "youth movement," see also Mosse. See also Lindner, 175, on the "masculine character" of New Objectivity.

30. Willet does not ignore important women artists like Hanna Höch and Käthe Kollwitz—or indeed the influential activity of women artists in the Soviet Union—yet by stressing the war without taking gender into account

Willett ends up with another version of the common masculinist narrative about Weimar.

31. At a conference at Hollins College in Virginia on Weimar film (March 1996), Anton Kaes asserted that Weimar cinema can be read as a (not necessarily conscious) attempt to deal with the trauma of World War I. Given the huge numbers of German dead and wounded and the omnipresence of the wounded in postwar society, it is clear that any discussion of "male crisis" in Weimar must take this into account. Cf. Rickels and Sloterdijk (v. 2, 791–814; English version, 443–59).

32. In 1919 General von Hindenburg used this formulation in testimony, ascribing the original idea (that Germany had been "stabbed in the back") to an English general (cited in Kaes, Jay, and Dimendberg, 15–16). See also Wolfradt in Kaes, Jay, and Dimendberg, 17–18.

33. See Maria Tatar's comments on male resentment of women in the wake of the lost war (11–12), in her discussion of the historical context for the misogyny evident in the German fascination with "Lustmord" (sexual murder), which is the theme of so much popular and "high" culture of the 1910s and 1920s. Tatar's book explores this theme in painting, literature, and film; the idea was first suggested by Beth Irwin Lewis in an article focused primarily on one form of "high culture": painting. Lewis wanted to call attention to what had received almost no attention: the striking gender dynamics of the (well-known) paintings of sexual murders by George Grosz and Otto Dix.

34. Cf. also Fehrenbach, *Cinema,* 30. On the genesis in pre-1918 German cinema of the "Autorenkino," as art film production has often been labeled in German, see Schlüpmann, 247–51.

35. See again Elsaesser, *Weimar Cinema and After,* 3, on the incorrect labeling of Weimar cinema. The first art films produced in the Weimar Republic were not "Expressionist" at all but rather (pace Eisner) the big-budget historical epics/costume melodramas of Ernst Lubitsch: *Madame du Barry* (1919), released in 1920 as *Passion* in the United States, the first German film to be shown in the United States after World War I; and *Anna Boleyn* (1920), released in the United States as *Deception.* Both were big successes in the United States, where Lubitsch was called "the German Griffith" (ctd. in Hake, *Passions,* 122). He would of course soon (in 1922) accept an offer from Hollywood.

36. Of course, there was also a German melodramatic tradition; certainly one notes this in the "Kammerspiel" films of the early 1920s—and indeed in German film Expressionism proper, as Petro has demonstrated. This tradition also has roots in German theatrical Naturalism—and even earlier in the *bürgerliches Trauerspiel* (bourgeois tragedy) of the late eighteenth and nineteenth centuries.

37. On the "Kulturfilm," see Zglinicki (551–82) on the relationship of these conservative but nonetheless sometimes racy "educational films" to the "Aufklärungsfilm" ("enlightenment" film —meaning sexual enlightenment/education) of the early Weimar Republic. The latter, which helped bring on the first censorship laws of the republic, dealt with sexual enlightenment in sometimes more, sometimes less sensationalized ways. Cf. Bock and Töteberg on the 1925 Ufa "Kulturfilm" *Wege der Kraft und Schönheit* (152–55).

38. For an excellent discussion of the relationship of the New Woman to New Objectivity, see Barndt. She examines the former as a discursive phenomenon in the literary marketplace, and finds that it was by no means solely a symptom of modernity or a mere product of the "culture industry," but rather also represented a site at which women negotiated their own desires and anxieties with regard to modernity.

39. Of course this violence against women, while quite explicit in some painting and literature, is not as evident in the films of the era.

40. See the Hertha Thiele interview—and the discussion of *Mädchen in Uniform* in Chapter 6 below.

41. Another woman filmmaker in the middle and late Weimar years was Lotte Reiniger, famous for her experimental animated films. In early Weimar and especially in the late Wilhelminian era (before the film industry got too concentrated), there were more women directors—the actor/director Fern Andra was one of the most prolific. See Knight, 2–3.

42. On *The Blue Light,* see Rentschler, *Ministry of Illusion,* 27–51, and Schulte-Sasse, "Leni Riefenstahl's Feature Films."

43. Keun is discussed in Chapter 6; see also von Ankum, Kosta, Gleber, Barndt, Horsley, Rosenstein, among many excellent discussions of this writer that have appeared recently, as well as Vibeke Petersen's new book with Berghahn Press. See also the dissertations by Kautz, Sopcak, and Drescher.

44. See Koonz on the conservative women's attraction to "separate sphere" as propagated on Right (and by Nazis). One should also note the success of Riefenstahl and Mary Wigman, two artists who were, or at any rate became "reactionary modernists." Wigman was one of the main exponents of "Expressionist dance," or "Ausdruckstanz," and before acting in, let alone directing, mountain films, Riefenstahl had danced in Wigman's troupe. Both of these modernist artists were able to accommodate the shift toward a more romantic, essentialist (and reactionary) ideal of female identity—and to enjoy success in the Third Reich. On Wigman see Manning and Norton.

45. On the ruthless trivialization of female characters in the cinema of the Third Reich, see Gleber, "'Only Man.'" Cf. also Rentschler, qtd. in Fehrenbach, 48; there is of course extensive treatment of gender in his *Ministry of Illusion.* But see also Grossmann's "*Girlkultur*" about continuities as well as

breaks in National Socialist policy with regard to "rationalized" womanhood (76–77).

46. Cf. Rosenhaft "Lesewut," 119–21; note also Barndt's discussion of "das
Gutgemacht-Mittlere" in the era of New Objectivity (e.g., 30–69) in which
she insists on the emancipatory potential of a type of literary culture that
bridged the high vs. low culture dichotomy. Although this may have been
co-opted in the Third Reich, it is not of necessity "fascist," she asserts—persuasively, in my opinion. She also maintains that while some popular literature of the Weimar Republic was indeed "völkisch," this was by no means
the case for all of it. The situation was much more complex (44–45).

Chapter Four

1. "Hier schnitt sich die Nation auf Befehl zielsicher die Geschlechtsteile
ab . . . ." Franz Schauwecker, *Aufbruch der Nation* (1928), ctd. in Sloterdijk,
vol. 2, 758, my translation; cf. English version of Sloterdijk, 420.

2. See, e.g., Lethen, *Verhaltenslehren*, 95.

3. He hanged himself in his room at the Mayflower Hotel in New York on
May 22, 1939, a few days after Franco's triumphal parade in Madrid at the
end of the Spanish Civil War. Toller had spent much of his last years in
political activity on behalf of the international campaign in solidarity with
the Republican, anti-fascist forces in Spain, which Franco, with the support
of Hitler and Mussolini, defeated.

4. That this rebellion was more than a mere literary or cinematic motif is
made clear by the story of Otto Gross, a renegade psychoanalyst and writer.
This "rebellious son" was committed to an asylum by his authoritarian
father, the Austrian criminologist Hans Gross, with the help of the psychoanalyst Carl Jung and the Prussian and Austrian authorities, an affair that
became a *cause celebre* of avant-garde artists and intellectuals in 1913. See
Bathrick, "Speaking the Other's Silence," and Donahue.

5. See Frühwald, 87; see also Sokel (ctd. in Cafferty, n. 3, 57), who sees *Hinkemann* as marking a shift (or progression) to "Aristotelian" drama..

6. Kaes proposed this at a conference on Weimar cinema at Hollins College,
Virginia, in March 1996.

7. The German word *Rat* (plural: *Räte*) and the Russian word *Soviet* both
mean council, and in this context they refer specifically to worker-council.
It was to these councils that power was ideally supposed to be given as part
of a socialist revolution.

8. Act, scene, and page numbers refer to the 1971 Reclam edition of Toller's
Hinkemann, which is based on the second 1924 version, which Frühwald
calls "1924/II" (57).

9. This more pessimistic ending was eerily prophetic of Toller's own death by
hanging in 1939. Suicide was a longstanding concern of Toller's, apparently;

he dedicated his 1933 biography, published in exile, to his nephew, who had committed suicide at 18 in 1928 (*Eine Jugend,* v).

10. See Frühwald and Spalek, 142–43, on the various titles, from the earliest published sketches of 1922 to the performances of 1923 and 1924. On the reception of the play, see same, 142–55; also Frühwald, 57–70, and (in the latter's "Nachwort") 89–93. Toller's letter to the director of Deutsches Theater in Berlin in late 1923 asserting that the allegorical interpretation was false, cited both by Frühwald (57) and Cafferty (48), can be found in his *Briefe,* 152.

11. Original German: "Mich drückt die Maschine nicht. Ich bin der Herr und nicht die Maschine. Wenn ich an der Maschine stehe, packts mich mit Teufelslust: Du mußt den Knecht da fühlen lassen, daß du der Herr bist! Und dann treibe ich das heulende und surrende und stöhnende Ding bis zur äußersten Kraftleistung, daß es Blut schwitzt . . . sozusagen . . . und ich lache und freue mich, wie es sich so quält und abrackert. So mein Tierchen, rufe ich, du mußt gehorchen! Gehorchen! Und das wildeste Stück Holz laß ich die Maschine verschlingen und laß es sie formen nach meinem Befehl! Sei ein Mann, Eugen, dann bist du der Herr."

12. Theweleit has of course elucidated the concept of the male body-armor; see also Lethen's remarks on Jünger, e.g., *Verhaltenslehren,* 202.

13. See, e.g., "Dramaturgie der Beschämung," Lethen, *Verhaltenslehren,* 23–26, also 38.

14. See above, Chapter 3.

15. Also in that play, castration is a motif, in the scene where the doctor proudly displays the amputees with artificial limbs to whom he has also restored "reproductive capacity" ("Fortpflanzungsmöglichkeit").

16. This may have had something to do with the strong desire of many German and Austrian Jews (including Toller himself) to enlist in World War I: to prove both their patriotism and their "manhood," elements essential to a complete German national identity that was denied them. On Jews as "feminized," see, e.g., Mosse.

17. See, e.g., Willibrand (16). This American critic, writing in 1941, develops a Christian, anti-Communist interpretation of Toller's life and works that seems itself to be somewhat grounded in a subtle, Christian anti-Semitism.

18. Heide Schlüpmann believes that early German cinema, especially before 1914, was more subversive in terms of sexual politics than German cinema in later periods.

19. Anton Kaes has stressed that much of Weimar cinema can be read as an attempt to work through the trauma of World War I, and that indeed much of the depicted trauma in the cinema is an unconscious representation of shell shock (e.g., in his talk at Hollins College, March 1996). This suggests a reading of *Variety* that I will not pursue in greater depth here, but I want nonetheless to remark that such a reading would indeed fit the narrative frame of *Variety* uncannily: Boss has spent ten silent years in prison before

he can talk about his traumatic experience; thus, in 1925 (assuming that the "present" in the frame of the story refers to the year in which the film appeared), Boss has been "imprisoned" in trauma since 1915.

20. The discussion of social mobility in Weimar cinema is indebted to Thomas Elsaesser, who began discussing this topic in his 1982 essay, "Social Mobility and the Fantastic." See also his new book, *Weimar Cinema and After.*

21. Ufa's material for *Variety* in the *Illustrierter Film-Kurier* no. 378 (1925)—uses the phrase "Nach Motiven des Felix Holländerschen Romans 'Der Eid des Stefan Huller.'" The motifs on which the film is based are contained in the very beginning of the novel, which focuses not primarily on the story of the cuckolded circus performer but rather that of his son, who grows up haunted both by his father's crime—the murder of his mother's lover—and his father's subsequent suicide. The novel too is about upward mobility, but the son's more successful version is solidly bourgeois. The sexual politics are interesting, because the son grows into a man enlightened enough to forgive his wife's one sexual "transgression."

 The 1927 American translation of Holländer's novel, titled *The Sins of the Fathers,* was no doubt occasioned by the film's success in the United States.

22. At just about the same time, production was beginning for Fritz Lang's *Metropolis,* which Pommer also produced. Whereas *Variety* succeeded at the box office in Germany and America, Lang's epic film would result in a monumental financial disaster that bankrupted Ufa and in many ways killed the big-budget art film; it also caused Pommer to leave Ufa and go to Hollywood for his first stint as a producer there. Upon his return to Germany to work for Hugenberg's Ufa in the late 1920s, the second phase of his career as a producer began, in which he would attempt a more American style of film production (Saunders, 248–49). This resulted among other things in the development of the German musical (or operetta film) in the early sound cinema. On Pommer's career, see Hardt, Jacobsen, and Elsaesser (*Weimar Cinema and After*).

23. On the genesis of the "Autorenfilm" in the 1910s, see Diederichs.

24. Esser gives a great deal of credit for the film's artistic quality to Dupont (165), as does Eisner (278–84), but I think Combs may be correct in his assertion that Dupont seems merely to have been at the right place at the right time to make this film, which is his most famous and most successful.

25. See the 1926 German report from Los Angeles by Reda on the "American" version, as well as the 1926 article, "*Varieté* in 2 Fassungen," which reports that both the "German" and "American" versions were shown in Chicago. Gerstein and Hall (of the *New York Times*) saw the "German" version in New York; Gerstein comments on rumors that (accurately) predict how the film will be cut for more prudish areas of the United States.

 It might be asked why Famous Players Lasky would cut the film this way in 1926, when a film like *The Blue Angel* in 1930 would not have problems with such pre-emptive censorship. One possible reason for this difference was that by the early 1930s Hollywood was much more willing to take risks, struggling to make money in the Depression with the production of sound films, which was more expensive. This was a time of many "excesses," which in turn led to the much stricter enforcement of self-censorship via the Hays Code beginning in mid-1934 (on "pre-Code" Hollywood, see, e.g., LaSalle) . Also significant, as Gertrud Koch reminds us (70), is the fact that *The Blue Angel* wasn't as popular in the United States as it was in Germany, and indeed its Hollywood distributors did not even release it in the United States until after the success of von Sternberg's first American film with *Morocco* (1930), which is what first made Dietrich famous in the States—not *The Blue Angel.*

26. Indeed, there are other versions besides the two I discuss here—the version at the Deutsche Institut für Film in Frankfurt is an Italian version more or less the same as the original, except that it does not use the prison sequences to frame the main flashback. Instead it has them together at the end of the film, thus eliminating the flashback and creating a narrative entirely linear in its chronological progression. This situation reminds us how much artistic "autonomy" counted for in the international marketing of silent films during the 1920s—even for the so-called "art films" of the German film industry. The most famous example is of course Fritz Lang's *Metropolis;* its American distributors authorized massive cuts and re-editing for the American audience, and its German producers agreed that the new version was more marketable and then released basically the same version in Germany. The original version is completely lost today. Such conditions create a situation for researchers today studying films produced in the 1920s that I imagine is somewhat comparable to what scholars studying medieval manuscripts face.

27. Eisner calls it "Impressionism" (282), stressing the fluidity of the boundary between subjective impressions of the external world and the externalized expressions of internal, subjective reality. Kracauer makes a similar point in contrasting *The Last Laugh*'s use of mobile and subjective camera to depict the doorman's internal reality to *Variety*'s use of the same techniques to "penetrate" external reality (*Caligari*, 127). In fact, both films use these techniques ultimately in the service of narrative realism and of enhancing identification with the protagonists—and these techniques (albeit in a more restrained fashion and limited to certain genres) will become part of the repertoire of classical narrative cinema as surely as Freund will end up as a cinematographer in Hollywood.

28. Many film historians, more or less following Eisner, consider all German art cinema of the Weimar Republic to be "expressionist." Obviously this is partly a question of definitions. Nonetheless, of the stylistic techniques often associated with "German expressionism" in the cinema, only the

emphasis on excessive or exotic mise-en-scene and the chiaroscuro lighting techniques (the famous expressive use of shadows) actually date from the period in the early 1920s when there was an attempt to adapt Expressionism for the cinema. Other techniques such as the mobile camera, optical print-ing and other special montage effects date from the mid-1920s and are arguably more a part of the "New Objective"/futurist/constructivist cele-bration of technology than Expressionist interiority. See Chapter 3 above for more discussion of the contrasts (and underlying similarities) between Expressionism and New Objectivity.

29. See, e.g., "Der dokumentarische Impuls: literarische Formen der 'Neuen Sachlichkeit,'" in Kaes, *Weimarer Republik,* 319–345.

30. The first cinematic productions ever screened in Germany were made by the Skladanowksy brothers and shown in the fall of 1895 in Berlin's Win-tergarten, and the films they exhibited depicted—appropriately enough—variety acts. On the Wintergarten's development into a hall that became devoted especially to the increasingly popular variety shows in the late 1880s, see Jelavich, 21–22.

31. Their choreographed routines were bemoaned by German intellectuals as the epitome of American mechanization. See Kaes, *Weimarer Republik*, n. 5, 242 ; also Kracauer, "Ornament der Masse" and "Girls und Krise." On the Tiller Girls specifically, see Jelavich, 175–86.

32. Melodrama, of course, had long played a role in German film, including the art film; melodrama can be found in Expressionist films and "chamber play" films, as Petro's *Joyless Streets* stresses. At one point, however, Petro aligns melodrama with American films—contrasting "American melodrama" with German Expressionism (218). While the melodramatic style of American cinema was influential, melodrama had already had a long history in Ger-many; it is arguably already to be found within the German "bourgeois tragedy" of the eighteenth century.

33. This is indeed a fair summary of the plot of Karl Grune's *The Street,* the 1923 film Kracauer cites as the prototype of the genre (*Caligari,* 125); Petro problematizes the genre in her discussion of Bruno Rahn's film *Dirnen-tragödie* (1927), 160–64. Miriam Hansen has commented how Kracauer continually used Grune's film to make larger (and quite different) arguments from the mid-1920s into the period after 1945 ("Decentric Perspectives").

34. Outside of some documentary footage of the city in the impressive mon-tage at the beginning of *The Street,* it is predominantly a studio film.

35. In the American version, Boss's "friends" petition for clemency.

36. According to the film's censorship cards, this is one of the few scenes where the censors demanded some cuts—during de Putti's belly dance (the inter-title calls it "Der fremde Zauber"). There were only 5 cuts demanded, 4 of which were in the Hamburg sequence, all involving Berta-Marie's body—including a close-up of her abdomen in the belly dance scene; the last

instance of cut footage occurs at the end of the knife fight, when apparently the dead Artinelli was shown next to a bloody knife.

37. Cited in Ufa's program for the film's premiere at the Ufa-Palast am Zoo, 16 November 1925.

38. In her reading of the film, Jan Wager focuses on the agency and power the film grants Berta-Marie as a femme fatale. While not denying that the film is male-centered, she stresses that this power, in its potential address to female desires, might well have been read differently by female spectators (Wagers, 36–51). This is a persuasive argument, although I would maintain that the film's narrative as a whole works against this effect.

39. Wager (41–43) suggests such a reading. Her discussion of the two male characters in terms of their desirability to female spectators is very nuanced and complex.

40. I am thinking of anti-French stereotypes in films like *The Old and the Young King* (Hans Steinhoff, 1935) as well as *Fräulein von Barnhelm* (Hans Schweikart, 1940), similar in many ways to the anti-Semitic traits embodied in the title role of *Jew Suess* (Veit Harlan, 1940).

41. I place the term "feminization" in quotes to stress again that the term has no "essential" validity and to underscore my conviction that it is an ideological term within patriarchal belief systems—to mean simply any deviation from some ideal valorization of "masculinity," that is, anything marked as less important, less powerful, less valuable than a certain ideal construction of masculinity. The psychoanalytical term with the same basic meaning would be "castration." The idealized ("uncastrated") concept of masculinity, certainly in Weimar, is almost always misogynistic, but it can also be seen as "männerfeindlich," that is, anti-male, in the sense that patriarchal constructions of masculinity are ultimately inimical to actual male human beings. Ultimately these constructions of "masculinity" and "femininity" are complementary parts of one (oppressive) system.

42. See, e.g., the chapter on "Mass Culture as Woman" in Huyssen's *After the Great Divide* (44–62).

43. Cf. Rosenhaft, "Lesewut," 140, on how for men (in this case working-class men) being the object of the gaze is destabilizing—all the more so when the gaze in question is that of a woman.

44. Many in the audience in the Wintergarten are actually depicted as wealthy, and thus their desiring gazes (at Berta-Marie, Boss, and Artinelli) are actually less "vulgar" than "decadent"—but they are clearly marked as negative by means of a reactionary populism according to which upward mobility is earned by catering to the illicit desires of the decadent.

45. Again, this is all the more interesting now that we know, according to Miriam Hansen, that Kracauer was gay (173).

46. At least this is the case at the level of the ideology of the film text itself. One might, however, speculate as to whether the film's popularity in Ger-

many and America might imply a reaction on the part of what Janet Staiger calls "perverse spectators"—a popular reception at odds with the apparently intentional conservatism of the text itself. To pursue such a reading, however, would demand more empirical evidence about the film's reception.

47. Original: "An die Ehemänner,—welche besonders in dieser Hinsicht Führer ihrer Gattinnen sein müssen—weil es ihnen häufig nicht nur an den richtigen Führer-Eigenschaften gebricht, sondern sogar an den Qualitäten eines guten Partners. Sie haben von ihren Unvollkommenheiten keine Ahnung."

48. See, e.g., Zglinicki, 580–81, and the reviews in *Der Film, Die Filmwoche,* and the *8 Uhr Abendblatt.*

49. On the "Kulturfilm" and its relationship to earlier "Aufklärungsfilme" ("enlightenment films"), see Zglinicki (e.g., 579–80); he maintains that such educational films often mobilized the same interest in erotic subjects on the part of the public that earlier had been satisfied by "Aufklärungsfilme," while at the same enjoying a veneer of cultural legitimacy that the earlier genre had never achieved, in spite of its pretension to "enlightenment." See also Töteberg and Dyer (25–26) on Ufa's 1925 *Kulturfilm, Wege zur Kraft und Schönheit (Ways to Power and Beauty).*

50. The background of the film's production is well documented in Atwell and Friedberg, who focuses in detail on the interaction between figures in the psychoanalytical community: Freud was against the film, but Abraham and Sachs were involved in the film project as consultants. She also indicates the limitations of Atwell's exclusive focus on the English version of the film by comparing the two exhaustively (n. 28, 246). Her synopsis is very thorough, more so than the one I provide here. I have only two relatively minor disagreements with her synopsis. First, it is the husband, not the wife, who tries at the beginning of the film to initiate a kiss (cf. Friedberg, 46). Second, the husband is able to use the letter opener in his lab the first day (i.e., before the dream); only on the second day is he unable to use it and instead must use his hands to open a letter (cf. Friedberg, 47). Her central arguments about excess and spectator positioning in the film are persuasive.

51. See also Friedberg, n. 21, 245. Colin Ross was famous for his travel documentaries in the 1920s, both as books and as films. He represents the more conservative wing of the "documentary" trend of New Objectivity; in the Third Reich he would work for the state. See Plonien. Interestingly enough, Ross appears in a pith helmet in his own travel documentary of 1925, *Mit dem Kurbelkasten um die Welt*—just as the cousin in *Secrets of A Soul,* of whom the film's protagonist is jealous. This is an interesting conflation of dreams about phallic potency with the trappings of colonial power.

52. On the film's reception, see note 48 above.

53. Friedberg makes the point that his career thus took him from "Caligari to Freud" (45). But since he would continue acting in the Third Reich, including his portrayal of a number of Jewish roles in Veit Harlan's notori-

ously anti-Semitic film *Jew Suess* (*Jud Süß,* 1940), his career really does demand Kracauer's phrase "From Caligari to Hitler."

54. Atwell, in true auteurist fashion, while mentioning the others involved, seems to give all the credit for the dream sequence to Pabst, as Lotte Eisner did before him (31). Friedberg makes the same point about Eisner (n. 34, 246) and also notes that Atwell dates Pabst's involvement in the film earlier than is accurate, implying that he was a collaborator on the screenplay (n. 21, 245).

55. During his psychoanalysis he recounts the dream, and the tower is shown again. When the psychoanalyst asks him to identify the women, the memories that are then recreated seem to imply that the three women are his wife, the lab assistant, and the other woman in the lab who had exchanged glances with the assistant in his lab (that is, the mother of the child to whom the protagonist gave candy). But the three women actually depicted "in the bells" do not include this last woman; the third woman depicted is his maid.

56. Friedberg notes that "Orth" means in Greek "the correction of deformities," as in "orthodontia" (n. 25, 245–46). It is of course also an older spelling of a German word meaning "place" or "location," and Orth's office becomes the site at which memory and dream images are recalled and analyzed. In any case, Friedberg's assertion that the doctor remains unnamed in the German version of the film is not correct; he is unnamed in the credits (as are all the characters), but in the intertitles he is identified as "Herr Dr. Orth" by one of the staff at the club.

57. For instance, the many superimpositions that required use of the optical printer (or if Atwell is correct, appear to result from optical printing but were actually done in the camera: 42). One example would be one of the train images, in which two variously distorted trains appear, over which an enlarged image of the cousin appears, apparently "riding" one of them, and waving at the protagonist, who in countershots appears trapped behind a crossing gate. As for the scenes that have been re-staged—Friedberg's article contains a photo that documents the restaging of one of them (the man shaving his wife's neck: 50)—it is important to note that there are at times significant differences between an image as it first appears and as it is restaged later, during the analysis. For example, during the scene early in the film in which the main character offers candy to a child, the child's mother and the man's female lab assistant exchange glances. While it is unclear what this exchange might mean when it is first shown (indeed, it is unclear whether or not the protagonist even noticed it—or could have noticed it), in its restaging, shown as a memory apparently recounted to the psychoanalyst, the women are clearly sneering at him. Thus, regardless of what the glances may originally have meant, it is clear that the protagonist remembers them as insults to his masculinity—hitting him "at his weakest point," as the analyst responds.

58. See Friedberg (42–45). Pavsek connects this to the "Bilderverbot," the Biblical prohibition against image-making one notes in the thinking of Freud and other Jewish intellectuals—notably Adorno.

59. Eisner, as befits a critic who valorizes the Expressionist cinema, criticizes it for being "superficial" (i.e., in its use of psychoanalysis, 295).

60. Original: "der . . . zum willenlosen Sklaven seiner Ur-Instinkte wird."

61. In fairness to Pabst, one must probably add that in his case the gaze was much less "surgically" cold and much more open about its voyeuristic fascination with the "others" it surveyed.

62. See Lethen on the "magical" aspect of the word "armor" in Weimar culture and for his discussion of related concepts in Otto Rank, Wilhelm Reich, and Alfred Adler (*Verhaltenslehren,* 202–04).

63. Again, if Kracauer was gay (cf. Hansen, "America, Paris . . . ," 173), why did he, at least in his famous postwar book on Weimar cinema, condemn any signs of "effeminate" decadence and weakness in the Weimar Republic and make them seem at least in part to blame for the triumph of Nazism?

64. On the Mitscherlichs and others involved in this problematic interpretation, see Linville, *Feminism,* e.g., 3–5; also her "Retrieving History," n. 10, 457. See also Hewitt's discussion of the conflation of narcissism, male homosexuality, and fascism in much post-1945 discourse, including some important works by the Frankfurt School, 1–78.

65. Original: "daß alle erotischen Symbole—Geburtswasser, Gebärmutter, phallische und vaginale Bilder u.a.—in diesem Film sichtbar enthalten waren, aber nicht gedeutet werden durften . . . ."

66. Rickels goes on to provide evidence in support of his main argument: that the fear of homosexuality "breaking out" and disturbing the homosocial harmony of the military unit motivated German psychology under the Nazis to experiment with "cures" for homosexuality. These cures included ideas that originated in Freud's work on shell shock and other traumas of the soldiers in World War I—paradoxically enough, given the Nazi view of the "Jewish" science.

Chapter Five

1. Maria Riva, in her 1992 biography of her mother, *Marlene Dietrich,* 419.

2. *Fabian,* 21; all further references in text. Original: "'Hält sich Ihre Gattin einen männlichen Harem? Mein Name ist Fabian.'

. . . . Fabian setzte sich. Irene Moll rutschte auf die Armlehne, streichelte ihn und sagte zu ihrem Mann. 'Wenn er gefällt dir nicht, brech ich den Kontrakt.' 'Aber er gefällt mir ja,' antwortete der Rechtsanwalt. 'Sie reden über mich, als wär ich ein Stück Streuselkuchen oder ein Rodelschlitten,' meinte Fabian. 'Ein Rodelschlitten bist du, mein Kleiner!' rief die Frau und preßte seinen Kopf gegen ihre volle, schwarz vergitterte Brust.'

3. Original: "Nein", sagte er, "ich fahre zu meiner Mutter."
   "Du verdammter Esel", flüsterte sie ärgerlich. "Soll ich vor dir niederknien und dir eine Liebeserklärung machen? Ist dir eine dumme Gans lieber? Ich habe es satt, nach der ersten besten Hose zu greifen. Du gefällst mir. Wir begegnen uns immer wieder. Das kann kein Zufall sein." Sie faßte seine Hand und streichelte seine Finger. "Ich bitte dich, komm mit."

4. E.g., Christa Anita Brück's novel *Schicksale hinter Schreibmaschinen (Destinies Behind Typewriters,* 1930). For a discussion of this novel, see e.g. Kautz.

5. For an overview of nightlife in Weimar Berlin, from glamorous revues, to Bohemian cabarets, and cheaper nightclubs (*Tingeltangel*) and bars, and the overlap between these various venues, see Jelavich, especially Chapters 5, 6, and 7. Jelavich (197–98; n. 17, 305) points out that one particularly sadistic "cabaret" visited by Fabian and Labuse in Kästner's novel, "Das Kabarett der Anonymen," was actually the "Kabarett des Namenlosen" ("Cabaret of the Nameless One") in Berlin; this latter name was also the title of an article by Kästner in the *Magdeburger General-Anzeiger* in 1929. In *Fabian* (see 67–76), Kästner changes the name of the actual owner, Elow (Erwin Lowinsky), to Caligula. (Jürgs notes that much in the novel consists of re-worked newspaper articles by Kästner: 199; n. 15, 210.)

6. Original: "Verein unchristlicher junger Männer," which, at the most obvious level, is probably just a play on the German term for the YMCA: "Der Verein christlicher junger Männer." Nonetheless, given the anti-Semitism of the times, one wonders about other connotations. The disparaging remarks about Russian and Hungarian Jews (99) are more explicit. One then begins to suspect descriptions such as the following from Fabian's dream: "Sitting at other tables were fat men, half-naked, hairy as gorillas, with top hats . . . ("An anderen Tischen saßen dicke Männer, halbnackt, behaart wie Gorillas, mit Zylindern . . ."; 149). By the standard of his day, Kästner was no anti-Semite; indeed, according to Wagener (13), the actual model for the character Labude was Kästner's Jewish friend Ralph Zucker. But the novel itself—especially in these passages—does not make the author's position with regard to anti-Semitism so clear.

7. In the English translation of Sloterdijk: 519–20.

8. Cf. Keun's *The Artificial Silk Girl (Das kunstseidene Mädchen)*: the main character Doris finds that men want to borrow money from her: 18–19, 41. The latter instance is with Hubert, her first lover. What makes Doris want to vomit, however, is not that he asks her for money, but rather his obvious disappointment when he learns that she has nothing, too, even though she has offered to stay with him and combine their efforts to survive.

9. This is an interesting reproach: the woman who symbolizes for Fabian "masculinized" sexual aggression accuses him of passivity with a metaphor that alludes to consumerism—and to consumers who in the popular mind were women.

10. To criticize this dynamic within *Fabian* is not to criticize Kästner for writing so many novels for children, which according to Last has condemned Kästner to critical neglect. I do not support any such "high culture" discrimination against children's literature, but I also cannot take any of Kästner's children's literature into account for this book.

11. This epilogue was written in 1931 but cut by the publisher; it was then published in the journal *Die Weltbühne*. Titled "Fabian und die Sittenrichter" ("Fabian and the Moral Judges"), it is appended to the edition of *Fabian* I used.

12. Original: Cornelia says: "Sogar der Mond scheint in dieser Stadt." Fabian replies, "Ist es nicht fast wie zu Hause?" Then he corrects her: "Aber Sie täuschen sich" (98).

13. Labude relates another anecdote in the text that bears some relation to incest, or anyway one that describes an odd and potentially somewhat incestuous situation (with an Oedipal twist). He tells of meeting an attractive young actress at a party who seemed to want to seduce him, and then learning over the course of their conversation that she is being kept by his father, a realization that causes him to flee (77–78). This bit of information about his father is introduced as follows: "The most he knew about his father he had learned once from a young actress" ("Das Meiste, was er über den Vater wußte, hatte er einmal von einer jungen Schauspielerin erfahren," 77).

14. Original: "Im Osten residiert das Verbrechen, im Zentrum die Gaunerei, im Norden das Elend, im Westen die Unzucht, und in allen Himmelsrichtungen wohnt der Untergang."

15. Original: Fabian: "Ich fürchte, die Dummheit." Cornelia: "In der Stadt, aus der ich bin, ist die Dummheit schon eingetroffen."

16. Indeed, if Lindner is correct, all of these positions—as well as the sensibility of New Objectivity itself—are subsumed within *Lebensideologie*, at least for bourgeois German intellectuals.

17. Only in the apparent celebration of "Lustmord" in Weimar paintings discussed by Beth Irwin Lewis and Maria Tatar is there no social critique—yet of course there is an implicit critique of modern women in these paintings, or at any rate evidence of very violent and defensive aversion to modern women.

18. See also Jürg's discussion of the presence of sentimentality in both *Fabian* and New Objectivity (207–09). Compare Klotz and Lethen: whereas for Klotz the critical perspective in *Fabian* is too superficial, not "deep" enough, Lethen (in *Verhaltenslehren*) critiques Kästner for his old-fashioned, moralizing stance that Lethen considers characteristic of the bourgeois cult of inwardness and "depth." In the end, Kracauer explains it best: Kästner (and New Objectivity) is *both* superficial *and* sentimental.

19. Pommer had made lots of money for Hugenberg. According to Pommer's son, John Pommer, Goebbels actually wanted Pommer to stay on in the

filmmaking business in Germany (see Fehrenbach, 45 and n. 105, 273) in spite of Pommer's Jewish descent. A similar offer to someone of (partial) Jewish heritage would be the one Goebbels made to Fritz Lang, or so the latter maintained (Kracauer, *Caligari,* 164). The filmmaker Reinhold Schünzel, probably most famous for *Viktor und Viktoria* (1933), directed films in Germany until 1937; he too was part Jewish, but was given special permission by Goebbels to make his popular musicals and comedies. In 1937, however, Goebbels turned against him, and Schünzel went to the United States. On Schünzel, see Aurich. Most interesting of all is the case of Erich Engel, who was also part Jewish and had worked in leftist theater in the Weimar Republic (with Brecht, for instance), and who like Detlef Sierck (Douglas Sirk) was then banned from the theater but was able to find work in the film industry in the Third Reich. Whereas the "Aryan" Sierck left Germany in 1937 out of concern for his Jewish wife, Engel managed to continue working in the German film industry up until 1945. Then, in 1948 and 1949, he made films for the East German Defa, but by 1951 was making films in West Germany.

20. Sternberg's film adaptation of the Dreiser novel was made in 1931.
21. Friedrich Hussong, a representative of the Hugenberg conglomerate, praised the film on the day before its premiere (April 1, 1930) as a film that was actually "in opposition to" ("gegen") Heinrich Mann. Both Pommer (in the *Film-Kurier*) and Heinrich Mann (reported in "Skandal um den Blauen Engel") denied this. On the other side of the political spectrum from Hussong and Hugenberg, "Celsus" in *Die Weltbühne* attacked the film but came to the same conclusion as Hussong: it is a film in opposition to ("gegen") Heinrich Mann.
22. This point has been made by Koch (69), Gregor and Patalas (140), and Meyer-Wendt (260).
23. The version of the film I am citing is one of at least two German-language versions with English subtitles. Another sub-titled version of the film opens to music and English credits over a static shot of the same poster. Since this second version has English credits, it seems more directed to an American audience; the greater emphasis on Lola/Dietrich (she gets star billing) also supports this impression. The first version (in which Jannings gers top billing) would appear to be the original German-language version of the film with subtitles added. The second version eliminates the shots of the rooftops, the women, and the rising blind, as well as the subsequent action: the woman who washes the window to which the poster appears to be attached. Among other slight differences between the two versions, the end-ings are significant: the first ends with Rath at his desk, while the second shifts Lola's final musical number so that it appears after the last shot of Rath. Ending with Rath's death places final emphasis on his tragedy, whereas ending with Lola stresses more the iconic vamp into which she has

been transformed—and of course Dietrich, who becomes a famous star in America. There is also an English-language version of the film, filmed simultaneously with the German version by the same cast and crew, which I have seen at the Bundesarchiv in Berlin; in it, Lola is an English-speaking performer touring a German town where Rath teaches English.

24. Mayne remarks on the washerwoman's mimicry of the poster of Lola: for all the film's emphasis on men ogling Lola, it introduces her "through the reaction of a woman" ("Marlene Dietrich," 38–39).

25. This film has long been (less accurately) called *Tragedy of the Street* in English. The best discussion of the film is by Petro (*Joyless* Streets, 160–74).

26. The films he produced in the late 1920s and early 1930s are quite different from the art films he produced in the early and mid-1920s. On Pommer's career see Hardt, Jacobsen, and Elsaesser, *Weimar Cinema and After.*

27. See Jelavich's book on Berlin cabaret for more information on Valetti and Gerron. Both were Jewish, but Gerron did not escape the Nazis, turning down an offer from Dietrich to come to the States after the German invasion of Holland. He performed in cabarets both at the Westerbork and Theresienstadt concentration camps before being sent to his death at Auschwitz (275–82). Jelavich also comments on the special role that the revue played in Weimar, and its affinity to film and montage (168).

28. The newspaper critic Herbert Ihering reviewed "Zwei Krawatten" on 6 September 1929. See also Sternberg ("Fun," 230–34) on his attempt to find an actress to play Lola (a role he says was inspired by Wedekind's Lulu) and his casting of Dietrich, who as he admits had been "discovered" long before he came to Berlin.

29. As Elsaesser writes in his new book, *Weimar Cinema and After,* "The German cinema of the Weimar Republic is often, but wrongly identified with Expressionism" (3).

Coates attempts to label all of German cinema—as well as the American horror film and film noir—"Expressionist," in what seems to be the attempt to make the term conform to what it has come to mean in film studies, thanks to Eisner. I do not consider this attempt successful, in spite of many persuasive film readings of great originality in Coates's book.

30. Another successor genre was the "Kulturfilm"—see Zglinicki, 575, 579–80, and also the section in Chapter 2 of this book that discusses Pabst's *Secrets of a Soul* (1926). On the street film as a genre, see Kracauer (*Caligari,* 157–60) and Petro (162–64).

31. Original: "Hollywood bewundert die Technik des 'Blauen Engel.'"

32. Mary Ann Doane first pointed out to me the obvious parody of femininity in Dietrich's costumes in her response to a paper I gave on Weimar film at Brown University in March 1990. Riva informs us that Dietrich (her mother) designed the costumes in *The Blue Angel* herself (65–67).

33. In Keun's *The Artificial Silk Girl* (*Das kunstseidene Mädchen,* 1932), Doris finds this book in Ernst's apartment. As Kaes points out ("Motor," 96), by 1932 Van de Velde's book was in its thirty-fourth edition. For a discussion of Keun's novel, see Chapter 6; for more on the sex reform movement in Weimar, see, e.g., Grossmann and Usborne.

34. I first heard Kaes make this point in a lecture in a course on Weimar cinema at the University of California, Berkeley, in 1986.

35. This does however seem to be a rehearsal. There is in any case a boisterous audience present.

36. Mayne ("Marlene Dietrich," 37) has also noted that it is the film's focus on the process of transforming Lola into the "ultimate fetish" for the male viewer that makes the film interesting—more than the end product.

37. This piece of business with a spotlight is repeated in one of Pommer's other productions of 1930, *The Three from the Gas Station* (*Die Drei von der Tankstelle,* dir. Wilhelm Thiele), the first of the true operetta films—and the biggest box-office hit of 1930. Lillian Harvey shines her car's headlight on Willy Fritsch to take a better look at him, and sure enough, he is the gas station attendant whom the rich young woman chooses to love. While it is here treated in a comic fashion, this thematization of a desiring female gaze brought to bear on a male object did harbor a threat, and indeed the resolution of the narrative in this film centers on the problem of how to trick Fritsch's character into agreeing to marry the wealthy and "aggressive" woman played by Harvey. Cf. Rosehaft, "Lesewut," 138–140, on the representation of a threatening female gaze of desire in leftist poetry addressed to proletarian males.

38. This is a gesture that Liza Minnelli repeats frequently in Bob Fosse's *Cabaret* (1972).

39. The "classical cinema" is supposed to avoid foregrounding either its own technique or its address to spectators. The idea that the transformation moves from the theatrical cabaret with its foregrounded spectators to a final more classically "cinematic" image was suggested by Mary Ann Doane in her response to an earlier version of this paper mentioned above. See also Mayne, "Marlene Dietrich," 35–37.

40. On the other hand, the film's New Objective origins implies a more cynical and/or "perverse" take on the sexual anxieties portrayed in Expressionist cinema.

41. An emblematic example of this approach to the film would be Baxter.

42. Similarly, in my experience, student audiences today generally enjoy the film's comedy and find the turn to "tragedy" after Rath's marriage to Lola heavy-handed.

43. Again, even more popular with that subculture than Sagan's *Mädchen in Uniform* (1931), according to the star of the latter film, Hertha Thiele.

44. See Riva, e.g., 58, 153–55, 485–86, 629.
45. Cf. the comment by Dietrich biographer Steven Bach about what she learned from her lesbian friend (and lover) Claire Waldoff in mid-1920s Berlin: "What she learned backstage was that her appeal to women was as great as her appeal to men. Kenneth Tynan would call it sex without gender: What it was sex with whatever gender one wanted to see or Marlene wanted to project—something for everyone."
46. Mayne discusses the ambiguity of Dietrich's screen persona, an image "contained by certain stereotypes of the *femme fatale,* and yet resistant to them" ("Marlene Dietrich," 42). She concludes her essay: "But for those not so readily seduced by the dominant visual and narrative momentum of the classical cinema, Marlene Dietrich embodies the possibility of other desires and other modes of performance" (44).
47. Both Coates and Levin have pointed out the Freudian pun in German about the "Eier" (eggs, but in German slang also testicles) that Kiepert cracks on Rath's forehead.
48. Kracauer's postwar reading of the film stressed the sadism in the film, and he read the humiliation of Rath—especially at the hands of the schoolboys— as proto-fascist, (*Caligari,* 217–18). But in 1930, the film was attacked in the Nazi newspaper, *Der Völkische Beobachter,* for the film's humiliation of the "Aryans" in the film, including the professor, but also the blond "teacher's pet" who is beaten up by the other schoolboys, including the character "Goldstaub." In other words, a Nazi reviewer in 1930 was bothered by the same "sadistic" schoolboys who later disturbed Kracauer. As mentioned above, Kurt Gerron, the Jewish actor who played Kiepert, actually would die in Auschwitz (Jelavich, 282).

Chapter Six

1. Christa Winsloe, *Girls in Uniform* (1930), 61.
2. Original: "Und also war ich genau das, was man treu nennt. Aber dann hatte er seinen Doktor und war fertig studiert—Physik und sowas. Und ging nach München, wo seine Eltern wohnen, da wollte er heiraten—eine aus seinen Kreisen und Tochter von einem Professor—sehr berühmt, aber nicht so wie Einstein, von dem man ja Photographien sieht in furchtbar viel Zeitungen und sich nicht viel darunter vorstellen kann. Und ich denke immer, wenn ich sein Bild sehe mit den vergnügten Augen und Staub-wedelhaaren, wenn ich ihn im Kaffee sehen würde und hätte gerade den Mantel mit Fuchs an und todschick von vorn bis hinten, dann würde er mir auch vielleicht erzählen, er wäre beim Film und hatte unerhörte Beziehungen. Und ich würde ihm ganz kühl hinwerfen: H_2O ist Wasser—das habe ich gelernt von Hubert und würde ihn damit in größtes Erstaunen setzen." In Keun, *Das kunstseidene Mädchen*, 13. All further references in the text.

3. For a study devoted to the humor in Keun's novel, see Sopcak.

4. See von Ankum, "'Ich liebe Berlin,'" 376, also her note 12, 386, about Kracauer's more sensitive consideration of working women as evidenced in his 1932 piece in *Querschnitt*, 12.4 (Apr. 1932): 238f, "Mädchen im Beruf" (transl. as "Working Women" in Kaes, Jay, and Dimendberg, 216–18). Besides von Ankum, other feminist discussions of Keun include Abel; Barndt; Gleber, *The Art of Taking a Walk*, 191–208; Frame; Horsley; Kautz; Kosta; Petersen; Rosenstein; Shafi; Sopcak; and Drescher.

5. Marlene Dietrich of course was "discovered" by von Sternberg in the sense that he decided to give her a starring role in his film, which then brought her a contract in Hollywood. But Dietrich was by no means a "nobody" when she met von Sternberg—she was an actress on the Berlin stage who had already had acted in many films.

6. This is a term he borrows from David Riesman.

7. Cf. Barndt, e.g, 217, on the reflexive process of Doris's writing and the way in which the discourse of the "New Woman" is therefore both described in all its social limitations but also modified in a way that engages the reader, especially the female reader of the time who wanted to negotiate her own identity in the midst of all the debates of the era about what roles for women were appropriate. Barndt also provides a thorough analysis of both the reception of this very popular novel by Keun and of the critical controversy that arose with regard to the charge of plagiarism that was levied against her by Robert Neumann (201–209); her comparison of the two not only demonstrates how the charge is false, but demonstrates the uniqueness of Keun's text without resorting to traditional notions of authorial "genius." Instead she describes—and valorizes—the text's intertextuality, accessibility, and engagement with popular discourses and popular literature.

8. For a feminist discussion of *Pandora's Box* that contextualizes it against early twentieth-century psychological discourses linking women's sexuality with crime, see Hales.

9. Martina Anderson first demonstrated this to me in a seminar paper she wrote for a film seminar I taught. This position contradicts Elsaesser, "Lulu," and Doane, "The Erotic Barter."

10. Irmgard Keun was born in 1905 (see Roloff, 45, n. 3; Krechel, 126, n. 1), and not in 1910 as some critics (Harrigan, Serke) have asserted. She died in 1982. Keun herself began listing her age as five years younger while she was still an actress; according to Kreis (70), Keun was advised to do this by her future husband, Johannes von Tralow. Thus Keun was thought to be twenty-two in 1932, much closer in age to her protagonist Doris.

11. Cf. Lindner, 86: vitalistic "Lebensideologie" is of course an intellectual constellation that includes Wedekind.

12. See Jelavich on the significance of the revue in Weimar entertainment; he asserts that it was the main theatrical competition with film in the 1920s,

and that both forms of entertainment were considered especially suited to urban modernity (165–69).

13. Besides Kracauer, "Lulu," see, e.g., Ihering, Wille, Blaß, and Lustig. It is odd to find Kracauer in 1929 siding with the brooding inwardness of Schoen and not the "superficial" Americanism of Brooks—perhaps it is once again gender, and not cultural sensibility, that is here decisive. Ihering missed the more theatrically expressive Asta Nielsen, who had played Lulu in Leopold Jessner's 1923 film adaptation *Erdgeist*. But today it would seem that the uniqueness of Brooks's performance is much more crucial to Pabst's film than is its narrative. For a recent discussion of Brooks's performance that takes such a position, see Hake, "The Continuous Provocation."

14. Lulu appears to have no parents, although Schigolch acts as a sort of "father figure" (but also as a pimp). Significantly, there is no "mother figure" at all. In contrast, Doris feels close to her mother but not to her adoptive father, and her biological father has been declared impossible to identify by a court of law.

15. Note also Gleber's discussion of this, both in "Female Flanerie" and in *The Art of Taking a Walk*.

16. There are of course some autobiographical parallels: the city is specified as being in the Rhineland (59); Keun's first novel, *Gilgi* (1931), takes place explicitly in Cologne. There is however an obvious class difference between Keun and Doris. Keun was much better educated and from a much more comfortable middle-class background. She had also had success as an actress, a profession that Doris also tries (without much success). In addition, she had had experience doing office work. See, e.g., Roloff, Krechel, Serke, Kreis, Barndt.

17. I am considering each "entry" to be marked by the space that separates it from other "entries." These entries vary in length from one sentence to a number of pages. Doris does not want to write a traditional diary but rather to capture the moments of her life as in a film, as she states famously early in the novel (6).

18. Original: "Ich trete ihn gegens Schienbein von wegen Loslassen und frage: 'Nun Sagen Sie mal, Sie blödsinniger Rechtsanwalt, was denken Sie sich eigentlich? Wie kann ein Studierter wie Sie so schafsdämlich sein und glauben, ein junges hübsches Mädchen wäre wild auf ihn. Haben Sie noch nie in den Spiegel gesehn? Ich frage Sie nur, was für Reize haben Sie?'"

19. See passage on 52–53; cf. 31.

20. Original: "Wenn eine junge Frau mit Geld einen alten Mann heiratet wegen Geld und nichts sonst und schläft mit ihm stundenlang und guckt fromm, dann ist sie eine deutsche Mutter von Kindern und eine anständige Frau. Wenn eine junge Frau ohne Geld mit einem schläft ohne Geld, weil er glatte Haut hat und ihr gefällt, dann ist sie eine Hure und ein Schwein."

21. In Wedekind's original "Lulu" plays of the turn of the century, *Earth Spirit* and *Pandora's Box,* the first play follows Lulu's rise to power and the second her decline. Pabst begins his film adaptation more or less at the end of *Earth Spirit,* when Lulu is nearing the peak of her power, thus placing emphasis on her decline.

22. von Ankum persuasively makes the point that Doris's situation illustrates that the female counterpart to the male flaneur wandering the streets of the modern metropolis is quite different: no middle-class voyeur looking on secure in his social position above the masses, the "flaneuse" is either a prostitute or will be taken for one ("'Ich liebe Berlin,'" 370–74). But note also Gleber's discussion of this, both in "Female Flanerie" and in *The Art of Taking a Walk.* She makes a persuasive case that in spite of the limitations on the movement of women in public—and the continual mistaking of them for prostitutes by male viewers and critics—there were nonetheless pioneering examples of the activity of female "flaneurs"—and she sees Keun's *The Artificial Silk Girl* as one important piece of evidence for the creation of a discursive tradition of such "flanerie."

    Interestingly enough, the one scene in *Pandora's Box* in which Lulu is finally on the streets remains quite ambiguous. Is Lulu now a prostitute, or only now on the verge of becoming one (hence Alwa's jealous distress)? If so, then she never actually becomes one, since she does not sell, she offers herself to Jack the Ripper. Although the ambiguity here may be due to fears of censorship, it corresponds exactly to the situation of the modern woman on the street that von Ankum describes so well.

23. Original: "Ich bringe ihm Berlin, das in meinem Schoß liegt." Although this phrase is a variant of a common German idiom without any necessarily sexual connotation, its use by Doris in this context—as she narrates her relationship with Brenner, which consists mainly in telling him about her adventures in Berlin to him and then having sex with him—would seem to justify my interpretation.

24. But again, spectacle and performance—here, of course, the performance of Louise Brooks—may be much more decisive for the film than Lulu's narrative function.

25. Of course, those fantasies are not uncritically portrayed in Pabst's film either; they are more clearly represented by something like Anita Loos's American novel of the mid-1920s, *Gentlemen Prefer Blondes* (see von Ankum, "'Ich liebe Berlin,'" 374–75).

26. A similar unexamined dualism lives on in debates today: compare for example the views of Brockmann (177–78) with those of von Ankum ("Motherhood," 182) on another of Keun's characters: Gilgi, in her 1931 novel of the same name. Brockmann sees Gilgi at the end of the novel as a cold, egotistical "New Woman" who exemplifies a cynical age, whereas von Ankum sees her as a "New Mother" whose acceptance of motherhood at the end is

complicitous with the onset of fascism. Brockmann gives no credit to Gilgi's decision to raise her baby on her own (certainly a contrast to Gilgi's biological mother, a wealthy woman who chose not to raise her "illegitimate" child). Meanwhile von Ankum sees Gilgi's decision as a prelude to fascist maternalism, which is an especially charged ideological field, even more so than simple bourgeois sentimentalism. It is even more charged in the German context, given the Nazi cult of motherhood. But this is no reason for a blanket condemnation of motherhood in general, any more than Nazi "irrationalism" is any reason to condemn all human emotion and feeling. With regard to *Gilgi,* I would concur with Kosta, who suggests that in it Keun "alludes to the possibility of reimagining motherhood" (282).

27. The song "That's the Love of the Sailors" ("Das ist die Liebe der Matrosen)" that Doris mentions here is from a popular 1931 film musical by Hanns Schwarz called *Bombs on Monte Carlo (Bomben auf Monte Carlo*—with a famous cast that included Hans Albers, Peter Lorre, Heinz Rühmann, Kurt Gerron, and the Comedian Harmonists, among others). The song was written by Werner R. Heymann, and as Rentschler notes, it is also cited in Hans Steinhoff's film *Hitler Youth Quex* of 1933—there depicted negatively because the song writer was Jewish (*Ministry of Illusion,* 59, 323 n. 36).

    Original: "'Meine Frau konnte singen so ganz hoch und hell.'"

    "Sing ich——das ist die Liebe der Matrosen—wunderbarstes Lied, was man hat."

    "'Schubert,' sagt er. Wieso? 'Gesungen hat sie, wie Schubert komponiert hat.' Das ist die Liebe der Matrosen—ist vielleicht ein Dreck, so'n Lied, was? Was heißt Schubert, was besagt er? Das ist die Lie—aus dem Leben gegriffen ist das, wie meine Mutter bei richtigen Kinostücken sagt."

28. Original: "Ich hantiere mit dem Staubsauger—sssss—ich bin ein Gewitter. Aus Versehen mache ich das Bild von der Frau mal eben kaputt. Sie hätten so viele gemeinsame Worte gehabt, sagt er—und es gibt da so kleine zärtliche Erinnerungen, ganz belanglos an und für sich. Sag ich: 'Sie ist fort, und Sie müssen Ihren Sinn jetzt auf anderes lenken.'

    "Sagt er: 'Nichts macht mir mehr Freude, für wen lebe ich, für wen arbeite ich?'"

    "'Ihnen ist wohl noch nie richtig schlecht gegangen, was?'"

    "'Doch, auch schon,' sagt er. Na, ich will erst fragen, was er unter Schlechtgehen versteht. Gibt welche, die weinen vor Mitleid Tränen über sich, wenn sie mal zufällig um drei noch kein warmes Mittagessen hatten."

29. Original: "Sie sehen recht angegriffen aus," sage ich ihm, "heute wird um zehn schlafen gegangen."

    "Hach, ich schlaf ja doch nicht," stöhnt er.

    Werd ich aber wütend. "Bilden Sie sich keine Schwachheiten ein, welche Lügerei ist das, keine Nacht schlafen können wegen Kummer und so, wo ich Sie jede Nacht deutlich nebenan schnarchen höre."

30. Of course, Doris has for quite some time up to this point kept the wife's letter to Ernst hidden under the rug—the letter in which the wife hints at her
wish for reconciliation with him. This is another funny—and sad—piece of
deception by Doris, as before in the theater episode, when she fabricated an
affair with one of the most important men in the theater.

31. Blond hair is a characteristic often associated in the text (by the brunette
Doris) with the racist ideals espoused by many in late Weimar Germany,
including openly anti-Semitic ones (der rote Mond, Großindustrie). Doris
confronts anti-Semitism much more clearly—and admirably—than Fabian.
(Blond cinema, however, at one point alludes merely to the movie star Lillian Harvey—cf. Gleber, *The Art of Taking a Walk*, 204)

32. See Horsley for an analysis of Doris's language from a feminist-post-
structuralist perspective, with less emphasis on the modernist or New
Objective style Keun uses and more on the way Doris's deviations from the
linguistic norm mirror the "outsider" status women occupy with regard to
patriarchal language (on the other hand of course we ought not to forget
that this is a representation of a style consciously constructed by Keun).

33. Rosenstein asserts that the satiric and ironic humor of Keun's book is one
element that goes beyond the "objective" observation of New Objectivity—and that indeed some of the more trendy aspects of the cult of New
Objectivity are being satirized in the novel (278, 280–81).

34. For a discussion of texts written by women at the end of the Weimar
Republic specifically with regard to the demonization of working women
and the campaign against "double-earners," see Kautz.

35. Sexless at least at first—a parallel with her relationship with Ernst? With
him, it could be argued that his leaving her alone sexually was one of the
first motivations for her to fall in love with him.

36. In *Kuhle Wampe*, of course, the garden colonies are not portrayed at all as
positive, but rather the privatistic refuge of the corrupt, Social Democratic
reformists of the older generation.

37. Cf. von Ankum, "'Ich liebe Berlin,'" 384, also Krechel, 109.

38. For similar conclusions with regard to female desire and subjectivity, see
Shafi and also Harrigan's conclusion about Keun's *Gilgi*, 120; the emphasis
here on the flaneur's gaze is obviously indebted to Gleber, and the emphasis
on writing, popular culture and the engagement of female readers is
indebted to Barndt's discussion of Keun's *Artificial Silk Girl*, 189–238.

39. In the words of Doris, the first-person narrator/protagonist of Irmgard
Keun's 1932 novel *The Artificial Silk Girl* (122–23). Original quote: "Wir
haben zusammen im Kino gesessen, es war ein Film von Mädchen in Uniform. Das waren bessere Mädchen, aber es ging ihnen ja wie mir. Man hat
wen lieb, und das gibt einem manchmal Tränen und rote Nase. Man hat
wen lieb—das ist gar nicht zu verstehen, ist ja furchtbar egal ob einen Mann
oder Frau oder lieben Gott."

40. There has been an unfortunate (rationalist/masculinist) tendency on the Left to maintain that any emphasis on emotions results in the "trivialization" of "more important" issues. Given Kracauer's own sexuality, however, his complete silence on the subject of homoeroticism in the film is probably more complicated.

41. The author of the dissertation in question is Freiburg. Besides the latter and those I have mentioned above—Rich, Dyer, Kracauer, Eisner, Reinig, and Ohm—other critics who have written on this film include Reisdorfer, Scholar, Schoppmann, von der Emde, and Zimnik.

42. Froelich is sometimes listed as co-director of the film (e.g., Wendtland, *Jahrgang*, 1931, 222; Krusche, 339).

43. Original quote: "Man sprach vom besten Film des Jahres. Auch in den USA waren die Kritiker begeistert."

   In 1933, already in exile, Winsloe published a novel in Amsterdam that was called "das Buch zum Film" and titled *The Girl Manuela* (*Das Mädchen Manuela*). Von der Emde asserts that the novel appeared in 1930, before the stage or film versions, and Ohm treats the novel in the same way. Dyer (35) calls the novel *Mädchen in Uniform;* Reinig (242) calls it *The Girl Manuela,* the screenplay that she interprets as a book "against" the Film. Claudia Schoppmann uses both titles (cf. 112 & 115); on 115 she lists the 1934 Leipzig and Wien (Vienna) edition (not the 1933 Amsterdam one) with the same title as the film. Ohm calls it *The Child Manuela* (98).

44. Dyer (58), citing Nancy Scholar, notes that it is open to two interpretations, the one explained above, and another one: "a rallying call for anti-authoritarian forces in Germany and elsewhere."

45. Cited in the English translation of Winsloe's play (61).

46. This makes *Mädchen in Uniform*'s opening shots of Potsdam doubly meaningful: here Froelich was involved with a film negatively depicting the Prussian history embodied in Potsdam, the seat of the Prussian military, but in a little over a year he would direct a film glorifying the Prussian tradition. One should also compare *Mädchen*'s opening shots of Potsdam to similar ones at the beginning of Hans Steinhoff's *The Old and the Young King* (*Der alte und der junge König,* 1935), another film in the long series of films glorifying the Prussian king Frederick the Great.

47. Of course, Erika Mann (daughter of Thomas, sister of Klaus) acted in the film, and she was bisexual, if not lesbian. Mann played the teacher Fräulein von Atems, who directs the school play.

48. Original: "Die Sagan hatte damals im Theater das Stück auf rein lesbisch inszeniert."

49. Wieck apparently sided with Sagan, but Thiele herself liked Froelich better than Sagan (34).

50. Cf. also Krusche (339–40): the reference is also to a "misinterpretation" ("Misdeutung") by the principal (339).

51. It is important to remember that the Americanism and the modern mass culture so celebrated in New Objectivity meant above all three things: "sports, the movies, and jazz" ("Sport, Kino und Jazz," Lindner, 171).

52. This could be read as a "heterosexual" cover for the film, although in context it seems more "polymorphous" or bisexual (or queer): crushes on Albers and on Porten are debated as though they are equivalent.

53. Obviously cross-dressing has a very old tradition in the theater, but most famously for men and boys.

54. One could also read this as the innocent Manuela being appraised by Bernburg, as she is about to be drawn into the shadowy world—and spell—of this (closeted) older woman, the character Reinig calls a "dark lesbian" ("Dunkellesbe"). This will be dangerous to Manuela, almost fatal—but in the end it will be Manuela who draws Bernburg "into the light" with which the younger woman is associated.

55. There was also a real model for "Manuela," not Winsloe but a fellow schoolmate, who did throw herself out of a window (as in the original play). Pace Dyer, she did not die; in fact she attended the premiere of the film, according to Thiele (34).

56. There is also a montage juxtaposing a shot of a teacher's mouth giving orders with shots of the girls in the washroom obeying her, a sequence Rich emphasizes (82–83). There are also certain obvious breaks of the "180–degree rule" and some anticipatory pans that foreground editing and camera movement: for example, in the hallway when Manuela shakes Marga's hand, the girls flip position, and the camera then pans to the door to show Manuela's aunt and Kesten entering the hallway.

57. Twenty-five girls from secondary schools all over Germany were selected to portray the pupils in the film (other than the important speaking roles such as Manuela, Ilse, Edelgard). They were featured in a 1931 issue of *Uhu* ("Von der höheren Tochterschule").

58. In discussing polarization around 1930, it may be relevant again to consider Lindner's point that New Objectivity and Expressionism are much more similar than is usually acknowledged, and nowhere more so than with the rhetoric of crisis and polarity that betrays their common origin roots in Nietzschean vitalism, or what he calls "Lebensideologie."

59. Ihering's original German calls the film "Einer der besten, saubersten, klarsten Filme des Jahres," and labels it a "leicht lesbisch betonte Tragödie." At the same time, there was a good deal of incredulousness expressed by German critics when the film's censorship problems in the United States became known. The U.S. censors, of course, found objectionable precisely the sections of the film that Rich stressed in her famous essay reclaiming the film as a lesbian text.

60. On "in-betweenism" in a lesbian context , see Dyer, 41–49, on the "female-identified" model, see especially Dyer, 49–58. See also Hewitt on in-

betweenism vs. masculinism split among male homosexual activists in the early twentieth century.

61. Hewitt attempts to prove that homosexual "masculinism" in Germany was not invariably linked either to reactionary politics or to the homosocial "masculinism" of the Nazis. He argues that in fact this latter phenomenon is a predominantly *heterosexual* fantasy. But the very project of his book concedes that homosexual masculinism and Nazi masculinism have been linked; he tries to demonstrate that there is no essential link between the two, precisely because he wants to show that gay masculinism is not inevitably fascist. This I feel he proves, but this does not negate the point that a masculinist model was politically problematic in the Weimar Republic given its popularity on the nationalist, anti-Semitic Right (with straight and gay reactionaries).

62. It might be argued that Erich Washneck's 1932 film *Eight Girls in a Boat* (*Acht Mädels im Boot*) implies something like a "separate sphere" in a much more positive way. On this film, see Kracauer (*Caligari*, 256–57), Dyer (56–57), Gramann and Schlüpmann (30–31), and Thiele (40).

63. Ohm argues that the film reproduces anti-lesbian discourses of the 1920s (the medico-scientific ones). This is accurate, but the film puts these arguments in the mouths of totally unsympathetic characters.

64. Set to music, this psalm can be found in Lutheran hymnals, a piece of information for which I am grateful to Jonathan Clark.

65. Rich made this point first (112–13), and Dyer underscores it (36–38). Raham, following Reinig, disagrees, finding the cowardly role Bernburg plays in the other versions of the story (the play and the novel) to be the point of Winsloe's critique: the treachery of the "Dunkellesbe," the closeted teacher not willing to endanger her career and save the young girl whose love she has—seductively—awakened. To portray her as a heroine thus flies in the face of Winsloe's intentions. Nonetheless, while the film may disregard those intentions, it is a separate text. In the film Bernburg is portrayed differently—as a heroine—or at least as someone who realizes her error. (The girls are the true heroines of the film; Bernburg is only more articulate.) Rich and Dyer are quite right to evaluate the film's ending on its own merits and in comparison to the suicides so often found in lesbian narratives of the late nineteenth and early twentieth centuries.

66. Cf. Barndt, 44–45.

67. Zimnik, using a Lacanian approach to the film and arguing against Kracauer, comes to a very similar conclusion, finding the ending of the film democratic precisely in its valorization of the relationships among the girls and its elimination of the one character who represents authoritarian patriarchy: the headmistress (178).

Chapter Seven

1. In Kaes, *Weimarer Republik,* 265–66.
2. In Kaes, *Weimarer Republik,* 270.
3. Ctd. in Maase, 54–55.
4. Adam Shatz, "Bebop and Stalinist Kitsch," 25.
5. Stuart Hall, "On postmodernism," 132.
6. We should, however, remember that the idea of socialism originated in the desire for democratic control of the economy, nor should we forget that the realization of democracy in the United States and other capitalist countries has often been less than ideal, to put it mildly. For ultimately there is a clear tension between a truly democratic society and the consolidation of great wealth and power in the hands of a relatively small elite.
7. On the ambivalence of German reactions to "Americanism" in the Weimar Republic, see von Saldern and the volume in which it appears, (which she co-edited:) Lüdtke, Marßolek, and von Saldern, *Amerikanisierung.* As for the potential criticism that my concern with the "emancipatory" is somehow dated, again, I beg to differ: the project of radical democracy is a process of emancipation from the authority of tradition and hierarchical elites.
8. In a review essay written before September 11, 2001, Edward Said critiques this trendy formulation, for which he credits Benjamin Barber, as an example of the kind of simplistic narrative to which intellectuals need to create alternatives so that historical memory is not lost (Said, 34).
9. One only needs to mention the Reverend Jerry Falwell's reaction to the terrorist attacks on September 11, 2001—namely, that the sins of secularists, feminists, and homosexuals in the United States have brought this punishment upon us. One wonders if Reverend Falwell realizes that his position on these issues is uncannily similar to that of the Taliban in Afghanistan?
10. Again: Huyssen—like Peter Bürger—stresses the opposition of the avant-garde beginning with Dadaism to modernism, an emphasis that is important for his understanding of "postmodernism" as well (see "Mapping the Postmodern").
11. About democracy as a component of modernization, the German Right was less ambivalent, of course; it rejected it, although there is some concession to democratic ideals in fascist populism. The popular will in fascism, however, is supposed to be expressed in some magical way through the authoritarian leader, not through democratically elected representatives. And on the Marxist-Leninist Left there was positive rhetoric about democracy, but as developments in the 1920s and 1930s in the Soviet Union demonstrated, this was merely lip service; there the will of the people was supposed to be embodied in the Party—and of course in Stalin.
12. Original: "Diese enthüllende Einstellung ist ein Grundzug unserer Zeit, und wenn auch eine verbreitete Strömung in ihr den Ausdruck einer

unvornehmen Haltung, einer Respektlosigkeit sieht . . . , so darf man nicht vergessen, daß eine Epoche der Transformation, wie die unsrige, die mit so vielen, für uns bereits unerträglich gewordenen Hüllen und Formen bricht, diese Haltung notgedrungen auf sich nehmen muß."

13. Patrice Petro made a similar point in the conclusion to her 1989 book, *Joyless Streets* (225–26): namely, that our late twentieth-century fascination with the sexual ambiguity, androgyny, and/or bisexuality that pervades Weimar culture—that which we might now call its queerness—should not blind us to the actual power relations between different social groups, especially women and men. One should not forget, in other words, "how bisexuality is figured differently for men and for women within a patriarchal culture" (226). She is right: attention to actual power relations within a society is absolutely necessary.

14. Again, see Barndt's discussion of "Das Gutgemacht Mittlere," 46–52.

15. This distinction between the Nazis and the German tradition must be problematized somewhat, if only for the cultural mobilization of the eighteenth century in the Third Reich. For a thorough and incisive discussion of this mobilization, see Linda Schulte-Sasse, especially "The Never Was" but also *Entertaining the Third Reich*. A few cinematic examples of this appropriation in the culture of the Third Reich: the use of the bourgeois tragedy for *Jew Suess (Jud Süß)*; the films not only about Frederick the Great, depicting him as a solid German bourgeois—indeed petit-bourgeois—in conflict with a Francophilic, feminized, German aristocracy in films like Hans Steinhoff's *The Old and the Young King (Der alte und der junge König,* 1935), but also films about Schiller. In German architecture, there was an obvious allusion to classicism. The postwar attitude was of course that the Nazis had misappropriated—and thus sullied—the legacy of classical German humanism—but the postwar appropriation was itself hardly "disinterested," since one of its consequences was a marking-off of the Third Reich as an aberration.

16. In Staudte's film, a German war criminal is depicted as the only person in the film with an intact, bourgeois family life, and Mertens, the main character, acquires the same bourgeois normalcy as he is cured of his complex about war crimes by the love of a woman (played by Hildegard Knef, in her famous portrayal of a rather improbable concentration camp survivor). Until this redemption he is associated with Expressionist shadows and angles and with a decadent bar that is an obvious allusion to late Weimar's *The Blue Angel*.

17. Fehrenbach shows that church officials who condemned Forst's film played a large role in stirring up the controversy, which of course drew more people to the cinemas. See Fehrenbach's articles "The Fight" and "*The Sinful Woman*" for early formulations of the research and argumentation fully elaborated in her book *Cinema in Democratizing Germany*.

18. In films like Willi Forst's *The Sinful Woman* and Bernhard Wicki's *The Bridge* (*Die Brücke,* 1959) the Third Reich and/or Nazis are associated with dissolute morals. The association of homosexuality in particular with fascism and Nazism in postwar culture and cinema is not merely a German, but rather an international phenomenon. See Hewitt on "homo-fascism," as he calls this bizarre discourse. It is certainly not limited to German culture; it obviously can be seen in the Italian cinema as well, starting with Rosselini's *Rome Open City* and his Berlin film *Germany Year Zero,* but carried on by Bertolucci (in his adaptation of Moravia's *The Conformist*), and Visconti (*The Damned*), among others. As to the situation of actual gays in West Germany (as opposed to "homofascist" fantasies about them) there was a revival of efforts to legalize homosexuality in the 1950s, but it was not successful in this decade of strong "family values."

19. I cannot attempt to trace the GDR's specific development here, but it is fairly obvious that its "scientific socialism" and technocracy is comparable to New Objectivist scientism (but also of course Western rationalism in general). Similarly, the GDR's favored "socialist realism" had origins in debates not only in the Soviet Union but also on the German Left in the 1920s, debates that included concerns with documentary art and social realism that also influenced New Objectivity.

20. A typical example of the discourse on the "emasculation" of men from the GDR after reunification: a headline in the early 1990s in the periodical *Super,* one of the (Western-owned) tabloids directed at former East Germans, proclaimed the sensational story of an "Ossi" (Eastern) man killing a "promiscuous" Wessi (Western) "woman" because she laughed at his naked body (cited in Riehl-Heyse, 3).

21. In 1999, moderate reforms of these antiquated citizenship laws were made into law—with great difficulty.

22. While it would be silly to deny that the process of global media conglomeration poses an ever greater danger both to cultural diversity and democracy, nonetheless popular culture for the last century or two has managed to elude the control of elite forces often and in unpredictable ways. Undifferentiated pessimism on this score seems simplistic.

Works Cited ∽

Bibliography

8 Uhr Abendblatt. Rev. of *Secrets of a Soul,* 25 March 1926.

Abel, Brigetta Marie. "Identities in Flux: The Exile Novels of Adrienne Thomas, Irmgard Keun, and Anna Seghers." Ph.D. Dissertation, University of Minnesota, 1999.

Adams, Parveen. "Per Os(cillation)." In James Donald, ed., *Psychoanalysis and Cultural Theory: Thresholds.* New York: St. Martin's Press, 1991, 68–88.

Adorno, Theodor W. "Ein Titel." In *Noten zur Literatur, Gesamte Schriften,* Vol. 2. Frankfurt: Suhrkamp, 1974, 656–57.

Atwell, Lee. *G. W. Pabst.* Boston: Twayne, 1977.

Aurich, Rolf. "Lachen mit Sondererlaubnis: Reinhold Schünzel." In Bock and Töteberg, 350–355.

Bach, Steven. *Marlene Dietrich: Life and Legend.* New York: Da Capo, 1992.

Barndt, Kerstin. "Sentiment und Sachlichkeit. Schreib–und Lesewesen der Neuen Frau am Ende der Weimarer Republik." Ph.D. Dissertation, Free University of Berlin, 1999.

Bathrick, David. "Max Schmeling on the Canvas: Boxing as an Icon of Weimar Culture." *New German Critique* 51 (1990): 113–36.

———. "Speaking the Other's Silence: Franz Jung's *Der Fall Gross.*" In Huyssen and Bathrick. 19–35.

Baxter, Peter. "On the Naked Thighs of Miss Dietrich." *Wide Angle* 2.2 (1978): 18–25.

Becker, Sabina. "Neue Sachlichkeit im Roman." In Becker and Weiss, 7–26.

Becker, Sabina, and Christoph Weiss, eds. *Neue Sachlichkeit im Roman: Neue Interpretationen zum Roman der Weimarer Republik.* Stuttgart: Metzler, 1995.

Benjamin, Walter. "Rückblick auf Chaplin" (1929). In Kaes, *Kino–Debatte,* 173–75.

———. *Ursprung des deutschen Trauerspiels* (1928). Frankfurt: Suhrkamp, 1963.

Berghahn, V[olker]. R. *Modern Germany: Society, Economy, and Politics in the Twentieth Century.* Cambridge: Cambridge University Press, 1982.

Berman, Russell A. *Cultural Studies of Germany: History, Representation, and Nationhood.* Madison: University of Wisconsin Press, 1993.

Blaß, Ernst. "Die Film-Lulu." Rev. of *Büchse der Pandora. Berliner Tageblatt* (No. 71): 11 February 1929, 71.

Bock, Hans–Michael, and Michael Töteberg, eds. *Das Ufa–Buch: Kunst und Krisen, Stars und Regisseure, Wirtschaft und Politik.* Frankfurt: Zweitausendeins, 1992.

Borchert, Wolfgang. *Draußen vor der Tür* (1947). In English: *The Man Outside,* trans. David Porter. New York: New Directions, 1971.

Brecht, Bertolt. "Elephantenkalb: Ein Zwischenspiel für das Foyer." Interlude for his *Mann ist Mann* (1925). Frankfurt: Suhrkamp, 1968, 87–99.

Bridenthal, Renate, Atina Grossman, and Marion Kaplan, eds. *When Biology Became Destiny: Women in Weimar and Nazi Germany.* New York: Monthly Review Press, 1984.

Bridenthal, Renate, and Claudia Koonz. "Beyond *Kinder, Küche, Kirche.*" In Bridenthal et al., 33–65.

Brockmann, Stephen. Unpublished conference paper on *Hinkemann.* German Studies Association Conference, Washington, D.C., October 1993.

———. "Weimar Sexual Cynicism." In Kniesche/Brockmann, 165–80.

Bronnen, Arnolt. *Vatermord* (1920). Munich: text + kritik, 1985.

Brück, Christa Anita. *Schicksale hinter Schreibmaschinen.* Berlin: Sieben-Stäbe-Verlag, 1930.

Budd, Michael. "Modernism and the Representation of Fantasy: Cubism and Expressionism in *The Cabinet of Dr. Caligari.*" In Jan Hokenson and Howard Pearce, eds., *Forms of the Fantastic.* Westport, CT: Greenwood Press, 1986, 15–21.

Bürger, Peter. *Theorie der Avantgarde.* Frankfurt: Suhrkamp, 1974.

Butler, Judith. *Bodies That Matter: On the Discursive Limits of "Sex."* New York: Routledge, 1993.

———. *Gender Trouble: Feminism and the Subversion of Identity.* New York: Routledge, 1990.

Cafferty, Helen. "Pessimism, Perspectivism, and Tragedy: *Hinkemann* Reconsidered." *German Quarterly* 54.1 (1981): 44–58.

Calhoun, Craig, ed. *Habermas and the Public Sphere.* Cambridge, MA: MIT Press, 1992.

"Celsus." Rev. of *The Blue Angel. Die Weltbühne* (Berlin), 29 April 1930.

Clover, Carol J. "Her Body, Himself: Gender in the Slasher Film." *Representations* 20 (1987): 187–228.

Coates, Paul. *The Gorgon's Gaze: German Cinema, Expressionism, and the Image of Horror.* Cambridge: Cambridge University Press, 1991.

Combs, Richard. Rev. of *Variety. Monthly Film Bulletin* 46.546 (1979): 160–61.

Czaplicka, John, Andreas Huyssen, and Anson Rabinbach. "Introduction: Cultural History and Cultural Studies." *New German Critique* 65 (Spring–Summer 1995): 3–17.

Deak, Istvan. *Weimar's Left–Wing Intellectuals.* Berkeley: University of California Press, 1968.

de Lauretis, Teresa. *Alice Doesn't: Feminism, Semiotics, Cinema.* Bloomington: Indiana University Press, 1984.

Diederichs, Helmut H. "The Origins of the 'Autorenfilm." In Paolo Cherchi Usai and Lorenzo Codelli, eds., *Before Caligari: German Cinema, 1895–1920.* Pordenone: Edizioni Biblioteca dell' Immagine, 1990, 380–401.

Doane, Mary Ann. *The Desire to Desire: The Woman's Film of the 1940s.* Bloomington: Indiana University Press, 1987.

———. "The Erotic Barter: Pandora's Box (1929)." In Rentschler, *The Films of G. W. Pabst,* 62–79.

Döblin, Alfred. *Berlin Alexanderplatz: Die Geschichte vom Franz Biberkopf,* (1929). Munich: Deutscher Taschenbuch Verlag, 1987.

Dollenmayer, David B. *The Berlin Novels of Alfred Döblin.* Berkeley: University of California Press, 1988.

Donahue, Neil H. "Unjustly Framed: Politics and Art in *Das Cabinet des Dr. Caligari.*" *German Politics and Society* 32 (Summer 1994): 76–88.

Doty, Alexander. *Making Things Perfectly Queer: Interpreting Mass Culture.* Minneapolis: University of Minnesota Press, 1993.

Drescher, Barbara. "The Vanishing Female Protagonists in the Weimar, Exile, and Postwar Fiction of Irmgard Keun, Dinah Nelken, and Ruth Landshoff–Yorck." Ph.D. Dissertation, University of Minnesota, 2001.

Dyer, Richard. "Lesbian and Gay Cinema in Weimar Germany." *New German Critique* 51 (Fall 1990): 5–60.

Eggebrecht, Axel. Rev. of *Mädchen in Uniform. Die Weltbühne* (Berlin), 26 December 1931.

Eisner, Lotte. *The Haunted Screen: Expressionism in the German Cinema & the Influence of Max Reinhardt.* (Orig.: *L'Ecran Démoniaque.* 1952; rev. 1965). Trans. from the French by Roger Greaves. Berkeley: University of California Press, 1969.

Eley, Geoff. "Nations, Publics, and Political Cultures: Placing Habermas in the Nineteenth Century." In Calhoun, 289–339.

———. "What is Cultural History?" *New German Critique* 65 (Spring–Summer 1995): 19–36.

Elsaesser, Thomas. "Film History and Visual Pleasure." In Patricia Mellencamp and Philip Rosen, eds., *Cinema Histories, Cinema Practices.* Frederick, MD: University Publications of America, 1984, 7–84.

———. "Lulu and the Meter Man: Pabst's Pandora's Box (1929)." In Rentschler, ed., *German Film and Literature,* 40–59. Another version of this essay is included in *Weimar Cinema and After.*

———. "Secret Affinities." *Sight and Sound* 58.1 (1989): 33–39. Another version of this essay is included in *Weimar Cinema and After.*

———. "Social Mobility and the Fantastic." *Wide Angle* 5.2 (1982): 14–25.

————. *Weimar Cinema and After: Germany's Historical Imaginary.* London: Routledge, 2000.

Elsaesser, Thomas, and Michael Wedel, eds. *The BFI Companion to German Cinema.* London: British Film Institute, 1999.

"Erste Ufaton-Großstaffel." *Film–Kurier,* 2 April 1930.

Esser, Michael. "Der Sprung über den großen Teich: Ewald Andre Duponts 'Varieté.'" In Bock/Töteberg, 160–65.

Fehrenbach, Heide. *Cinema in Democratizing Germany: Reconstructing National Identity after Hitler.* Chapel Hill: University of North Carolina Press, 1995.

————. "The Fight for the 'Christian West': German Film Control, the Churches, and the Reconstruction of Civil Society in the Early Bonn Republic." *German Studies Review* 14.1 (1991): 39–63.

————. "*Die Sünderin* or Who Killed the German Male? Early Postwar German Cinema and the Betrayal of the Fatherland." In Frieden et al., Vol. 2, 135–60.

Fickert, Kurt J. "Moral Ambiguity in the Weimar Republic: Kästner's *Fabian* Revisited." *Germanic Notes* 14.4 (1983): 51–54.

Die Filmwoche 15 (1926). Rev. of *Secrets of a Soul.*

Fleisser, Marieluise. *Mehlreisende Frieda Geyer* (1931). Rev. with new title: *Eine Zierde für den Verein. Roman vom Rauchen, Sporteln, Lieben und Verkaufen.* Suhrkamp: Frankfurt, 1972.

Frame, Lynne. "Gretchen, Girl, Garçonne? Weimar Science and Popular Culture in Search of the Ideal New Woman." In von Ankum, *Women in the Metropolis,* 12–40.

Fraser, Nancy. "Rethinking the Public Sphere: A Contribution to the Critique of Actually Existing Democracy." In Calhoun, 109–42.

Freiburg, Jeanne Ellen. "Regulatory Bodies: Gendered Visions of the State in German and Swedish Cinema." Ph.D. Dissertation, University of Minnesota, 1994.

Friedberg, Anne. "An *Unheimlich* Maneuver between Psychoanalysis and the Cinema: Pabst's *Secrets of the Soul* (1926)." In Rentschler, ed., *The Films of G. W. Pabst,* 41–51.

Frieden, Sandra, Richard W./Laurie McCormick, Vibeke Petersen, and Melissa Vogelsang, eds. *Gender and German Cinema: Feminist Interventions.* 2 vols. Providence, RI: Berg, 1993.

Frühwald, Wolfgang. 1971. Appendix, notes, and *Nachwort.* In Toller, *Hinkemann,* 56–93.

Frühwald, Wolfgang, and John M. Spalek, eds. *Der Fall Toller: Kommentar und Materialien.* Munich: Hanser, 1979.

Gay, Peter. *Weimar Culture: The Outsider as Insider.* New York: Harper & Row, 1968.

Geiger, Theodor. "The Old and the New Middle Classes." 1932. In Kaes, Jay, and Dimendberg, 191–94.

Gerstein, Evelyn. Rev. of *Variety. The New Republic,* 28 July 1926.

Giese, Fritz. *Girlkultur: Vergleiche zwischen amerikanischem und europaeischem Rhythmus und Lebensgefühl.* Munich: Delphin, 1925.

Gleber, Anke. *The Art of Taking a Walk: Flanerie, Literature, and Film in Weimar Culture.* Princeton, NJ: Princeton University Press, 1999.

———. "Female Flanerie and the *Symphony of a City.*" In von Ankum, *Women in the Metropolis.* 67–88.

———. "Das Fräulein von Tellheim: Die ideologische Funktion der Frau of in der nationalsozialistischen Lessing–Adaption." *German Quarterly* 56.4 (1986): 547–68.

———. "Only Man Must Be and Remain a Judge, Soldier and Ruler of State," trans. Antje Masten. In Frieden et al., Vol. 2, 105–16.

Gramann, Karola, and Heide Schlüpmann. "Vorbemerkung" to "Momente erotischer Utopie—ästhetisierte Verdrängung: Zu *Mädchen in Uniform* und *Anna und Elisabeth.*" *Frauen & Film* 28 (June 1981): 28–31.

Gregor, Ulrich, and Enno Patalas. *Geschichte des Films,* Vol. 1: 1895–1939. Reinbek: Rowohlt, 1976.

Grossman, Atina. "Abortion and Ecomomic Crisis." In Bridenthal et al., 66–86.

———. "*Girlkultur* or Thoroughly Rationalized Female: A New Woman in Weimar Germany?" In Judith Friedlander, Blanche Wiesen Cook, Alice Kessler-Harris, and Carroll Smith-Rosenberg, eds., *Women in Culture and Politics: A Century of Change.* Bloomington: Indiana University Press, 1986, 62–80.

———. *Reforming Sex: The German Movement for Birth Control and Abortion Reform, 1920–1950.* Oxford: Oxford University Press, 1995.

Habermas, Jürgen. *Strukturwandel der Öffentlichkeit: Untersuchung zu einer Kategorie der bürgerlichen Gesellschaft.* Darmstadt: Luchterhand, 1962.

Hake, Sabine. "Chaplin Reception in Weimar Germany." *New German Critique* 51 (1990): 87–111.

———. "The Continuous Provocation of Louise Brooks." *German Politics and Society* 32 (Summer 1994): 58–75.

———. "Girls and Crisis: The Other Side of Diversion." *New German Critique* 40 (1987): 147–64.

———. *Passions and Deceptions: The Early Films of Ernst Lubitsch.* Princeton, NJ: Princeton University Press, 1992.

———. "Urban Paranoia in Alfred Döblin's *Berlin Alexanderplatz.*" *German Quarterly* 67.3 (Summer 1994): 347–68.

Hales, Barbara. "Woman as Sexual Criminal: Weimar Constructions of the Criminal *Femme Fatale.*" *Women in German Yearbook* 12 (1996): 100–121.

Hall, Mordaunt. Rev. of *Variety. New York Times,* 28 June 1926.

Hall, Stuart. "On Postmodernism and Articulation: An Interview with Stuart Hall," ed., Lawrence Goldberg. Orig. in *Journal of Communication Inquiry* 10.2 (1986): 45–60. Rpt. in David Morley and Kuan-Hsing Chen, eds., *Stuart Hall: Critical Dialogues in Cultural Studies.* London: Routledge, 1996, 131–50.

Hansen, Miriam. "America, Paris, the Alps: Kracauer and Benjamin on Cinema and Modernity." In Lüdtke, Marßolek, and von Saldern, *Amerikanisierung,* 161–98.

————. "Decentric Perspectives: Kracauer's Early Writings on Film and Mass Culture." *New German Critique* 54 (Fall 1991): 47–76.

————. "Early Silent Cinema: Whose Public Sphere?" *New German Critique* 29 (Spring–Summer 1983): 147–84.

————. Foreword. Negt/Kluge. *The Public Sphere and Experience.*

Hardt, Ursula. *"From Caligari to California: Eric Pommer's Life in the International Film Wars.* Providence: Berghahn Books, 1996.

Harrigan, Renny. "Novellistic [*sic*] Representation of *die Berufstätige* during the Weimar Republic." *Women in German Yearbook* 4 (1988): 97–124.

Hasenclever, Walter. *Der Sohn* (1914). In *Dramen.* Berlin: Die Schmiede, 1924, 9–148.

Hausen, Karin. "Mother's Day in the Weimar Republic." In Bridenthal et al., 131–52.

Henseleit, Felix. Rev. of *The Blue Angel. Reichsfilmblatt* (Berlin), 5 April 1930.

Herf, Jeffrey. *Reactionary Modernism: Technology, Culture, and Politics in Weimar and the Third Reich.* Cambridge: Cambridge University Press, 1984.

Hermand, Jost, and Frank Trommler. *Die Kultur der Weimarer Republik.* Munich: Nymphenburger, 1978.

Hewitt, Andrew. *Political Inversions: Homosexuality, Fascism, and the Modernist Imaginary.* Stanford, CA: Stanford University Press, 1996.

Holländer, Felix. *Der Eid des Stefan Huller* (1912). In English: *The Sins of the Fathers,* trans. Sara J. I. Lawson. New York: Payson & Clarke Ltd., 1927.

"Hollywood bewundert die Technik des 'Blauen Engel.'" *Film-Kurier* (199): 23 August 1930. "2. Beiblatt."

Holmlund, Christine. "When Is a Lesbian not a Lesbian? The Lesbian Continuum and the Mainstream Femme Film." *Camera Obscura* 25/26 (January–May 1991).

Horsley, Ritta Jo. "'This Number Is Not in Service:' Destabilizing Identities in Irmgard Keun's Novels from Weimar and Exile." In Elke P. Frederiksen and Martha Kaarsberg Wallach, eds., *Facing Fascism and Confronting the Past: German Women Writers from Weimar to the Present.* Albany: State University of New York State Press, 2000, 37–60.

Hussong, Friedrich. Statement on *The Blue Angel. Montag* (Berlin), 31 March 1930. Cited in "Skandal um den Blauen Engel."

Hutcheon, Linda. *A Poetics of Postmodernism: History, Theory, Fiction.* New York: Routledge, 1988.

Huyssen, Andreas. "Mapping the Postmodern." In *After the Great Divide: Modernism, Mass Culture, Postmodernism.* Bloomington: Indiana University Press, 1986, 179–221.

————. "The Vamp and the Machine." In *After the Great Divide,* 65–81.

Huyssen, Andreas, and David Bathrick, eds. *Modernity and the Text: Revisions of German Modernism.* New York: Columbia University Press, 1989.

Ihering, Herbert. "Jack unterm Mistelzweig." Rev. of *Büchse der Pandora. Berliner Börsen–Courier* (71), 12 February 1929.

————. Rev. of *The Blue Angel*. *Berliner Börsenkurier,* 2 April 1930.

————. Rev. of "Zwei Krawatten." *Berliner Börsenkurier,* 6 September 1929. Rpt. in *Film und Fernsehen* 12 (1980): 34.

Illustrierter Film–Kurier 7.378 (1925): Ufa's promotional material for *Variety.*

Isherwood, Christopher. *Goodbye to Berlin.* New York: Random House, 1939.

Jacobsen, Wolfgang. *Erich Pommer: Ein Produzent macht Filmgeschichte.* Berlin: Argon, 1989.

Jelavich, Peter. *Berlin Cabaret.* Cambridge, MA: Harvard University Press, 1993.

Jürgs, Britta. "Neusachliche Zeitungsmacher, Frauen und alte Sentimentalitäten: Erich Kästners Roman 'Fabian: Die Geschichte eines Moralisten.'" In Becker/Weiss, 195–211.

Kaes, Anton. "Film in der Weimarer Republik: Motor der Moderne." In Wolfgang Jacobsen, Anton Kaes, and Hans Helmut Prinzler, eds. *Geschichte des Deutschen Films.* Stuttgart: Metzler, 1993, 39–100.

————. "German Cultural History and the Study of Film: Ten Theses and a Postscript." *New German Critique* 65 (1995): 47–58.

Kaes, Anton, ed. *Kino–Debatte: Texte zum Verhältnis von Literatur und Film 1919–1929.* Tübingen: Max Niemeyer, 1978. English translation of the introduction: "The Debate about German Cinema: Charting a Controversy (1919–1929)," trans. David J. Levin. *New German Critique* 40 (1987): 7–33.

———— . *Weimarer Republik: Manifeste und Dokumente zur deutschen Literatur 1918–1933.* Stuttgart: Metzler, 1983.

Kaes, Anton, Martin Jay, and Edward Dimendberg, eds. *The Weimar Republic Sourcebook.* Berkeley: University of California Press, 1994.

Kaplan, Marion. "Sisterhood under Siege." In Bridenthal et al., 174–98.

Kästner, Erich. *Fabian: Die Geschichte eines Moralisten* (1931). With 1950 foreword. Munich: Deutscher Taschenbuch Verlag, 1989. English trans. by Cyrus Brooks. Evanston, IL: Northwestern University Press, 1990.

————. "Kabarett des Namenlosen." *Magdeburger General–Anzeiger,* 7 April 1929.

Kautz, Elisabeth. "The Fruits of Her Labor: Working Women and Popular Culture in the Weimar Republic." Ph.D. Dissertation, University of Minnesota, 1997.

Keun, Irmgard. *Gilgi—eine von uns,* (1931). Munich: Deutscher Taschenbuch Verlag, 1990.

————. *Das kunstseidene Mädchen* Ergl: (*The Artificial Girl*) (1932). Munich: Deutscher Taschenbuch Verlag, 1991.

————. *Nach Mitternacht* (1937). Munich: Deutscher Taschenbuch Verlag, 1995.

Kinematograph (Berlin). Rev. of *Mädchen in Uniform,* 28 November 1931.

Klotz, Volker. "Forcierte Prosa. Stilbeobachtungen an Bildern und Romanen der Neuen Sachlichkeit." In Rudolf Wolff, ed., *Erich Kästner: Werk und Wirkung.* Bonn: Bouvier, 1983, 70–90.

Kniesche, Thomas, and Stephen Brockmann, eds. *Dancing on the Volcano: Essays on the Culture of the Weimar Republic.* Columbia, SC: Camden House, 1994.

Knight, Julia. *Women and the New German Cinema.* London: Verso, 1992.

Koch, Gertrud. "Between Two Worlds: von Sternberg's *The Blue Angel.*" In Rentschler, *German Film and Literature,* 60–72.

Koonz, Claudia. *Mothers in the Fatherland: Women, the Family, and Nazi Politics.* New York: St. Martin's Press, 1987.

Kosta, Barbara. "Unruly Daughters and Modernity: Irmgard Keun's *Gilgi—eine von uns.*" *German Quarterly* 68.3 (Summer 1995): 271–86.

Kracauer, Siegfried. *Die Angestellten* (1929/30). In Siegfried Kracauer, *Schriften* 1. Frankfurt: Suhrkamp, 1971, 205–304.

———. *From Caligari to Hitler: A Psychological History of the German Film.* Princeton, NJ: Princeton University Press, 1947.

———. "Girls und Krise," (1931). *Frankfurter Zeitung,* 26 May 1931. In English: "Girls and Crisis." In Kaes, Jay, and Dimendberg, 565–66.

——— "Die kleinen Ladenmädchen gehen ins Kino" (1927). In Kracauer, *Das Ornament der Masse.* Frankfurt: Suhrkamp, 1963, 279–94.

———. "Lulu." Rev. of *Büchse der Pandora.* "Stadt–Blatt," *Frankfurter Zeitung,* 17 February 1929.

———. "Das Ornament der Masse," (1927). In *Das Ornament der Masse: Essays.* Frankfurt: Suhrkamp, 1963, 50–63.

Krechel, Ursula. "Irmgard Keun: die Zerstörung der kalten Ordnung. Auch ein Versuch über das Vergessen weiblicher Kulturleistungen." *Literaturmagazin* 10 (1979): 103–28.

Kreis, Gabriele. *"Was man glaubt, gibt es": Das Leben der Irmgard Keun.* Zürich: Arche, 1991.

Krusche, Dieter, with Jürgen Labenski. *Reclams Film–Führer.* 9th rev. and expanded ed. Stuttgart: Reclam, 1993.

Kuzniar, Alice A. *The Queer German Cinema.* Stanford, CA: Stanford University Press, 2000.

Landes, Joan. *Women and the Public Sphere in the Age of the French Revolution.* Ithaca, NY: Cornell University Press, 1988.

Laqueur, Walter. *Weimar: A Cultural History, 1918–1933.* London: Weidenfeld and Nicholson, 1974.

Last, R. W. *Erich Kästner.* London: Oswald Wolff, 1974.

Lavin, Maud. *Cut with the Kitchen Knife: The Weimar Photomontages of Hannah Höch.* New Haven, CT: Yale University Press, 1993.

Lensing, Leo. "Cinema, Society, and Literature in Irmgard Keun's *Das kunstseidene Mädchen.*" *Germanic Review* 60 (1985): 129–34.

Lenssen, Claudia et al. "From Hitler to Hepburn: A Discussion of Women's Film Production and Reception." *New German Critique* 24/25 (1981–1982): 172–85.

Lethen, Helmut. *Neue Sachlichkeit 1924–1932: Studien zur Literatur des "Weißen Sozialismus."* Stuttgart: Metzler, 1970.

———. *Verhaltenslehren der Kälte. Lebensversuche zwischen den Kriegen.* Frankfurt: Suhrkamp, 1994. In English: *Cool Conduct: The Culture of Distance in Weimar Germany,* trans. Don Reneau. Berkeley: University of California Press, forthcoming.

Levin, David J. Unpublished conference paper on *The Blue Angel*. German Studies Association Conference, Washington DC, September 1993.

Lewis, Beth Irwin. "*Lustmord:* Inside the Windows of the Metropolis." In Charles W. Haxthausen and Heidrun Suhr, eds. *Berlin: Culture and Metropolis.* Minneapolis: University of Minnesota Press, 1990, 111–40.

Lindner, Martin. *Leben in der Krise: Zeitromane der neuen Sachlichkeit und die intellektuelle Mentalität der klassischen Moderne.* Stuttgart: Metzler, 1994.

Linville, Susan E. *Feminism, Film, Fascism: Women's Auto/Biographical Cinema and West German "Postwar" Culture.* Austin: University of Texas Press, 1998.

———. "Retrieving History: Margarethe von Trotta's *Marianne and Juliane*." PMLA 106.3 (May 1991): 446–58.

Livingstone, Rodney. Intro. to English trans. of Kästner's *Fabian*, vii–xxiii.

Lüdtke, Alf, Inge Marßolek, and Adelheid von Saldern, eds. *Amerikanisierung. Traum und Alptraum im Deutschland des 20. Jahrhunderts.* Stuttgart: Franz Steiner, 1996.

Luft, Herbert G. Rev. of *Variety. Films in Review* (June–July 1977).

Lungstrum, Janet. "*Metropolis* and the Technosexual Woman of German Modernity." In von Ankum, *Women in the Metropolis,* 128–44. (Note: this author now publishes under the name Janet Ward.)

Lustig, Hanns G. "Wedekinds 'Lulu' im Film: Der Fall der verwitweten Frau Schön." *Tempo* (Berlin, No. 35), 11 February 1929.

Maase, Kaspar. *BRAVO Amerika: Erkundungen zur Jugendkultur der Bundesrepublik in den fünfziger Jahren.* Hamburg: Junius, 1992.

Makela, Maria. "The Misogynist Machine: Images of Technology in the Work of Hannah Höch." In von Ankum, *Women in the Metropolis,* 106–27.

Makholm, Kristin. "The Höch Papers: Film, Portraiture, and Primitivism in the Art of Hannah Höch." Ph.D. Dissertation, University of Minnesota, 1999.

Mannheim, Karl. *Ideologie und Utopie* (1929). Frankfurt: F. Cohn, 1930 (2nd ed.).

Manning, Susan A. *Ecstasy and the Demon: Feminism and Nationalism in the Dances of Mary Wigman.* Berkeley: University of California Press, 1993.

Mason, Tim. "Women in Germany, 1925–1940: Family, Welfare and Work," pt. 1. *History Workshop* 1 (1976): 74–113.

Mayne, Judith. "Dracula in the Twilight: Murnau's *Nosferatu*." In Rentschler, *German Film and Literature,* 25–39.

———. "Feminist Film Theory and Women at the Movies." In *Profession 87,* 14–19. New York: Modern Language Association, 1987.

———. *Framed: Lesbians, Feminists, and Media Culture.* Minneapolis: University of Minnesota Press, 2000.

———. "Marlene Dietrich, *The Blue Angel,* and Female Performance." In Dianne Hunter, ed., *Seduction and Theory: Readings of Gender, Representation, and Rhetoric.* Urbana: University of Illinois Press, 1989, 28–46. Also included in Mayne, *Framed.*

McCormick, Richard W. "From *Caligari* to Dietrich: Sexual, Social, and Cinematic Discourses in Weimar Film." *SIGNS: Journal of Women in Culture and Society* 18.3 (1993): 640–68.

————. "Private Anxieties/Public Projections: 'New Objectivity,' Male Subjectivity, and Weimar Cinema." In *Women in German Yearbook* 10. Lincoln: University of Nebraska Press, 1995, 1–18.

Meyer–Wendt, Jochen. "Die Fassade der Moral: Josef von Sternberg's "Der blaue Engel." In Töteberg and Bock, 260–63.

Mitscherlich, Alexander and Margarete. *Die Unfäehigkeit zu travern. Grundlagen Kollektiven Verhaltens.* Munich: Piper, 1967. In English: *The Inability to Mourn: Principles of Collective Behavior.* Trans. Beverly Placzek. New York: Grove Press, 1975.

Mizejewski, Linda. *Divine Decadence: Fascism, Female Spectacle, and the Makings of Sally Bowles.* Princeton, NJ: Princeton University Press, 1992.

Mosse, George. *Nationalism and Sexuality.* New York: Howard Fertig, 1985.

Mulvey, Laura. "Afterthoughts inspired by *Duel in the Sun*" (1981). In *Visual and Other Pleasures.* Bloomington: Indiana University Press, 1989, 29–38.

————. "Changes: Thoughts on Myth, Narrative and Historical Experience" (1985). In *Visual and Other Pleasures.* Bloomington: Indiana University Press, 1989, 159–76.

————. "Visual Pleasure and Narrative Cinema" (1975). In *Visual and Other Pleasures.* Bloomington: Indiana University Press, 1989, 14–26.

Munby, Jonathan. "Screening Crime in the U.S.A., 1929–1958: From Hays Code to HUAC; From *Little Caesar* to *Touch of Evil.*" Ph.D. Dissertation, University of Minnesota, 1995. See also his book: *Public Enemies, Public Heroes: Screening the Gangster from Little Caesar to Touch of Evil.* Chicago, University of Chicago Press, 1999.

Murray, Bruce. "The Role of the Vamp in Weimar Cinema: An Analysis of Karl Grune's *The Street.*" In Frieden et al., Vol. 2, 33–41.

Negt, Oskar, and Alexander Kluge. *The Public Sphere and Experience: Toward an Analysis of the Bourgeois and Proletarian Public Sphere* (1972), trans. Peter Labanyi, Jamie Owen Daniel, and Assenka Oksiloff. Minneapolis: University of Minnesota Press, 1993.

Norton, Sydney. "Early German Modern Dance and the Avant–Garde." Ph.D. Dissertation, University of Minnesota, 1998.

Ohm, Lisa. "The Filmic Adaptation of the Novel *The Child Manuela:* Christa Winsloe's Child Heroine Becomes a *Girl in Uniform.*" In Frieden et al., Vol. 2, 97–104.

Pavsek, Christopher. Unpublished paper on Freud and *Secrets of a Soul.* Durham, NC: Duke University, 1993.

Penley, Constance, and Sharon Willis, eds. and intro. *Male Trouble.* Minneapolis: University of Minnesota Press, 1993.

Petersen, Klaus. "'Neue Sachlichkeit': Stilbegriff, Epochenbezeichnung oder Gruppenphänomen?" *Deutsche Vierteljahreszeitschrift für Literaturwissenschaft und Geistesgeschichte* 56.3 (1982): 463–77.

Petersen, Vibeke Rützow. *Women and Modernity in Weimar Germany: Reality and its Reflection in Popular Fiction.* Oxford: Berghahn Books, forthcoming.

Petro, Patrice. "Modernity and Mass Culture in Weimar: Contours of a Discourse on Sexuality in Early Theories of Perception and Representation." *New German Critique* 40 (1987): 115–46.

————. *Joyless Streets: Women and Melodramatic Representation in Weimar Germany.* Princeton, NJ: Princeton University Press, 1989.

Peukert, Detlev J. K. *Die Weimarer Republik: Krisenjahre der Klassischen Moderne.* Frankfurt: Suhrkamp, 1987. In English: *The Weimar Republic: The Crisis of Classical Modernity.* New York: Hill and Wang, 1992.

Pinthus, Kurt. "Männliche Literatur" (1929). In Kaes, *Weimarer Republik,* 328–33.

Plonien, Klaus. "Re–Mapping the World: Travel Literature of Weimar Germany." Ph.D. Dissertation, University of Minnesota, 1995.

Pommer, Erich. Statement on the "Hussong–Polemik." Cited in *Film–Kurier,* 1 April 1930.

Raham, Rebecca. "Reinig's *Die ewige Schule* as Film Critique and Lesbian Theory." Unpublished paper. Women in German Conference, Great Barrington, MA, October 1993.

Ratchye, Ellen. *"Metropolis,* Thea von Harbou, Critical Feminism." M.A. thesis, University of Minnesota, 1991.

Rauch, Angelika. "The *Trauerspiel* of the Prostituted Body, or Woman as Allegory of Modernity." *Cultural Critique* 10 (Fall 1988): 77–88.

Reda, Ernst E. "Wie *Varieté* in Amerika aussieht." *B. Z. (Berliner Zeitung) — Mittag* (183), *Film–B.Z.,* 9 July 1926.

Reinig, Christa. "Christa Reinig über Christa Winsloe." In Christa Winsloe, *Mädchen in Uniform: Roman.* Munich: Frauenoffensive, 1983, 241–48.

Reisdorfer, Kathryn. "Seeing Through the Screen: An Examination of Women in Soviet and German Popular Cinema in the Inter–War Years." Ph.D. Dissertation, University of Minnesota, 1993.

Rentschler, Eric, introd. and ed. *The Films of G. W. Pabst: An Extraterritorial Cinema.* New Brunswick, NJ: Rutgers University Press, 1990.

Rentschler, Eric, ed. *German Film and Literature: Adaptations and Transformations.* New York: Methuen, 1986.

Rentschler, Eric. *The Ministry of Illusion: Nazi Cinema and Its Afterlife.* Cambridge, MA: Harvard University Press, 1996.

————. "Mountains and Modernity: Relocating the *Bergfilm.*" *New German Critique* 51 (1990): 137–61.

Rich, B. Ruby. "From Repressive Tolerance to Erotic Liberation: *Girls in Uniform*" (1984). In Frieden et al., Vol. 2. Providence, RI: Berg, 61–96.

Rickels, Laurence. "The Demonization of the Homefront: War Neurosis and Weimar Cinema." In Kniesche and Brockmann, 181–93.

Riehl–Heyse, Herbert. "Mit Zeitungspapier Aggressionen anheizen." *Süddeutsche Zeitung* 23 (May 1991): 3.

Riesman, David. *The Lonely Crowd: A Study of the Changing American Character.* New Haven, CT: Yale University Press, 1950.

Riva, Maria. *Marlene Dietrich.* New York: Knopf, 1992.

Riviere, Joan. "Womanliness as a Masquerade." Orig. in *The International Journal of Psychoanalysis* 10 (1929). Rpt. in *Formations of Fantasy,* eds. Victor Burgin, James

Donald, and Cora Kaplan. London: Methuen, 1986, 35–44.

Rodowick, D. N. *The Difficulty of Difference: Psychoanalysis, Sexual Difference, and Film Theory.* New York: Routledge, 1991.

Roloff, Gerd. "Irmgard Keun—Vorläufiges zu Leben und Werk." *Zur deutschen Exilliteratur in den Niederlanden 1933–1940. Amsterdamer Beiträge zur neueren Germanistik* 6 (1977): 45–68.

Rosenhaft, Eve. "Lesewut, Kinosucht, Radiotismus: Zur (geschlechter–)politischen Relevanz neuer Massenmedien in den 1920er Jahren." In Lüdtke, Marßolek, and von Saldern, *Amerikanisierung,* 119–43.

———. "Women, Gender, and the Limits of Political History in the Age of 'Mass' Politics." In Larry Eugene Jones and James Retallack, eds., *Elections, Mass Politics, and Social Change in Modern Germany: New Perspectives.* Washington, DC: German Historical Institute; Cambridge: Cambridge University Press, 1992.

Rosenstein, Doris. "'Mit der Wirklichkeit auf du und du'? Zu Irmgard Keuns Romanen 'Gilgi, eine von uns' und 'Das kunstseidene Mädchen.'" In Becker and Weiß, 273–90.

Roth, Joseph. "Schluß mit der 'Neuen Sachlichkeit!'" (1930). In Kaes, *Weimarer Republik,* 653–55.

R.P. Rev. of *The Blue Angel. Münchener Neueste Nachrichten,* 3 March 1930.

Rühle–Gerstel, Alice. "Zurück zur guten alten Zeit?" (1933). In Kaes, *Weimarer Republik,* 359–60.

Ryan, Mary. "Gender and Public Access: Women's Politics in Nineteenth–Century America." In Calhoun, 259–88.

Said, Edward W. "The Public Role of Writers and Intellectuals." *The Nation,* 17/24 September 2001, 27–36.

Sarris, Andrew. *The Films of Josef von Sternberg.* New York: Museum of Modern Art, 1966.

Saunders, Thomas J. *Hollywood in Berlin. American Cinema and Weimar Germany.* Berkeley: University of California Press, 1994.

Schlüpmann, Heide. *Unheimlichkeit des Blicks. Das Drama des frühen deutschen Kinos.* Frankfurt: Stroemfeld/Roter Stern, 1990.

Schmied, Wieland. "Neue Sachlichkeit and the German Realism of the 1920s," trans. David Britt and Frank Whitford. *Neue Sachlichkeit and German Realism of the Twenties.* Arts Council of Great Britain. London: Arts Council of Great Britain, 1978, 7–32.

———. *Neue Sachlichkeit und Magischer Realismus in Deutschland 1918–1933.* Hannover: Fackelträger Verlag Schmidt–Küster, 1969.

Scholar, Nancy. Rev. of *Mädchen in Uniform* (1975). Rpt. in Patricia Erens, ed., *Sexual Stratagems: The World of Women and Film.* New York: Horizon, 1979, 219–23.

Schoppmann, Claudia. "Portrait: Christa Winsloe." In Schoppmann, ed., *Im Fluchtgepäck die Sprache: Deutschsprachige Schriftstellerinnen im Exil.* Berlin: Orlanda Frauenverlag, 1991, 110–16.

Schulte–Sasse, Linda. *Entertaining the Third Reich: Illusions of Wholeness in Nazi Cinema.* Durham, NC: Duke University Press, 1996.

————. "Leni Riefenstahl's Feature Films and the Question of a Fascist Aesthetic." *Cultural Critique* 19 (Spring 1991): 123–48.

————. "The Never Was as History: Portrayals of the Eighteenth Century in National Socialist Film." Ph.D. Dissertation, University of Minnesota, 1985.

————. Notes on *Der blaue Engel.* In Thomas G. Plummer et al., eds., *Film & Politics in the Weimar Republic.* Minneapolis: University of Minnesota, 1982, 67–68.

Sedgwick, Eve Kosofsky. *Tendencies.* Durham, NC: Duke University Press, 1993.

Serke, Jürgen. *Die verbannten Dichter.* Weinheim: Beltz and Gelberg, 1977.

Shafi, Monika. "'Aber das ist es ja eben, ich habe ja keine Meinesgleichen': Identitätsprozeß und Zeitgeschichte in dem Roman *Das kunstseidene Mädchen* von Irmgard Keun." *Colloquia Germanica* 21 (1988): 314–25.

Shatz, Adam. "Bebop and Stalinist Kitsch." Rev. of Michael Denning, *The Cultural Front: The Laboring of American Culture in the Twentieth Century. The Nation,* 10 March 1997, 25–28.

Silverman, Kaja. *Male Subjectivity at the Margins.* New York: Routledge, 1992.

"Skandal um den Blauen Engel." *Der Abend,* Spätausgabe des *Vorwärts* (Berlin), 31 March 1930.

Sloterdijk, Peter. *Kritik der zynischen Vernunft.* 2 vols. Frankfurt: Suhrkamp, 1983. See also Sloterdijk, *Critique of Cynical Reason,* trans. Michael Eldred. Minneapolis: University of Minnesota Press, 1987.

Sneeringer, Julia. "'Who Will Be the Party of Women?' Mobilizing Women for Politics in Germany." Unpublished paper, German Studies Association Conference, Dallas, TX, October 1994.

Sopcak, Lorna. "The Appropriation and Critique of the Romance Novel, Film, and Fashion in Irmgard Keun's Weimar Prose: Humor, Intertextuality, and Popular Discourse." Ph.D. Dissertation, University of Minnesota, 1999.

Staiger, Janet. *Perverse Spectators: The Practices of Film Reception.* New York: New York University Press, 2000.

Tatar, Maria. *Lustmord: Sexual Murder in Weimar Germany.* Princeton, NJ: Princeton University Press, 1995.

Tax, Meredith. "World Culture War." *The Nation,* 17 May 1999, 24–28.

Theweleit, Klaus. *Männerphantasien.* Vol. 1. Reinbek: Rowohlt, 1980. See also Theweleit, *Male Fantasies,* Vols. 1 & 2, trans. Stephen Conway. Minneapolis: University of Minnesota Press, 1987, 1989. (Conway trans. based on orig. ed.: Theweleit, *Männerphantasien,* 2 vols. Frankfurt: Roter Stern, 1977, 1978.)

Thiele, Hertha. "Gestern und Heute: Gespräch mit Hertha Thiele." Interview with Heide Schlüpmann, Karola Gramann, et al. *Frauen & Film* 28 (1981): 32–41.

Toller, Ernst. *Briefe aus dem Gefängnis. Gesammelte Werke,* Vol. 5, eds. Wolfgang Frühwald and John M. Spalek. Munich: Hanser, 1978.

————. *Hinkemann: Eine Tragödie.* (1924) Ed. Wolfgang Frühwald. Stuttgart: Reclam, 1971. In English: *Brokenbrow,* trans. Vera Mendel; illustr. Georg Grosz. London: Nonesuch, 1926.

————. *Hoppla, wir leben!* (1927). Stuttgart: Reclam, 1978.

————. *Eine Jugend in Deutschland.* Amsterdam: Querido, 1933.

————. *Die Maschinenstürmer* (1922). Leipzig: E.P. Tal, 1927.

————. *Masse Mensch* (1920). Berlin: Kiepenhauer, 1930.

————. *Die Wandlung* (1918). Potsdam: Kiepenhauer, 1925.

Töteberg, Michael. "Schöne nackte Körper: *Wege zu Kraft und Schönheit.*" In Bock and Töteberg, 152–55.

Trask. Rev. of "*Varietee*" [sic]. *Variety,* 20 January 1926.

Usborne, Cornelie. *The Politics of the Body in Weimar Germany: Women's Reproductive Rights and Duties.* Ann Arbor, MI: University of Michigan Press, 1992.

van de Velde, Th. H. *Die vollkommene Ehe: eine Studie über ihre Physiologie und Technik* (1926). Leipzig: Benno Konegen, 1927 (11th ed).

"*Varieté:* Der grosse deutsche Film." *Kinematograph* 979 (1925): 21.

"*Varieté* in 2 Fassungen." Rev. of *Variety. Film Kurier,* 23 November 1926.

Variety. Ufa's program for the film's premiere. Ufa-Palast am Zoo, 16 November 1925.

Völkischer Beobachter (Munich ed.) (210), 29 July 1931. Rev. of *Blue Angel.*

von Ankum, Katharina. "'Ich liebe Berlin mit einer Angst in den Knien': Weibliche Stadterfahrung in Irmgard Keun's *Das kunstseidene Mädchen.*" *German Quarterly* 67.3 (Summer 1994): 369–388.

————. "Motherhood and the New Woman: Vicki Baum's *stud. chem. Helene Willfüer* and Irmgard Keun's *Gilgi — eine von uns.*" *Women in German Yearbook* 11 (1995): 171–88.

von Ankum, Katharina, ed. *Women in the Metropolis: Gender and Modernity in Weimar Culture.* Berkeley: University of California Press, 1997.

von der Emde, Silke. "'Mädchen in Uniform.' Erotische Selbstbefreiung der Frau im Kontext der Kino-Debatte der Weimarer Republik." *Kodikas/Code: Ars Semiotica* 14 (1991): 35–48.

"Von der höheren Tochterschule zum Film: Ein Querschnitt durch fünfundzwanzig junge Mädchen von heute." *Uhu* (12) (1931): 34–42.

von Hindenburg, Paul. "The Stab in the Back" (1919). In Kaes, Jay, and Dimendberg, 15–16.

von Saldern, Adelheid. "Überfremdungsängste. Gegen die Amerikanisierung der deutschen Kultur in den zwanziger Jahren." In Lüdtke, Marßolek, and von Saldern, *Amerikanisierung,* 213–44.

von Sternberg, Josef. *The Blue Angel, a Film by Josef von Sternberg.* "Authorized Translation of the German Continuity." New York: Simon and Schuster, 1968.

————. *Fun in a Chinese Laundry.* New York: Macmillan, 1965.

"W." Rev. of *Secrets of a Soul. Der Film* (13), 28 March 1926.

Wagener, Hans. *Erich Kästner.* (W.) Berlin: Colloquium, 1973.

Wager, Jan B. *Dangerous Dames: Women and Representation in the Weimar Street Film and Film Noir.* Athens: Ohio University Press, 1999.

Ward, Janet. *Weimar Surfaces: Urban Visual Culture in 1920s Germany.* Berkeley: University of California Press, 2001. (Note: this author formerly published under the name of Janet Lungstrum.)

Wedekind, Frank. *Erdgeist* (1895) and *Büchse der Pandora* (1904). Munich: Goldmann, 1995.

Wegner, Hart, ed. and intro. *Der blaue Engel* ("The Blue Angel"). New York: Harcourt Brace Jovanovich, 1982.

Wendtland, Karlheinz. *Geliebter Kientopp: Sämtliche deutsche Spielfilme von 1929–1945 mit zahlreichen Künstlerbiographien. Jahrgang 1929/30 and Jahrgang 1931.* Berlin: Medium Film, 1990.

Wille, Hansjürgen. Rev. of *Büchse der Pandora. 8 Uhr-Abendblatt* (35), 1 February 1929.

Willett, John. *Art and Politics in the Weimar Period: The New Sobriety, 1917–1933.* New York: Pantheon, 1978.

———. *The Weimar Years: A Culture Cut Short.* New York: Abbeville, 1984.

Williams, Linda. *Hard Core: Power, Pleasure, and the Frenzy of the Visible.* Berkeley: University of California Press, 1990.

Willibrand, W. A. *Ernst Toller: Product of Two Revolutions.* Norman, OK: Cooperative Books, 1941.

Winsloe, Christa. *Gestern und Heute (Ritter Nérestan): Schauspiel in Drei Akten.* Vienna: Georg Marton, 1930. In English: *Girls in Uniform: A Play in Three Acts,* trans. ("Adaptation") Barbara Burnham. Boston: Little, Brown, 1933.

———. *Das Mädchen Manuela: Der Roman von "Mädchen in Uniform."* Leipzig: E. P. Tal, 1933. In English: *The Child Manuela: The Novel of "Mädchen in Uniform,"* trans. Agnes Niel Scott. London: Chapman & Hall, 1934.

Wittmann, Livia. "Der Stein des Anstoßes: Zu einem Problemkomplex in berühmten und gerühmten Romanen der Neuen Sachlichkeit." *Jahrbuch für Internationale Germanistik* 14.2 (1982): 56–78.

Wolfradt, Willi. "The Stab-in-the-Back Legend?" (1922). In Kaes, Jay, and Dimendberg, 16–18.

Zglinicki, Friedrich von. *Der Weg des Films: Die Geschichte der Kinematographie und ihrer Vorläufer.* Berlin: Rembrandt, 1956.

Zimnik, Nina. "No Man, No Cry? The Film *Girls in Uniform* and Its Discourses of Political Regime." *Women in German Yearbook* 15 (2000): 161–83.

Filmography

Primary Films

The Blue Angel (Der blaue Engel). Dir. Josef von Sternberg. Germany, 1930. 99 min. U.S. dist.: Facets Multimedia and West Glen Communications.

Mädchen in Uniform (a.k.a. Girls in Uniform). Dir. Leontine Sagan. Germany, 1931. 87 min. U.S. dist.: Facets Multimedia.

Pandora's Box (Die Büchse der Pandora). Dir. Georg Wilhelm Pabst. Germany, 1929. 133 min. (Restored Version). U.S. dist: Facets Multimedia.

Secrets of a Soul (Geheimnisse einer Seele). Dir. Georg Wilhelm Pabst. Germany, 1926. 97 min. U.S. dist.: Facets Multimedia and West Glen Communications.

Variety (Varieté). Dir. Ewald André Dupont. Germany, 1925. German version: 90 minutes; U.S. version: 59 min. U.S. dist.: Facets Multimedia.

Films Cited

An American Tragedy. Dir. Josef von Sternberg. USA, 1931. 96 minutes.

Asphalt. Dir. Joe May. Germany, 1929. 90 min. U.S. dist.: Facets Multimedia and West Glen Communications.

Backstairs (Hintertreppe). Dir. Leopold Jessner and Paul Leni. Germany, 1921. 42 min. U.S. dist.: Facets Multimedia and West Glen Communications.

The Battleship Potemkin (Bronenosets Potyomkin). Dir. Sergei M. Eisenstein. USSR, 1925. 80 min. U.S. dist.: Facets Multimedia.

Berlin, Symphony of a (Big/Great) City (Berlin, Symphonie einer Großstadt). Walter Ruttmann. 1927. 65 min. U.S. dist.: Facets Multimedia.

The Blue Light (Das blaue Licht). Dir. Leni Riefenstahl. Germany, 1932. 70 min. U.S. dist.: Facets Multimedia.

Bombs on Monte Carlo (a.k.a. *The Bombardment of Monte Carlo;* orig. German title: Bomben auf Monte Carlo). Dir. Hanns Schwarz. Germany, 1931. 111 min. U.S. dist.: International Historical Films.

The Bridge (Die Brücke). Dir. Bernhard Wicki. West Germany, 1959. 105 min. U.S. dist.: Facets Multimedia and West Glen Communications.

Cabaret. Dir. Bob Fosse. USA, 1972. 124 min. U.S. dist.: Facets Multimedia.

The Cabinet of Dr. Caligari (Das Kabinett des Doktor Caligari). Dir. Robert Wiene. Germany, 1920. 71 minutes. (18 fps) U.S. dist.: Facets Multimedia and West Glen Communications.

The Conformist (Il Conformista). Dir. Bernardo Bertolucci. Italy, 1970. 110 min. U.S. dist.: Facets Multimedia.

The Damned (La Caduta degli dei). Dir. Luchino Visconti. Italy, 1969. 155 min. U.S. dist.: Facets Multimedia.

Deception (German title: *Anna Boleyn*). Dir. Ernst Lubitsch. Germany, 1920. 100 min. U.S. dist.: Facets Multimedia.

Diary of a Lost Girl (Das Tagebuch einer Verlorenen). Dir. Georg Wilhelm Pabst. Germany, 1929. 100 min. (restored version) (24 fps) U.S. dist.: Facets Multimedia.

Dr. Mabuse: The Gambler (Dr. Mabuse, der Spieler). Dir. Fritz Lang. Germany, 1922. 2 Parts: 270 min. [Berlin film festival 2001 restored version: 155 min. (part 1) + 115 min. (part 2)] U.S. dist.: Facets Multimedia and West Glen Communications.

Eight Girls in a Boat (Acht Mädels im Boot). Dir. Erich Washneck. Germany, 1932. 81 min.

The Eternal Jew (Der ewige Jude). Dir. Fritz Hippler. Germany, 1940. 62 min. U.S. dist.: Facets Multimedia.

Das Fräulein von Barnhelm. Dir. Hans Schweikart. Germany, 1940. 91 min.

Germany Year Zero (Germania anno zero). Dir. Roberto Rosselini. Italy, 1947. 78 min. U.S. dist.: Facets Multimedia.

Hitler Youth Quex (Hitlerjunge Quex). Dir. Hans Steinhoff. Germany, 1933. 95 min. U.S. dist.: Facets Multimedia.

The Hymn of Leuthen (a.k.a. *The Anthem of Leuthen;* original German title: Der Choral von Leuthen). Dir. Carl Froelich and Arzén von Cserépy. Germany, 1933. 91 min.

Jew Suess (Jud Süß). Dir. Veit Harlan. Germany, 1940. 98 min. U.S. dist.: Facets Multimedia.

Joyless Street (Freudlose Gasse). Dir. Georg Wilhelm Pabst. Germany, 1925. 125 min. / 175 min. (restored version of the Filmmuseum Munich from 1997). U.S dist.: Facets Multimedia.

Kuhle Wampe. Dir. Slatan Dudow. Screenplay: Bertolt Brecht. Germany, 1932. 71 min. U.S. dist.: West Glen Communications.

The Last Command. Dir. Josef von Sternberg. USA, 1928. 85 min. U.S. dist.: Facets Multimedia.

The Last Laugh (Der letzte Mann). Dir. Friedrich Wilhelm Murnau. Germany, 1924. 90 min. U.S. dist.: Facets Multimedia and West Glen Communications.

The Love of Jeanne Ney (Die Liebe der Jeanne Ney). Dir. Georg Wilhelm Pabst. Germany, 1927. 113 min. U.S. dist.: Facets Multimedia.

Metropolis. Dir. Fritz Lang. 1927. Germany: 115 min. / 150 min. (restored version, Filmmuseum Munich) / 153 min. (original release) / 210 min. (original director's cut at premiere). U.S. dist.: Facets Multimedia.

Mit dem Kurbelkasten um die Welt. Dir.: Colin Ross. Germany, 1925.

Morocco. Dir. Josef von Sternberg. USA, 1930. 90 min. U.S. dist.: Facets Multimedia.

Mother Krause's Journey to Happiness (Mutter Krausens Fahrt ins Glück). Dir. Piel Jutzi. Germany, 1929. 121 min. U.S. dist.: Facets Multimedia.

The Murderers Are Among Us (Die Mörder sind unter uns). Dir. Wolfgang Staudte. Germany, 1946. 85 min. / 91 min. (re-issue). U.S. dist.: Icestorm and West Glen Communications.

Nosferatu, a Symphony of Horror (Nosferatu, eine Symphonie des Grauens). Dir. Friedrich Wilhelm Murnau. Germany, 1922. 75 min. / 94 min. (Restored Version Cannes 1995) U.S dist.: Facets Multimedia and West Glen Communications.

The Old and the Young King (Der alte und der junge König). Dir. Hans Steinhoff. Germany, 1935. 91 min. U.S. dist.: Facets Multimedia.

Passion (Madame Dubarry). Dir. Ernst Lubitsch. Germany, 1919. 85 min. U.S. dist.: Facets Multimedia and West Glen Communications.

People on Sunday (Menschen am Sonntag). Dir.: Robert Siodmak, Edgar G. Ulmer ; Screenplay: Billy Wilder, Fred Zinnemann, Edgar Ulmer. Germany, 1929. 60 min. U.S. dist.: Facets Multimedia.

Rome Open City (Roma, città aperta). Dir. Roberto Rosselini. Italy, 1946. 105 min. U.S. dist.: Facets Multimedia.

The Sinful Woman (Die Sünderin). Dir.: Willi Forst. West Germany, 1950. 100 min.

The Street (Die Straße). Dir. Karl Grune. Germany, 1923. 74 min. U.S. dist.: Facets Multimedia.

Stresemann. Dir. Alfred Braun. West Germany, 1957. 105 min.

The Three from the Gas Station (Die Drei von der Tankstelle). Dir. Wilhelm Thiele. Germany, 1930. 99 min. U.S. dist.: West Glen Communications.

Thunderbolt. Dir. Josef von Sternberg. USA, 1929. 85 min.

Tragedy of a Prostitute (a.k.a. Tragedy of the Street; original German title: Dirnentragödie). Dir. Bruno Rahn. Germany, 1927. 85 min. U.S. dist.: West Glen Communications.

Triumph of the Will (Triumph des Willens). Dir. Leni Riefenstahl. Germany, 1935. 114 min. U.S. dist.: Facets Multimedia.

Viktor and Viktoria (Viktor und Viktoria). Dir. Reinhold Schünzel. Germany, 1933. 100 min.

Ways to Strength and Beauty (Wege zur Kraft und Schönheit). Dir. Wilhelm Prager. Germany, 1925. 100 min.

Index ～